Ra

'Jaideep Hardikar has lived Ramrao's life for some time to write this searing biography of a farmer in Vidarbha. Through the protagonist, the book, in a sense, projects the everyday tribulations of the agrarian community in India, for whom death, not life, has become the favoured option. It is a resounding answer to a question that we often casually ask: why do farmers commit suicide? Ramrao is a throbbing cry from the ground, the anti-heroic story of an ordinary man who almost succumbs to near-fatal despair but survives to tell the tale.'

MEENA MENON, INDEPENDENT JOURNALIST AND AUTHOR

'Jaideep masterfully narrates a story about the life of the Indian farmer over the past few years, intricately weaving in the string of policy failures on an unprecedented scale that have brought things to such a pass. Even while painting its bleakest moments, the book captures the prevailing rustic humour and spirit in equal measure. It does not pre-judge but allows the readers to figure out for themselves who is responsible for the trajectory of tragedies: the politicians, the bureaucracy or the people themselves for the choices they make at the elections.'

AJAY VIR JAKHAR, CHAIRMAN, BHARAT KRISHAK SAMAJ

'Jaideep could have easily penned the extraordinary life of the rich and famous. Instead, he chose the plebian tale of an Indian farmer and, through him, the story of India's rural half. Ramrao survives and continues in the chilling commonness, like countless others, of debt and drudgery. Jaideep's book is a quietly searing of our billionaire-obsessed nation and tells us that the problem is not with the farmer or farming but with the exploitative system that refuses to allow farmer-friendly policies. It is an important work that must be read by those who want to understand the ABC of agriculture as well as by policy planners.'

VIJAY JAWANDHIA, FARMERS' LEADER AND CO-FOUNDER OF THE SHETKARI SANGHATNA

'Jaideep Hardikar tells the agonising story of what keeps farmers perpetually indebted. Through the life of a small farmer, he explores the depth and extent of the misery that farmers are faced with—their everyday struggles, untiring efforts, the restless nights and how they hope against hope that tomorrow may turn out to be a better day. Gripping and engrossing, the book takes you deep into India's agrarian distress.'

DEVINDER SHARMA, FOOD, POLICY AND AGRICULTURE ANALYST AND COMMENTATOR

Ramrao

THE STORY OF INDIA'S
FARM CRISIS

Jaideep
Hardikar

HarperCollins *Publishers* India

First published in India in 2021 by
HarperCollins *Publishers*
A-75, Sector 57, Noida, Uttar Pradesh 201301, India
www.harpercollins.co.in

2 4 6 8 10 9 7 5 3 1

P-ISBN: 978-93-5422-301-3
E-ISBN: 978-93-5422-309-9

Typeset in 12/16.2 Adobe Garamond Pro at
Manipal Technologies Limited, Manipal

Printed and bound at
Replika Press Pvt. Ltd.

To

The Indian peasant-farmer

CONTENTS

Prologue

A FARMER'S EULOGY

'Something is terribly wrong in the countryside.'

—PROFESSOR M.S. SWAMINATHAN, 2005

TWO DAYS BEFORE HANGING himself to death on 24 March 2008, fifty-year-old farmer Shrikrishna Kalamb penned his own eulogy—all of six lines—and put it in his shirt's pocket.

In chaste Varhadi, a dialect of Marathi spoken in the western Vidarbha region that the British called Berar, it begins thus:

Me aagala vegala, mahi nyarich jindagani;
mahye maran bhi aahe, jase avakali paani.

I am unique; my life an uncommon odyssey;
My death will also be like untimely rain.

Kalamb, a 5-acre, atypical, dry-land farmer from Vidarbha, a region in the news since 1995 for farmers' suicides, wrote that his cotton was precious to him, like his poems. He likened its roots to the sweetness of sugarcane. In the poem, he built an image of his body hanging from a door—he had made up his mind to commit suicide.

Symbolism and emotion mark Kalamb's poignant poems; he ended his life at his sister's home in Murtijapur town, 30 kilometres from his native village Babhulgaon (Jahangir) in Akola. It is one of the six districts in Maharashtra—all in western Vidarbha—with high incidence of farmer suicides. He left behind five daughters and a bereaved wife.

Like most farmers, he had unpaid debts from banks and private lenders, and worried about the impending costs of his daughters' weddings. A few years earlier, a devastating accident had left him with a limp. He could no longer physically work the way he used to in his heyday, which added to his frustration and financial woes.

In another poem, titled 'Vasare' (Calves), he writes:

Amhi vasare vasare, muki upasi vasare.
Gaya panhavato amhi, chor kalatat dhar
Tapa tapa gham unarato, unarato bhuivar
Moti pikavato amhi, tari upasi lekare.

We are calves—dumb, hungry calves
We tend to cows, but thieves walk away with the milk and cream
We sweat and sweat on fields, we cultivate pearls,
but our children go hungry.

Kalamb was a sensitive man. A Dhangar (shepherd) by caste, a nomadic tribe in Maharashtra, his poems are rooted in the region's rustic culture and offer invaluable insights into an average Indian farmer's life. They are a reflection of the changing socio-economic, political and ecological landscape of rural India.

In another poem titled 'Lek' (Daughter), he showcases the worries of a father who is a farmer. While the poem carries deep patriarchal undertones, it explains the structural social problems of Vidarbha, which once was a feudal region; though things have changed or are changing, caste and class animosities still subtly prevail. In 'Itihaas' (History) he questions time for preserving only the glorious history of the rich, while wilfully burying the resilient struggles of the poor.

He wrote for farmers, and he wrote about them. It is a pity that his identity as a farmer quashed the poet in him. But he will, one can only hope, live on in his verses of revolt.

Kalamb wrote on small chits of paper, never preserving his work. He memorized all his poems and would sing them lyrically whenever his friends urged him to. After he was gone, his eldest daughter, Usha, meticulously searched for those chits in his trunk, bags and at his friends' homes. She could find only fifty-odd verses of the several he wrote. Most of these bring to us the small universe of a Berar farmer, forced to perpetually borrow money for all his needs, and who lives with the angst of being unable to repay it. Kalamb was pained by his tribe's crumbling lives: a farmer lives and dies in debt, exploited by the market and the political class, beleaguered by fledgling farms, where even when production goes up the income rarely does. He was, as his poems strongly indicate, also intrigued and agitated by the social ills and superstitions pervading rural life, the slow pace of much-needed social reforms. Usha would tell me days after his death that her father wrote whenever he was in a pensive mood.

She was, and remains, sorrowful that her father did not give her a chance to financially support the family. She eventually got a government job to support the household.

It is not the event of Kalamb's death that I seek to chronicle in this book, but the harrowing life of a farmer, which is what his poems portray. His deep, philosophical musings aptly capture the acute distress plaguing vast sections of the Indian peasantry. In over two decades of my journeys into Vidarbha and across the country's dusty countryside, I stood witness to human grief, struggle, brave fight-backs and several complex, crumbling worlds within that world—things that I hope to show in this narrative.

Around the mid 1990s, a liberalized and globalized economy engulfed great many unsuspecting farmers in problems that were beyond their comprehension, triggering suicides that surged in the early 2000s. In the cotton hinterland, I was waking up to life and living against the backdrop of premature deaths of young and old farmers and a new India taking shape in the new millennium. India's economy was now fuelled by sectors other than agriculture, like services. Local farmers' markets were invaded by global markets, like that of cotton or food. Rapid upward economic mobility of sections of the population was creating newer inequalities, leading to a perception among the peasantry that they were losing out. The fast-changing economic conditions were also altering long-held social equations. Landed farmers, once among the respected classes in a village economy, were now unable to meet their ever-growing needs, while the non-landed classes, absorbed in the unorganized service economy, migrated out of their villages to urban centres for better wages and work, doing marginally better than they once did as farm labourers.

There was a growing perception among the rural peasantry in Vidarbha that the new economic realities were doing them more harm than good. Cotton farmers, for example, saw their production costs multiply many times as energy, inputs and fertilizer prices soared. While generally the cost of living—health, education, and so on—went up, their real incomes stagnated. Government subsidies were tweaked or withdrawn. The declining incomes and the rising cost of living, they rued, were by design and not coincidental. The villages I saw held that the state and central governments were biased in favour of the rich, and that living in villages had become difficult.

In protest, they came up with sensational—at times weird—ideas of protests to draw the attention of authorities. There were villages that put themselves up for sale—lock, stock and barrel. Some residents put up signboards saying that they were willing to sell their kidneys. Thousands of farmers took to the streets just to be heard. They still do, not only in Vidarbha but now increasingly across the country.

The dawn of 2021, for instance, brought droves of farmers in their tractors to the borders of Delhi to protest against the passage of three contentious laws that the Narendra Modi government claims will reform the farm sector. The farmers from Punjab, Haryana and western Uttar Pradesh are unconvinced. They are sceptical that the new legal regime will bulldoze the old architecture which provided them some support in terms of an assured minimum support price and timely procurement. They fear that the new laws will help big corporations usurp their only asset: their land. Instead of expanding the security net, the government is doing away with the existing support to farming, they argue. The way the laws were passed in Parliament in September 2020—without a debate and despite opposition from several political parties—also came in for criticism and questioning.

A pan-Indian farmers' fightback is finally happening. Over the last two decades, though, I witnessed what agrarian distress really looks like, up close and in the isolation of individual households. I met villagers who pooled in money to cremate the dead because their families could not afford to do so. I read farmers' suicide notes addressed to district collectors, chief ministers, even prime ministers and presidents. There was one in which a newly married young farmer asked his soon-to-be-widowed wife to get remarried but not to a farmer. I witnessed a village coming together to celebrate a wedding and perform three funerals within a span of twenty-four hours, a young farmer in Washim who watered his orange orchard for days with a bucket and a mug when his well ran dry, a widow who witnessed the suicides of four men in the family—her father-in-law, husband and two younger brothers-in-law—but fought to resurrect the family farm, repay her debts and become a progressive farmer. I also reported on women farmers' suicides, suicides by young children.

The prevailing agrarian distress has a context with many factors: a giant interlinked global economy; commercialization of farming and life itself; a rural population unable to withstand the new economic order in the absence of safety nets; an upwardly mobile and new affluent India disconnected from its villages; and the struggling poor even in the urban spaces. Thirty years of liberalization, privatization and globalization have helped a class of Indians live the dream life, but for vast sections of the peasantry and rural populations this has been a tumultuous and deathly period, like a never-ending recession.

The chasm has grown so vast that the former does not care if it does not rain one season, affecting farm yields and pushing inflation. One glaring example of this disconnect was on display in the summer of 2020, when during the Covid-19 lockdown announced by the Indian government millions of poor migrants struggled to reach home. They walked long distances—often hundreds of kilometres in the punishing sun, with many dying along the way—while affluent Indians stayed indoors, enjoying a long vacation with minor inconveniences.

There was a time when, as my father recalls, the middle classes would keep an eye on the monsoon because it had a bearing on their own family budgets. Not any more. Today, these two worlds are starkly different. The universe of the top 10 per cent and that of the bottom 50 are sharply unequal. One example is how much gold upwardly mobile urban Indians buy every year while farmers sell or mortgage it—one to invest surplus money, the other to generate desperately needed cash to keep farmlands productive.

The countryside is, to put it in the words of Palagummi Sainath, India's foremost rural affairs journalist, a different planet today, not a third, fourth or fifth world. And this world is unable to run the household with its abysmal farm incomes. I had hoped, both as a reporter and as a citizen, that things would get better for the agrarian masses over time, the way they have for the rest of us. My wish hasn't come true so far.

It is of course true that some things have changed, where there have been public or private capital investments, since the country opened its economy in 1991. But life in villages in Vidarbha and many other regions in India, even if they are just a stone's throw away from the big cities, has grown more cumbersome. Exceptions are few and far between. Economic distress continues to haunt the peasantry, particularly small and marginal farmers in rain-fed regions.

Nearly 4,00,000 farmers committed suicide in India between 1995 and 2018, if we collate the data from the annual reports of the National Crime Records Bureau (NCRB) on 'Accidental Deaths and Suicides in India'. What happened to them? Why did they kill themselves? How do the farmers survive hunger, debts, sudden and extreme climate events, price volatility, poverty, structural inequalities? What drives them? What are their—if at all they have any—dreams?

SINCE I FIRST REPORTED on a cotton grower's suicide in a Yavatmal village over two decades ago, the story of agrarian distress is turning stale. Political parties promise doles, shiny new schemes. Economists call for more reforms. State and central governments, while shedding crocodile tears, push for new technologies and call for embracing modern systems even as farmers quietly carry on with work—all the while sinking deeper into debt, year after year.

The purpose of writing this book is not to recount the deaths or the grim statistics, or to write a historic account of how the cotton country has turned into a farmers' graveyard. The purpose is to tell, as the tagline at the People's Archive of Rural India reads, the everyday life of an everyday farmer. To remind us that amidst acerbic debates and arguments, cries for reforms of one kind or the other, many theoretical prescriptions, and attempts to bring in new programmes for the poor and the peasantry conceptualized by those in positions of power, a farmer's life hangs by a thread. To understand the process that leads a farmer to take that extreme step. There are many stories from across the country that speak of tragedy as well as of human grit in the midst of acute agrarian distress. This is merely one.

This is not Kalamb's story, though, as I said. He is not alive, like thousands of other farmers who are no more, to tell it to us. This is the story of a survivor, the kind of farmer Kalamb's poems are about—the extraordinary struggle of an ordinary soul. It is the story of life in an unequal world, one that rides on perpetual hope—hope that hangs like a mirage.

I

CORAGEN

HE RANG THE TEMPLE bell, applied a saffron mark to his forehead, folded his hands and bowed his head to offer one last prayer to Hanuman, the deity he would often turn to for succour, and fainted.

Darkness descended on him as if daylight had been switched off. His eyelids fluttered. He felt light-headed, as if in a trance. His mountainous worries melted away, then his brain stopped battling what felt like a faraway need to stay awake.

When he opened his eyes, he saw an old, motionless ceiling fan above him, its white blades grimy black with cobwebs and layers of dirt. It had not been cleaned in ages. Disoriented, his vision blurry, he took a while to regain consciousness. He was lying on a bed with a worn-out mattress and a dirty bed-sheet. A saline bottle hung from a rusty iron stand, transporting fluids and injections into his veins, drip by every drip. The ECG monitor mounted on a shelf behind the bed blipped, making haphazard lines in quick succession and a rhythmic tic-tic-tic sound. The digital screen displayed his blood pressure and pulse rate. He quietly studied the large, high-ceilinged room. He found himself relaxing. But at the same time his anxiety started coming back. He felt strained, his heart constricted.

Alongside him were eight or ten people in the room, a couple of them writhing in pain, fidgeting in their beds. Some others lay listless, almost dead. Two short, stout women in their fifties, clad in white, went in and out of the room, recording temperatures of the ailing men on the beds, administering medicine and yelling at the gathered crowds to wait outside.

For him, the surroundings were unnerving. It was not until he saw both his married daughters and a few familiar faces by his side that he felt reassured. It was a hospital and not the afterlife! His younger daughter told him he was in the Intensive Care Unit (ICU). It was maddeningly noisy and crowded because it was a public hospital. When he regained full consciousness, a thought ran through his mind—it may have been his first since he opened his eyes. Flashes of faces came to him, haunting him one by one. Those faces were of his lenders. Then he remembered: a dead cow, electrocuted by the barbed-wire fence on his field. He felt burdened by every breath he took.

He was still alive. He wanted to cry but could not; there were people around. For, Ramrao Panchleniwar, a cotton grower in his late forties, had meant to end his life by swallowing pesticide.

A DISHEVELLED RAMRAO IS teary-eyed and, because of the heavy burdens he carries, he is exhausted, physically weak and constantly sighing. His stomach burns. He has no appetite.

Ramrao has been a farmer for as long as he remembers. And, like millions of Indian farmers, he is trapped in a vicious circle of debt and despair. We have been chatting for I don't know how long now in his home in Hiwara village, a fifteen-minute drive from Pandharkawda, a town off National Highway 44—earlier called NH7—in Yavatmal district in eastern Maharashtra's cotton belt of Vidarbha. Yavatmal has been in the news for an unabated spell of farmers suicides since 1996, the year I began as a cub reporter with an English daily in Nagpur. During this period, while reporting on rural distress, I have not met or known of many farmers who survived serious attempts to take their own lives.

Some months earlier, I met a young, educated Dalit farmer, a Neo-Buddhist, and his frail wife in a village in Washim district, north-west of Yavatmal and part of the cotton–soybean belt. They too had survived a suicide pact, an act they had committed in a fit of rage, a result of accumulated despondency—momentarily forgetting about their three children, all aged below seven. The couple, in their early thirties, was in anguish, hassled by loans, caught in a constant struggle to make their petty ends meet, unable to give their children a meaningful life.

Year after year they suffered losses from their arid, rain-fed, 3-acre farm. That year, when the children insisted on getting firecrackers and new clothes for Diwali, something the well-to-do in cities frequently splurge on, the young wife asked her husband if they could get the kids what they wanted. On hearing his blunt no, a brawl ensued between the two childhood sweethearts over their unending financial woes. The furious husband, distraught by his inability to fulfil his children's small, legitimate wishes, swallowed a small bottle of Monocrotophos, an insecticide. In a fit of rage, his wife too quickly consumed another bottle kept in the house. They were lucky to survive the attempt—because they didn't want to die.

Still struggling with trauma and guilt over what they had done, they told me that all they wanted was a decent life for their children—the good 'convent school' education they themselves never got, the clothes they themselves could not afford as kids, and three square meals.

Around the same time, a husband and wife in Deonala village, Yavatmal, took their lives because of mounting debts and declining incomes. The couple had taken loans from banks, micro-finance institutions, relatives. They hadn't been able to meet their modest needs from their farm income—they had a 3-acre rain-fed plot on a hilly tract adjoining the village. They were Banjaras, the nomadic tribe known once for their primary occupation as cotton transporters. They had two teenaged sons, who migrated to a city to work as daily wagers in order to support the family, but the mountain of debt still proved to be too much.

For the scores of farmers attempting suicide, a few survive. Ramrao did.

In early April 2014, Ramrao and I have our first meeting. It is around 2 in the afternoon—the sun is belching heat, the kind one swears will cook an egg if one did crack it open on a tar road. A week from then, eleven revenue districts spread over two administrative divisions in Vidarbha with some 2 crore people would cast their votes in the Lok Sabha election that would see Narendra Modi rise to power. I see anger and frustration all over the dusty countryside where cotton is often referred to as 'white gold'.

Hiwara—actually Hiwara Barasa according to census records—shows no hint of election fervour. Men and women here have other worries. Torrential rains accompanied by hailstorms in January partially damaged the standing winter crop. Not all farmers in the village have the luxury of water to plant a winter crop but some do. The previous year, an erratic and uneven monsoon had caused cotton and soybean yields to take a hit, pushing commodity prices down. And within five years of a ₹59,000 crore loan waiver doled out by the United Progressive Alliance (UPA) government at the Centre, cotton farmers are back to square one. They have defaulted on bank loans, thousands are in the grips of informal moneylenders, and farm incomes are in free fall, further aggravating the socio-economic problems of rural households.

Having survived his suicide attempt, Ramrao doesn't stop talking. It is as if he has been waiting for me to come, sit down and listen to him.

'Why should I live? You tell me. What is left in my life?' he says.

Ramrao's bitter, defiant tone stems from a deep depression afflicting his mind and heart. Aware that he isn't fully out of it, I nod in agreement as he spews anger. He is bitter that providence has been unfair to him.

'Since childhood I have been suffering.'

Standing in a corner, Suman, his younger sister, stares at us, clenching her sari's pallu, feeling helpless at her brother's misery. Two years younger than him, she has come from her village in Jagtial district, Telangana, to support him. Ramrao's elder daughter, Alakya, was with him until the last evening; she left for her husband's home in Telangana's Adilabad district but will be back with her father soon. Anuja, his younger daughter, got married the previous year to a young farmer in Hiwara's big landholder family, the Bolenwars. Vimalbai, Ramrao's wife, died of a prolonged illness in 2012.

Suman is filling in for Alakya as Ramrao can't be left alone. Anuja drops in through the day. It has only been a couple of weeks since he returned home from hospital. With big eyes, long, thick hair and a fair complexion that contrasts her brother's, Suman shares a special bond with Ramrao.

Two young men are sitting on the bed to my left, staring at us, not saying a word, just quietly listening to our conversation. I don't know who they are. A village is like an open house. You can't stop people coming in and going out of your home here, especially if there has been a death or a near-death event. Everyone is family.

Ramrao lives in a thatched hut he managed to raise along the walls of his elder brother Ashokrao Panchleniwar's concrete house just before Alakya's wedding in 2011. He could only afford to cement the floor. He couldn't build the brick walls, he had no money left. So, he put up bamboo thatch held up by round and thick wooden logs to split the space into two rooms and covered it from all sides. The house has a tin roof. Two beds, a rusty cooler, two plastic chairs, a few personal items—there isn't much else. The other room is sans sunlight, so it is dingy and dark.

Ramrao is wobbly and impatient. One moment he sits in a brown plastic chair, the next he stands up. He is not stable. I gently force him to sit down, take a deep breath and talk. He obeys.

'I WAS EATING AN orange,' Ramrao says, straining his memory.

'Any particular reason?' I ask, curious.

'I felt like eating something sour, I don't know why,' he says, recounting in an incoherent manner what happened that fateful morning when he came perilously close to death. If the farmers who died by suicide could speak to us about the moments leading up to their death, I think they would sound a lot like Ramrao does at this moment.

The day he consumed poison was Holi, 17 March 2014, a Monday. The night before Holi, villagers had lit a bonfire symbolizing the torching of the demoness Holika and the burning of all societal ills. The next day, they celebrated the festival of colours, which also signals the end of a farming season. That day, the week-long Bhagavata Saptah, the programme retelling myths about Lord Vishnu's incarnations, including the Shri Krishna Leela, was ending. It had been a few years since Hiwara had hosted a kirtankar, a balladeer, for this event leading up to Holi. For the village, this religious event served both as entertainment and a way to salvation.

Ramrao was lucky. By some chance, four people were on the spot when it mattered the most. Bhaskar Hiraman Chahare, Ramrao's regular farmhand, was passing by when he was inching towards death.

Ramrao points to one of the two men sitting to my left. 'He is the one—Bhaskar,' he says. Bhaskar, an unlettered, slim but sturdy man in his late-thirties belonging to the Gowari tribe, mostly a landless community whose traditional occupation is to rear livestock, stares at me and feigns a smile. The other man sitting on the bed with Bhaskar is, I am informed, a visiting relative of his neighbour's. He is here for gossip.

Sadhana, the petite, talkative but doughty wife of the carpenter-cum-electrician Waman Jagtap, was in the front yard of their recently reconstructed house opposite the Hanuman temple, hanging laundry.

Anuja's matrimonial house was a few yards away from the temple.

And the only auto driver in the village, Pramod Nellawar, a landless Marathi- and Telugu-speaking, tall, well-built man in his forties, had not yet set out for the day. He was getting ready for work. Pramod ferries commuters from the surrounding villages to the town of Pandharkawda in his nine-seater for a living. He has driven at least a hundred farmers from around this village to hospital in similar situations and, barring two or three of them, most survived the suicide bid. He has been, in a sense, a saviour of sorts. He had recently bought the new auto—people in this part of India call the vehicle Dukkar, or pig—on a loan.

'I woke up early,' says Ramrao, trying to piece together the chain of events. It was still dark. He took a bath and went to the Hanuman temple to offer his morning prayers. From there he walked back home, wore his cotton bandana and headed for his farm. His farm, which lies across the main road skirting the village, surrounded by a teak and shrub forest, is a five-minute walk from his home. That's his routine: Wake up early. Bathe. Go to the temple. Head for the farm. Return in an hour to the cattle shed. Give fodder to the cows and goats. And go home for an early lunch. After his wife passed away and his daughters got married, his considerate neighbour, a landless Gond household, feeds him and in return Ramrao pays them some money every month.

Ramrao had been under immense strain. It had been another bad kharif season, made up of poor yields and abysmal monetary returns. When he reached his farm that morning, he spotted the temple cow—he had reared her as if she were his own—trapped in the wired fence, electrocuted.

How did the cow reach there? He has no idea.

He had erected a temporary fence in the middle of his field to protect his green gram and vegetable crop from wild boars. In January, hailstorms had destroyed the crop partially, but he had turned it around with hard work. The village is surrounded by a forest, and herds of wild boars and blue bulls often stray into farms at night and devour the crop. Farmers have had to resort to shocking measures to keep the animals away. One of these is to attach a hook on the electric lines and steal power to electrify their fences. Animals get an electric shock when they come in contact with the fence and run away. At times they die, trapped in the fence. But farmers do it to teach them a lesson. They bribe the foresters to turn a blind eye and bury the animals without a fuss. Indian wildlife protection laws are strict and people may end up in prison if they are caught on the wrong side of the law. The region is also tiger territory, with a wildlife sanctuary close by. The wild cats pass through the farms at times.

'The night before, I had switched on the electricity to keep the wild boars away from my green gram and brinjals, but the temple cow got stuck in the fence instead and died,' Ramrao says.

The brinjals were ready for harvest but prices in the market had collapsed. Ramrao decided he would pluck them in a few days, hoping that the prices would recover. The green gram crop, sown on a few acres of his leased land, was reasonably better and could fetch him good returns. It would help him repay part of his outstanding loans.

He is overcome by the guilt of accidentally killing the cow. 'I could not stand that sight. I had committed a horrible sin.'

The event pushed him over edge. He had lost his wife to a prolonged illness; her treatment costs had bled him dry. His daughters' weddings had further drained his savings. For four years, crops had been below par and he owed a lot of money to his creditors, most of whom were his friends and relatives. The wretchedness was too much; life had lost meaning, he says.

Feeling light-headed at the sight of the dead cow, Ramrao scurried back home. He passed by the huts of the Kolams, a particularly vulnerable tribal group found only in this part of Maharashtra, and then the Zilla Parishad school, with its beautiful playground and five decorated classrooms, which was closed on account of the public holiday. He went straight to his shed—a mud-floored, tarpaulin-covered dingy storage space opposite his home, across an open yard, where his family had once lived and where his farming implements were stored now. The barn gave off a putrid smell—a mix of fertilizers, seeds, chemicals, dung, dirty clothes, shoes, rubber and farm garbage. 'I sat there, thinking.'

The sun had come up. He heard the splashing sounds of women cleaning their courtyards with water. People were starting their day. Reeling under the guilt of what had happened and the unrelenting burden of loans, he wanted to destroy whatever was left of him. He had never even deliberately killed an ant. How could he accidentally kill a cow? In a flash he remembered his dead wife, daughters, friends, relatives. He owed most of them money.

'What would they say? *Karu ka nahi karu?* Should I or should I not do it?'

He finally turned his anger inwards. That is perhaps what most farmers go through before they kill themselves—anger and helplessness, then the violence turned inwards.

'Angry?' I ask. 'Why? With whom?'

'I don't know. I don't know if it was anger or guilt or both. I could not save my wife. I could not educate my daughters. I could not repay my loans. And I feared seeing my friends and relatives, asking for their money back when I have none.'

Standing in that seedy barn all alone, confronted by the dilemma of whether to kill himself or not, a medley of thoughts ran through Ramrao's mind. Talking about those fervent moments, he gets agitated, even now. Perhaps if somebody had been around to talk to him in that moment, he wouldn't have done what he did.

'I grabbed a bottle of insecticide and drank all of it.'

Ramrao felt a slow burning sensation envelop his body as the liquid chemical slithered down his throat.

'Then I felt very cool. As if there was ice melting in my stomach.'

He describes the sensation but cannot remember the taste.

'Then I swallowed the second bottle.'

Two 150 ml doses of Coragen, an insecticide meant to be sprayed on his standing brinjal crop. Two bottles, dissolved in two large drums of water, would cover 2 acres. He had bought the expensive chemical on credit only the previous day from Kashinath Milmile, an agriculture inputs dealer in Pandharkawda whom I have known for years. An ever-smiling man in his early sixties and an agriculture graduate of the late 1970s, he advises farmers on crop and pest management. Vidarbha in general and Yavatmal in particular are a high input-consuming region, where farmers, irrespective of the size of their landholdings, aggressively use expensive chemicals and fertilizers in the hope of higher yields from the medium-quality soil.

'Two bottles!' I exclaim.

'Just in case the first one did not accomplish the task.'

Ramrao's quip is in line with the searing dark humour that is characteristic of the Vidarbha countryside. I am reminded of a farmer's blunt reply to a fact-finding team of the erstwhile Planning Commission that came on a tour of Vidarbha in March 2006. One of its erudite members asked a group of farmers in a village in Wardha district, 'Why do you consume alcohol? Why do you drink so much?' An old farmer present at the gathering shot back, 'You can't drink Monocrotophos neat!'

Ramrao cackles at his awkward joke, which lightens the mood. I notice Bhaskar shaking his head in disapproval. He didn't like the joke.

'*Bas, peun taklo.* I just swallowed it,' he says this to me in a self-deprecating manner, as if his life had little value.

'Then?'

He had sat in the shed, his mind calm, not knowing what to expect.

'I waited for my death.'

I feel a distinct sense of unease when he talks about waiting for death. In those moments he had been all alone, tired and deeply sad.

After a while, he stepped out of the shed and went home, where he picked up oranges from the kitchen and walked towards the Hanuman temple for one last darshan before death embraced him. Bajrangbali had always been his go-to deity. The small temple is a few hundred metres from his home. He walked past the Bolenwars' old sprawling house, now his daughter Anuja's home. It was a three-minute walk.

Four alleys converge at the temple, behind which is the community hall that has been under construction forever. When donations flow into the collection box, a few bricks go up here and there.

At the temple he gonged the bell, folded his hands before the deity, and no sooner did he turn back and trudge a few steps than he collapsed. 'After that, I don't remember anything.'

SADHANA WAS THE FIRST one to see Ramrao fall, in front of their home, an unplastered structure of bricks with a sprawling front yard, guava trees standing on both sides of the bamboo gate. She used to run a shop opposite the temple but had shut it down because they made no sales. That mud-brick structure has now partially caved in. Sadhana thought Ramrao had fainted. Maybe, he hadn't eaten. She stopped her chores and ran to him.

Ramrao was babbling, but he seemed listless. Sensing something was wrong, she raised an alarm. She called her husband, who hurried out, wondering why she was shouting. Waman saw Ramrao lying on the road. He tried waking him up and was able to make him sit up, but Ramrao was not in his senses. He was foaming at the mouth and his body was jerking. It looked like he was nearing his end.

Bhaskar, who was walking along, noticed the frenzy and came running. He spotted his employer; a white fluid was oozing out of his mouth. He noticed a familiar strong odour, putrid but heady. Bhaskar was supposed to spray Coragen on Ramrao's vegetable farm that afternoon. He suspected Ramrao had consumed it.

Time was the crucial factor. If Ramrao did not reach the hospital in time, he would not survive. This was an emergency for the entire village. Hiwara had already lost two farmers to suicide.

One had hung himself from a tree in his fields, the other had consumed pesticide. Ramrao was a beloved figure in the village, a good Samaritan, he couldn't be allowed to die like this. For Bhaskar, nothing was more important than saving the life of his shet maalik, the farm owner. Ever since he was a child, he had worked on Ramrao's farm. Ramrao had looked after his family—wife, three daughters, a son—like they were his own.

'I came running to inform Ashok bhau.' As he recounts those tense moments, Bhaskar's eyes grow bigger.

Ashokrao had felt his heart pound when he heard his younger brother had consumed poison and collapsed. He had been sitting on the swing, sipping tea. He had seen him step out just a few minutes ago. Ramrao had not left for his farm like he did every day. It was 7.30–8 a.m. when he saw Ramrao exit the gate. He knew his brother had financial worries but he hadn't noticed anything particularly wrong with him that day. He assumed his brother was headed to the temple for the Bhagavata Katha. Ramrao attended it on all days without fail. The katha started at 9 a.m. Ashokrao thought Ramrao went there early that day to help with the puja arrangements.

Bhaskar rushed to call Pramod Nellawar and asked him to bring his auto to the temple.

Next, he ran to inform Anuja. She had just started her day. When he broke the news to her, she began to tremble. But she quickly regained her composure, changed and rushed to the temple, where a barely conscious Ramrao lay surrounded by villagers. His daughters were aware of his unpaid loans.

There was a flurry of activity as the village woke up to the news of what Ramrao had done. It is a small village after all, just about a hundred or so households. Anuja's husband, Suraj, a nephew of Munna Bolenwar, an old activist friend of mine, quickly intimated his uncle in Pandharkawda over the phone. Munna had connections everywhere—in the hospital, in government offices.

Ashokrao, Anuja, Bhaskar and Pramod were by Ramrao's side in minutes. By then, Sadhana and Waman had got a few more people to help. Pramod and Bhaskar lifted Ramrao into the auto; Ashokrao sat inside holding his unconscious brother. Anuja insisted on coming along and sat holding her father from the other side, sobbing uncontrollably. Before stepping out, Ashokrao had instructed his son Pravin to follow them to the tehsil hospital on his bike as he might be required there. Pravin, a short, introverted, soft-spoken man in his late twenties, recently married, had changed his job the previous month. He had moved to the Godrej company after working as a farm inputs salesman for seven years. With a diploma in agriculture, he knew most agriculture products.

Pramod started his auto and raced towards the town of Pandharkawda. Throughout the journey, he kept chatting with Ramrao, asking him to stay awake and hang in there. He repeatedly assured Ashokrao that they were about to reach the hospital. Ramrao, though, couldn't hear him.

The upgraded tehsil hospital is on the outskirts, about 12 kilometres from Hiwara. One has to cross seven small villages, inhabited by marginal farmers of all castes and creed, to get there. The road is flanked by cotton and soybean fields on both sides and, by mid to late March, they stand barren or are bursting with cotton stalks.

Meanwhile, Pravin went looking for clues at Ramrao's shed. He wanted to find out what his uncle had consumed—that crucial information could help doctors administer the right antidote to him. He saw two empty bottles of Coragen lying on the floor by the door. That confirmed his fears. He wasted no time in calling the higher officials of his company in Yavatmal, seeking their help. He then telephoned Alakya, Ramrao's elder daughter who lived with her husband Rahul Ranganeniwar in Adilabad. She and her husband immediately left on their bike for Hiwara, 50 kilometres from Adilabad. A distraught Alakya began praying for her father, hoping he would survive the calamity.

Ramrao's body kept jerking and he kept foaming at the mouth all the way. Munna was at the hospital, coordinating with Ramrao's brother and nephew. Once there, the doctors made Ramrao vomit most of what he had consumed—they pushed a long tube down his mouth to empty his stomach. Stomach wash or gastric lavage is an important first aid in cases of pesticide poisoning, a standard operating procedure. The doctors then advised to shift him to a better equipped centre—the district government hospital 90 kilometres away in Yavatmal. The doctors at the cottage hospital assured Ashokrao that his brother had a very good chance of surviving.

Within an hour of reaching the tehsil hospital, where the doctors did not have the necessary antidote, Ashok, Pravin and other villagers were on the road to Yavatmal in an ambulance, with Ramrao battling for his life. Tensions heightened further when, near a village called Jodmoha, it suddenly seemed like he was slipping away. For Ashokrao, it felt like an arduous, never-ending journey. Pravin's colleagues had alerted the doctors at the Yavatmal hospital and explained about the patient who would reach there soon.

Ramrao was admitted to the ICU on the fourth floor of the vast hospital. The doctors administered atropine doses to him after repeating the stomach wash procedure. By late evening, his vital statistics stabilized and his blood reports suggested he was out of danger. The doctors told the family that Ramrao would be kept under observation for two days.

The Yavatmal district general hospital gets poisoning cases every day, most of them cotton growers or farm labourers from across the district or neighbouring ones. After all, it is a region notorious for farmers' suicides. Ramrao's case was no exception. More than a decade ago, when farmers' bodies started pouring into the hospitals across Vidarbha and rural Maharashtra due to suicides, the Maharashtra government passed a resolution to keep mortuaries in rural hospitals open round the clock to facilitate quick post-mortems and handing over of bodies to their families.

The poison that raced in his veins had not been flushed out completely yet but Ramrao would be okay, the doctors told the worried family members, who were relieved to hear the update. It had been a long, tortuous day for all of them—twelve eventful hours. But Hiwara had managed to save one of its own.

Back in the village that evening, villagers burnt the Holika, symbolizing the end of all ills. The Bhagavata Katha was over too. The following day, no adult in Hiwara celebrated with colours; only the children played Holi.

'WHY DID YOU DO it?' Alakya asked her father when he seemed a bit settled. She was upset with him.

He was exhausted. 'How did I survive after consuming two bottles of pesticide?'

The company perhaps sold him adulterated insecticide. He was going to sue them, Ramrao jokes again.

This time Bhaskar smiles.

'It was a close call. *Mamla bighadla hota ji*,' Bhaskar says. He speaks Varhadi, which in these parts has a strong Telugu influence. 'The case was about to be shut.'

With Ramrao indisposed, it is Bhaskar and a few other farm hands who are tending to his farm. They harvested his green gram and brinjals, sold them to the traders and handed him the money after keeping their wages. From that income, he will repay a small chunk of his loans.

Ramrao got the necessary medical aid in time. Not many farmers are as lucky. He came back to his senses after twenty-four hours. The first thought that struck him while staring at the ceiling fan of the ICU after regaining consciousness was his debt and his lenders. He had borrowed more than he could repay. He had borrowed it for his farm, for the treatment of his ailing wife, whom he was not able to save. He had drained out his assets during the weddings of his two daughters. He was completely broke.

'How much do you owe?' I check with him.

'₹25 lakh or so!'

When a farmer's average debt of a hundred thousand rupees is defined as a crushing burden, this is a stunningly high amount.

Ramrao asks me to follow him inside. I do. He opens an old almirah. I glance at the framed photo of a woman that rests on the only table in his house. That's his departed wife, Vimal. A few steel utensils and other household items lie scattered on the floor. The house clearly belongs to a struggling farmer of modest means.

From the top shelf he removes neatly tied bundles of paper. Four of them. These are unpaid bills, he tells me, owed to inputs dealers. Bills he has not been able to pay off in years—of seeds, chemicals, fertilizers, pumps. He then reaches out to a register and hands it to me, prodding me to find a long list of lenders and how much he owes them. I flip through the pages. Some entries are in Marathi, others in Telugu—names, dates, amounts—in his neat handwriting. Ramrao is uneducated but not unlettered. It seems to me he has exhausted his options.

He shakes his head in disbelief. 'It's a lot of money to be repaid,' he says.

Ramrao's finances, it seems, went astray the way his life did. He could no longer support his exigencies from his farm income. He can't sell his farm. Nor does he have any other assets.

Suman, listening to him patiently, mutters in both Marathi and Telugu that things will get better. Her eyes never leave him. 'No one is pushing you to pay up immediately,' she tries to reason with him again. 'They all know you won't ditch them. You are an honest man. You will pay back every dime you owe them.'

'I won't die with unpaid debts. Maybe,' Ramrao says intently, 'God wanted me to return to the mortal world to pay my bills.'

THE QUESTION IS HOW he will repay his loans.

He asks me, nervously looking at the register, 'How do I clear my burden?'

He does not want to farm again. He has no zeal left to do the same backbreaking work that he has been doing all his life. He can't sell his land to repay his debt because there are some legal problems with its title.

We sit in silence, pondering over Ramrao's piercing question. Bhaskar and the other man are watching us. I avoid eye contact with him; I have no answer to his question, only more questions.

A few moments pass.

'How did you get into this mess, Ramrao?' I ask.

Ramrao takes a deep breath and sighs. Staring outside the door, he folds up his green lungi, tucks it into his waist, and starts talking.

2

ROOTS

RAMRAO IS FIVE-FEET-FIVE, STOUT and well-built. The shape of his face resembles a pentagon, his skin the colour of wheat. His palms are rough and heavy. Farmers' palms are alike—rough, with blurred lines—a sign of the gruelling heavy labour they do every day. Like most of his fraternity, he wears modest clothes—usually dark-grey pants folded up to his knees and a bush shirt. When I first met him, he had a beard growing on his face and looked a bit scruffy. But since then, I have never seen him dishevelled again. Whenever he steps out of his home, he wraps a cotton cloth around his head and ears as protection from the sun, wind and dust. When he walks, he swings his hands—almost in a rhythm. Even in his despair, he still has a sharp sense of humour. He never stops laughing at himself or cracking jokes at the community of farmers.

A kind man, Ramrao has no enemies in the village. Almost everyone you meet likes him. Villagers call him 'Shuddhatma', a pure soul. The women, especially, are rather fond of him; he is like a brother always ready to lend a helping hand. He often enquires about their health and well-being, whether it is Meenabai, his farmhand, or Ushabai, a woman whose son suffers from schizophrenia. He detests male chauvinism and gets furious when inebriated men beat up their women; he is himself a teetotaler.

Born into a very poor family, Ramrao remembers going several days without eating a good, satisfying meal in his younger days. This was during the 1970s and '80s, when villages in this part of the world weren't connected by all-weather roads, bullock carts were the only mode of transport, and life moved at a snail's pace. There was no hurry. Nobody had anywhere to go.

Ashokrao is the eldest of the siblings. Ramrao has two sisters: the elder Sulochana and the youngest Suman, with whom he shares the strongest bond. The two sisters married into landed families and live in Telangana. All of the siblings were born two years apart, in Hiwara. Ramrao lost his mother, Vatsala, when he was about ten. He hardly has any memory of her. His father, Narayan, died after he got married. The two brothers rarely talk about their parents and have no photographs to remember them by. After the father died, the sisters took over the household duties. They cooked, cleaned and helped with farm work before Ashokrao got married and brought home a wife, who then took charge of the responsibilities.

Ashokrao took to farming at fourteen. To keep the household running, he tilled farms for big landowners and also cultivated their poor-quality land. He got married when he was eighteen, and within his clan. They needed a woman to cook for him and his siblings and, of course, to look after the old man. Vimal, his wife, must have been fifteen then. Dark, slim, with curly hair and an affable smile, she has glasses now. Despite appearances she isn't very old, neither is Ashokrao, but the backbreaking work that they have done throughout their lives has taken a toll on their faces and their bodies. Ramrao's wife's name was also Vimal. The two brothers addressed them as vajnya, the elder one, and mardalu, the younger one, until the latter died in 2012.

Ramrao learnt farming from Ashokrao but the two brothers rarely talk with each other now. When they do, it's usually in short, staccato sentences, spoken mostly in Telugu. Ramrao does not look directly at Ashokrao when they interact, maybe out of fear or respect.

As a child, Ramrao remembers eating mahua flowers or its soup in summers when they didn't have any rations. They would bring handfuls of edible greens from their rain-fed farm, where they grew cotton and pigeon pea. In the years when they had good rainfall and the black soil held the moisture until October or November, they would plant green gram. Those were the days, Ramrao remembers, when farmers still used their own seeds—desi varieties of cotton, lentils or sweet sorghum. Hybrid cotton was not yet heard of and genetically modified seeds were not on the horizon. Farmers coated their seeds with cow-dung before sowing them. They believed it helped them get high-quality cotton and shoo away unfriendly pests. On an acre, they would harvest two, sometimes three, quintals of cotton. They would eat the farm-fresh greens with coarse jowar or bajra rotis.

Once the monsoon receded, their farms would turn dry and barren and then that would not be possible. The two brothers would go foraging in the surrounding forest with their cousins or friends to bring home wild greens, vegetables and fruits that were in abundance then. The village forests—which once had bamboo, teak and a variety of flora and fauna—have now diminished, felled for money by the villagers and stripped off their natural wealth for decades by the forest department. School was out of question. None of the siblings went to school after seventh class. But both Ramrao and Ashokrao can read and write well.

'Dada would tell me do this and do that and I would do it, without asking any questions,' Ramrao says. The elder brother was both father and mother to him. Summers came and went, so did winters and rains. Life in Hiwara was one uninterrupted cycle. There was little change. The hut never got a touch-up, the blue tarpaulin did not get replaced, the only thing that remained constant was their small plot of arid land and the daily grind.

There was no fun in his life, Ramrao says with remorse. 'I only thought of the farm and nothing else.' Even today, Ramrao gets restless reliving his growing-up years.

When he was thirteen or fourteen, Ramrao went to Nagpur with the help of a fellow villager and worked as a cleaner on a truck for a year. Things had become so dire that the family felt it would be better if Ramrao went to the city to work and remitted money home. The older acquaintance worked in Nagpur, the Orange City, that was once the capital of the Central Provinces and Berar and Vidarbha's major industrial and textile town. Ramrao took his help to find work there. He got food to eat and free lodging; he lived and slept in the truck, which transported building materials.

That whole year, he roamed all over the country loading and unloading goods, working to the bone. But Ramrao soon got bored of a trucker's life. He yearned for his village, his people. Most of the other truckers drank a lot and slept with sex workers, but Ramrao was different. He was—and remains—a sensitive man with a modest lifestyle. Drinking and swinging did not fit into his idea of life. He tried drinking, he ate meat, but he drew the line at women. Eventually he got tired of that life and returned to his native village to lend a helping hand to his elder brother.

'It was a good experience,' he says, recalling those days. 'It taught me a lot. But I did not like city life and I did not make enough money to send back home.'

Once he returned to Hiwara, he picked up the plough and decided to turn the barren, boulder-riddled land that fell into his share fertile and green.

I MET RAMRAO BY chance, thanks to an activist friend. Bhimrao Atram was insistent I meet Ramrao in Hiwara. Since the late 1990s, I had visited Hiwara several times but had never met Ramrao or his family. Two previous suicides, one of a young Yelmi man who was related to Ramrao and another of Chakkarsingh Bais, a Thakur farmhand who had migrated to Hiwara some years ago, had taken me there. I was investigating the cause of these suicides. Later, in 2009, Mrs Bais, a frail but talkative woman in her late fifties, was fielded as a candidate in the Maharashtra legislative assembly elections by the Vidarbha Jan Andolan Samiti (VJAS), a farmers' movement in south Yavatmal led by activist-politician Kishor Tiwari, to draw the attention of political parties and policy makers to the problems of farm widows. Bais bai went on to win a few hundred votes.

A large map of Vidarbha hangs on the wall in Tiwari's VJAS office in Pandharkawda town. For Hiwara—which falls in the Fifth Schedule of the Constitution, marked by a majority of tribal population—and most villages in its vicinity, Pandharkawda, one of the oldest cotton markets in south Yavatmal, is the nearest major town. 'Pandhar' in Marathi means white and 'Kawda' implies cotton. It got its name from the blooming white cotton that farmers around the town grew for ages and brought in cart loads to the local markets. Historically, the town has been an important cotton trading centre in south Yavatmal, which did not have a textile mill but had several landlord families owning endless tracts of cotton fields which were tended to by the downtrodden families, many of whom came from Andhra Pradesh and tribal communities. Entrenched then was a barter system: men got a monthly wage of ₹50 and 50 kg of jowar for all the backbreaking work they did on the fields; that came to less than ₹2 a day.

The map in Tiwari's office is marked with dots all over. These represent the areas where farmer suicides have happened. I have been to many of these farm suicide households in villages scattered all over Vidarbha. Activist and office boy Santosh Naitam has been doing a peculiar job for almost twenty years. A chronicler of sorts, he enters in a register the name, age and other details of farmers who have died by suicide, often collating the information from regional newspapers. The VJAS has ledgers containing year-wise records of farmers whose suicides were reported by newspapers. Around this town, there are hundreds; in Vidarbha, thousands.

Over time Bhimrao and I became friends. I first met him around 2000 during a trip to Pandharkawda for a story on the cotton crisis. A Gond tribal, Bhimrao is a short, well-built man with reddish eyes and sharp features. He has a keen nose for news, and even though he is unlettered he knows the local politics better than most people. He is like a bird that flies from one field to another, keeping an eye on everything without being noticed. He brings small bits of information to Tiwari, a Brahmin by caste whose father came to this cotton-trading town way back in the 1960s to set up the local unit of the Jan Sangh, the political offspring of the Rashtriya Swayamsevak Sangh (RSS) from which proliferated the Bharatiya Janata Party (BJP).

Tiwari calls himself '*Devane dhadlela garibacha manus*', a poor man's friend sent by God. His politics revolves around the native adivasi communities, mainly the Kolams, and the peasantry, and he is both friendly and unfriendly with all the political parties. His elder brother, Anil, was Pandharkawda municipality's chairman for a very long time and commands influence in local politics. In 2014, when the BJP rose to power both at the Centre and in Maharashtra, the new chief minister, Devendra Fadnavis, made Kishor Tiwari chairman of a task force to look into solutions to tackle the long-prevailing distress in the worst-affected districts of the state. After a point, though, it was largely perceived as a BJP ploy to keep him in good humour and reduce the trouble he might otherwise cause the government. Through the first decade of the 2000s, Tiwari had brought the issue of farmers' suicides to national attention with his dogged media campaigning and unsparing criticism of government policies which in a way politically helped the BJP and the Shiv Sena, the main opposition then, to keep the ruling alliance of the Congress and the Nationalist Congress Party (NCP) under constant pressure.

Tiwari the BJP–Sena government's offer to head the task force thinking he would be able to do something useful for the farmers. He would later quit the post just before the Maharashtra assembly elections of October 2019, disillusioned with his own government He then joined the Shiv Sena.

Kishor Tiwari's presence in Yavatmal has been important for the farm widows, though. Often, he helps them with their financial problems and children's education, roping in generous donors willing to support the families in the crisis. The widows see in him a saviour brother, a moral support. They go to him whenever they are in trouble and, over the years, he has steadfastly stood by their families.

Bhimrao, father of four sons, sometimes brings juicy gossip, but most of the times he is the bearer of serious news. Whenever I am in Pandharkawda, he usually accompanies me to the villages. He is someone who takes me beyond the realm of a 300-word news report and introduces me to the real rural world. The moment he told me about Ramrao, I got curious. Bhimrao has a way of telling a story that generates curiosity and captures your attention.

'He consumed a full bottle of poison and survived. God knows if that's because of luck or adulterated insecticide.' These company-wallahs sell anything, he said, to make money. '*Sale thye gadhyayche mut suddha aushadh mhanun viktil*,' he said, bursting into laughter with a twinkle in his eyes, his hearty laugh baring his yellowish teeth. The farm-input companies can even sell donkey's urine as an insecticide.

That morning, we were driving to Chalburdi to meet Lacchu Patel. A dark-skinned figure in his mid-fifties, with big blood-red eyes and chubby cheeks, Lacchu—today a very rich man—is his pet name. No one knows him by his formal name, Laxman Ramanna Bolenwar. He takes weak cattle from hard up farmers and nourishes them to good health before returning them to their owners. This is his way of earning 'punya', or good karma, he told me. He spoke in Hindi with a Telugu accent. 'He accidentally killed a cow,' he said, as if explaining Ramrao's attempt to take his own life.

Ramrao struck me as a survivor I had to meet. Once we were done meeting with Lacchu, we headed for Hiwara.

'*Nahi bhau, tho paar karjat gadla ahe*,' my go-to man averred as we drove. 'He is completely broke and in debt.'

The truth is that either or both reasons could have been the trigger. As I discovered, the accidental death of the temple cow for which he considered himself responsible was the straw that broke the camel's back, but his suicide bid was a sum total of all those factors.

RAMRAO IS A YELMI, a close-knit landed community also known by the name of its clan deity, Velamma. They claim to be Rajputs. You find them in Telangana and the contiguous districts of Yavatmal and Nanded in Maharashtra. Most Yelmis in Hiwara have blood relatives in Telangana. Nine decades earlier, Ramrao's great-grandfather migrated to this part in Yavatmal from the erstwhile princely state of Hyderabad during a famine and worked on a local landowner's farm as a farmhand. He was a bonded labourer, or so goes their family legend.

India was on the verge of Independence when Ramrao's grandfather moved to Hiwara, then a small, sleepy hamlet in today's Jhari Jamni tehsil in the southern part of Yavatmal, after spending a few years in the neighbouring village of Chalburdi. Vidarbha was feudal; big landowners belonging to the Kunbi caste reigned over its social, political and agricultural structures. They still do—the reason they are addressed with the suffix of Patil.

Hierarchically, the Kunbi Patils are lower down the caste ladder, coming below the 'superior' Deshmukhs and Marathas, the subedars of the Bhonsles and the warrior clan respectively. The late Panjabrao Deshmukh, the agriculture minister in the first cabinet of Prime Minister Jawaharlal Nehru in 1952, who hailed from

Amravati, made sure that the Patils clearly mentioned their caste as Kunbi in their domiciles—this later helped them draw the benefits of reservations under the Other Backward Classes (OBC) category. The Kunbis fall under the rubric of OBC despite a majority of them being erstwhile landlords. A number of them retain a high social standing even today because of their long legacies in different parts of the region. However, most of them, irrespective of their landholder status, have today fallen on bad times. Tens of them have committed suicide or migrated to cities for work.

The steep economic and social downfall of the Patils and the massive exodus of landless OBCs, Dalits and adivasis from villages across Vidarbha post liberalization have gone hand in hand. Farming is non-lucrative, risky and too volatile. New services—food, real estate, financial institutions and even small trading—attracted landless farmers and provided them assured wages and proved to be more remunerative than working on farms round the clock.

Hiwara is a settlement of OBCs, Gonds and Kolams, an impoverished and particularly vulnerable tribal community that you find only in parts of Yavatmal, Wardha, Washim, Nanded and Hingoli districts. Yelmis you find only in the Jhari Jamni and Kelapur blocks of south Yavatmal, around the reserved forests. Legend is that Yelmis came from what is now Telangana, crossing the Godavari and then the Painganga during famines. They found the soils here similar to theirs and the local landlords welcoming. Following in the footsteps of Ramrao's grandfather, his brothers and cousins came to Hiwara and settled in the small hamlet. Some of Ramrao's direct and distant relatives live here and in the neighbouring villages and till their fields.

Chalburdi, a large village near Hiwara and a political epicentre of this region, had a big Patil landowning family, that of Krishnarao Patil, who was a member of the Maharashtra legislative assembly for many years in the 1960s and '70s and a Congress satrap greatly respected for his generosity. Ramrao's landless father—who reared sheep, goats and cows—worked on an annual wage and was among the farmhands taking care of the landowning family's vast swathes of cotton fields, some of which spilled into Hiwara, where a part of the Patil family had its palatial home, or Vada in local parlance. Big landlords in Vidarbha lived in majestic bungalows with pure teak windows and heavy doors which their owners would oil every Diwali when cotton was harvested—the seeds would be crushed and oil extracted while the white lint went to the ginning and spinning mills. Most Yelmi families that migrated here from the neighbouring southern states settled as farmhands taking care of the Patil lands. Even the Bolenwar family in Hiwara did the same, but in time became part of the legislator's trusted inner circle.

When Prime Minister Indira Gandhi brought in the land ceiling act and put a limit to how much land one could own—18 acres irrigated and 54 acres non-irrigated—Krishnarao Patil donated large swathes, mainly the degraded kind, to his farmhands instead of forfeiting them to the state. In a similar way, Vidarbha's landlords managed to keep large tracts of their lands intact and within their closed circles. This region was and remains a rain-fed, dry-land agricultural area unlike the western parts of Maharashtra, where old and new dams transformed thousands of acres of once-dry land into prosperous sugarcane fields and orchards. During that phase, Ramrao's father got about 10 acres of rain-fed, low-grade land, categorized in the administrative ledger as 'B-class'. Lands that got distributed under the land ceiling law could not be sold or purchased (until a Maharashtra government fiat in 2018 annulled that condition to bring long-awaited relief to the owners of such lands).

Ramrao's father was the eldest of his siblings. Then Laxmanna was born—now in his mid-seventies, he lives down the alley at the main square in Hiwara. Laxmanna once told me that his father actually bought their mother from her father and married her. When I asked him why, he told me that such was the poverty at the time that marrying a girl away meant losing the cheap manual labour she contributed, so men wanting to marry her needed to provide adequate compensation, a bride price, to her parents.

'Of course, it has all changed now.' The abject poverty of his childhood is a thing of past. Laxmanna believes that the younger generations through the decades have made a relative difference to their lives. When I asked him what had changed, he thought it over and said, 'Zameen.' They now owned land and over the years had managed to turn it productive.

Laxmanna has grown old, tough as betel nut, his rough palms and aching knees bearing testimony to his arduous life. He is very close to Ramrao, and when the latter tried to end his life the old man was crestfallen for days. Ramrao gives him small amounts in cash from time to time to buy liquor, one of the reasons why Laxmanna, I reckon, is so fond of his nephew.

Ramrao had two aunts, both of whom have passed away. One of them died around the time he tried to commit suicide. She had no children and would often lend him money to help him during times of financial strain. He owed her a couple of lakhs, and her old husband keeps checking on the status of that loan. But he never comes to Hiwara to demand the money; he knows he shouldn't be pushy. For a few months after her death, Ramrao sulked that she had died worrying about him and he was responsible for giving the old woman sleepless nights. That was not the case—age had finally caught up with her.

DEEP BLACK COTTON SOILS, rocky terrain and a teak forest make up the land in and around Ramrao's village; Hiwara falls between the Painganga and the Wardha river basins, an area that is replete with coal, iron ore and other minerals. In the Vidarbha region, Hiwara is a small village with a population of about a thousand people, 250 households and 75 per cent literacy.

Vidarbha has about 15,000 of Maharashtra's 48,000 village or gram panchayats, some of them with 10,000-plus population and traditional marketplaces that are suffering in the face of the burgeoning urban economy. Western parts have 8,000 villages; once predominantly cotton-growing, these villages now also grow soybeans.

The Painganga river, 50 kilometres south of Hiwara, flows further and merges into the majestic Godavari. This—the part on the edge of the Deccan—is a fertile cotton-growing belt, almost like the large swathes at the foothills of the Satpudas, where soils are so rich that they once earned Vidarbha or Varhad the metaphor of being a Golden Axe—so goes the Marathi saying, '*Varhad, sonyachi kurhad*'. For ages, cotton ruled and yet, as the respective district gazettes show, never occupied more than 40 per cent of the total cultivable land before Independence.

Yavatmal has a bustling population of Banjaras, a community categorized as a Nomadic Tribe in Maharashtra, and as a Scheduled Tribe in Andhra Pradesh and Telangana. The Banjaras, among the farmers using new farm inputs aggressively today, were mainly the cotton transporters—they carried cotton in their bullock carts, a system which was affected after the British laid railway lines.

In his book *Cotton and Famine in Berar*, Prof. Laxman Satya of Lock Haven University in the US discusses the checkered past of the region before and during the colonial period. Based on the accounts of travellers, he writes:

> The long trails of the Banjara carts originated from Purna valley and traversed in all directions carrying the famed *Oomra* cotton on their back—from Kartik (November) to Vaisak (May) of every year. Then when monsoons began in June, the mundane rhythm of the agriculture cycle year after year created a culture of its own which was quite unique to Berar. People were content, with lowly needs and small wants.

It was to transport cotton and teak that the British built railways here. During the American civil war in the nineteen century, they transported the 'white gold' to Bombay and Calcutta and from there to the Manchester and Liverpool textile factories. The remains of that railway infrastructure laid by Killick, Nixon and Company, set up in 1857, is the Shakuntala Express, the narrow-gauge train which still runs from Yavatmal to Badnera in Amravati, chugging through white-dotted cotton fields along the way. The railway tracks, otherwise idle, serve as a reminder of the raw cotton exports that fired the British textile industry, conquered global markets, filled the coffers of the Raj and, in the early twentieth century, animated Berar's textile mills.

After the 1970s, cotton acreage grew in Yavatmal and much of western Vidarbha mainly due to the introduction of the Monopoly Cotton Procurement Scheme (MCPS), a state intervention that was lifted in 2002 after three decades. The farmers grew cotton and the Maharashtra government, through its cotton marketing federation, bought every pound of it, made bales and then sold it to millers. The government bought cotton at the minimum support price (MSP) from the farmers and transferred profits after marketing it. The share in profits that farmers got from the federation was commonly called 'bonus'. Carts filled with cotton would line up outside the federation-run temporary cotton procurement centres all over Vidarbha before Diwali and the marketing season would continue late into March or April. Yavatmal was the epicentre of the cotton trade.

The idea was to develop a cotton-to-cloth chain in the region so that the value addition would stabilize the markets and expand the economy, but that remained a dream. Not only did Vidarbha fail to develop such a chain, it actually lost through the 1980s, '90s and the first decade of the 2000s whatever it once had—booming textile mills from Nagpur to Khamgaon to the west of Akola on the Mumbai–Nagpur route, and handlooms in the eastern parts of Vidarbha, from Nagpur to Gondia. With the processing sector collapsed, Vidarbha cottons lost their economic lustre. This had much to do with a new textile policy of the mid-1980s which incentivized powerlooms and a more decentralized and technologically advanced cotton processing. The emergence of powerlooms generally spelt doom for the integrated textile mills across India from the mid-1970s to the late 1990s. The Empress Mills in Nagpur—the historic textile mill of the Tatas, India's oldest—the Pulgaon cotton mills of Wardha district, and the textile mills of Khamgaon in Buldana district, all crumbled in the face of the emerging new disintegrated textile sector, fired by the cutting-edge automated technology, and stiff global competition.

While the textiles shifted to southern and western India, Vidarbha saw its textile sector bow out. Reticent trade unions, mismanagement by mill administrations, the inability of farmers to produce better-quality cotton, a visionless local leadership that refused to see the switch in the national and global economy, and generally the failure of the state government to bring about the necessary changes in the region's cotton-to-cloth process cumulatively meant that the old system of the processing industry—from ginning and spinning to yarn and garments—steadily folded up.

From the mid-1970s, western Vidarbha saw cotton monocultures being reinforced. The fields saw a sharp decline in jowar, or sweet sorghum, and horticultural plants such as mangoes, guavas and custard apples that would bring seasonal, if small, incomes. Cotton, the cash crop, nudged out food crops, largely also because the local food crops such as millets became non-remunerative, the public distribution system did not expand to include locally grown food crops, and farmers' growing financial needs pushed them to plant cotton, and subsequently soybeans, from the turn of the century on all of their fields as cash monocrops. This contributed slowly to the humanitarian, ecological and economic crisis that now goes beyond farmers' suicides.

In 2002, when the MCPS ran into huge losses, they were a result of international markets being flush with better-quality, cheap cotton imports. Between 1997 and 2004, India imported over 7.5 million cotton bales, more than its cotton imports in the preceding forty years. In 2004, the Vilasrao Deshmukh-led government discontinued the scheme and opened the cotton market for private buyers, limiting the cotton marketing federation's role to market intervention in case prices fell below the MSP announced by a central government agency called the Commission for Agriculture Costs and Pricing (CACP). The decision was forced by the shrinking coffers and other structural adjustments the state government had to make post liberalization.

Since that year the federation has barely procured even 10 per cent of the cotton Maharashtra grows, which stands at around 8 to 9 million bales, or 35 million quintals of cotton. Vidarbha grows around 3 million bales, or 10 to 11 million quintals. The 2013–17 five-year average for cotton area in India during the kharif season (July to October) was around 13 million hectares, a staggering figure when compared with the average of 8 or 9 million hectares a decade earlier. Maharashtra grows cotton on about 4 million hectares, a fourth of it in Vidarbha. The irony is in the abysmal per acre productivity of cotton in Vidarbha—a mere 146 kg as compared to Punjab's 800 kg per acre, according to various reports of the Cotton Corporation of India, the CACP and others. The reason: barely 3 to 4 per cent of Vidarbha's cotton area enjoys protective irrigation from ground or surface water sources, a fact underlined by several studies. The remaining 96 per cent or so is purely dependent on rains or, in some cases, where farmers have dug wells, groundwater.

Cotton is one of the few commodities for which the central government announces an MSP below which a buyer can't procure the produce, a price shock absorption mechanism to protect growers. The prices rarely fall below the MSP but the catch is that the support prices don't bring large dividends. They are no more remunerative, and prices are now linked with the global markets that are flooded with heavily subsidized cheap cotton from the developed world. Ditto for the other crops, including soybeans that Vidarbha farmers started cultivating as an alternative to cotton from 2002.

Yavatmal receives an average of about 800 mm of annual rainfall, enough to replenish its water sources, make its seasonal rivulets flow and keep the cotton smiling on farmlands. If it rains the way it should, Ramrao's well that he dug some time in 2007 or 2008 gets filled to the brim and he can fetch water by a bucket tied to a small rope. You can't grow any other crop in the absence of protective or canal irrigation and cotton is the only option for thousands of small and marginal farmers in the entire region. And in recent decades, the monsoon has become moody, non-uniform and at times furious. 'Crazy,' is how Ramrao puts it. In Marathi, he calls it 'Yeda'.

A stark statistic that shows how the fortunes of cotton have changed over the decades: in the 1970s—the decade of successive droughts in most parts of Maharashtra—the value of ten grams of gold equalled the price of a quintal or two of cotton, but that's a bygone era. Today a quintal of cotton is ₹5,500, while the price of ten grams of gold hovers at around ₹50,000.

3

LONELY

RAMRAO AND I ARE chatting on a languid day in May 2015. Since first meeting him in April the previous year soon after his suicide attempt, we have had regular phone conversations and I have been to his home on several occasions.

Every time, he has looked and sounded depressed.

Health problems can have debilitating effects, not only on the patient but the entire household. And if you happen to be a farmer, healthcare costs can tear your family apart. Farmers in Vidarbha have had to sell or mortgage their lands to foot spiralling medical bills. Even a viral fever epidemic could leave a village in tatters, as I saw during the chikungunya sweep of 2005, when several people died in the countryside all over Vidarbha. The more fatal the illness, the more severe the distress. Several national and local studies have termed health exigencies and private healthcare spending as a contributing factor in aggravating the agrarian crisis. This drew a policy response from the central government when the Manmohan Singh-led UPA rationalized rural health programmes to launch the National Rural Health Mission (NRHM) to improve the rural health apparatus and cut skyrocketing healthcare costs. But it was not enough. And of late, in stark contrast to the concept of universal healthcare, the BJP governments at the Centre and state have pushed for private, insurance-driven healthcare.

Vimalbai suffered from multiple illnesses. She inherited chronic asthma and later developed kidney complications that ultimately proved fatal. For years, Ramrao spent huge sums on her hospital stays and medicines, looked after her at home and brought up their two daughters but could not, as he laments, give them higher education. A large part of his borrowings was to pay the fat healthcare bills incurred at private hospitals in Yavatmal.

'If she were healthier, we would have been better off,' he once rued.

From 2000 to 2006, when Vidarbha's farmer suicides multiplied, Ramrao remembers his financial status being that of an average farmer's. The 2008–10 period even brought him good luck. Those were the best years for his farm and of his life.

'In 2008, my loans got waived off,' he vividly recalls.

That year, then Union Finance Minister P. Chidambaram announced a much-anticipated total loan waiver scheme in the Union budget, just a year before the UPA went into the 2009 Lok Sabha elections. The alliance comfortably returned to power, riding on the goodwill it had generated among the nation's peasantry with the waiver of outstanding bank loans and other important interventions to augment rural incomes. In fact, that decision had been prompted by vitriolic farm protests in Vidarbha and other parts of India.

In 2006, Prime Minister Manmohan Singh had toured Vidarbha and a few other regions that reported a high incidence of farmer suicides to draw up a strategy to mitigate the crisis. He was unequivocal in admitting that rural India was in a deep, deep crisis and farmers' suicides were a national shame. His visits yielded a series of policy steps for about three dozen districts spanning five states, including Maharashtra, with six of the districts in Vidarbha. There was a generous raise in the support prices of agricultural commodities, including cotton—the prices that year went up from ₹1,980 to ₹3,000 a quintal—and a total loan waiver, apart from money being pumped to augment irrigation projects in dry-land Vidarbha.

However, the Centre resorted to quick-fix schemes and programmes rather than providing a long-term plan for the rural peasantry. It undertook the guarantee of repayment of the outstanding loans of farmers as the Reserve Bank of India (RBI) asked nationalized and cooperative banks to erase all outstanding farm loans from their ledgers and make the indebted peasants creditworthy once again.

Ramrao had some ₹50,000 to ₹60,000 worth of outstanding loans waived off, got fresh loans at lower interest rates, and sold his cotton at a rate he had never earned in his entire life as a farmer.

With good monsoon backing and the slew of farmer-friendly policies, 2009 looked rosy. And buoyed by that year's success and his drive, Ramrao and his farm were on song the following year—2010 is etched in his memory as though the year was the pinnacle of his hard work and love for farming.

'I took every single farmland around me on lease.'

Cumulatively, he calculates, about 150 acres.

Momentarily, Ramrao looks happy as he travels down memory lane, looking as if he would want to live every day of 2010 again.

With optimism that he hadn't allowed himself ever, Ramrao aggregated small lands in 2010 and paid a lot of money as rent. The future of his two daughters, who would soon be of marriageable age, was on his mind and he knew he would need money.

'Karru Soyam's 30 acres, Ghagru Kinnake's 10 acres, Arjun Kinnake's 10 acres, Yadgirwar saheb's 30 acres, Nilesh Panchleniwar's 10,' he goes on listing the people whose farmlands he leased that year. 'Jhambai Pendore, she came to me and said—Ramrao, why have you left out my land, what have I done wrong? So, I took hers too—3 acres … then, my farmhand Fulabai also asked me to help her cultivate the land, so I said okay, let us do your land too … Bhimrao came, Bhimrao Tekam, he lives in Borgaon, and told me, "Ramrao, I am old and unable to work my land, I heard you have taken Jhambai's land, will you take mine too? I need some cash for my health," so I decided to till his land too.'

Vimalbai, he says, cautioned him, for she thought it was too much of a burden. But that year he was in a mood to go all out.

'*Juyat rahte na, sappa paise takun dete, tassas.*' Like in gambling, he threw everything he had in the pot.

'Why did the other farmers not want to cultivate their lands? They also must have gotten a loan waiver,' I check with him.

'Some of them did, but a lot of small farmers did not have bank accounts or funds to cultivate their lands. Many of them or their children had left for the cities for work because they got better wages there, so most of the old farmers didn't have the labour to till their lands—I mostly cultivated such lands.'

The catch was that the banks lent money only for the land in your name. For the leased or rented lands, Ramrao had to borrow money from private lenders at higher interest rates.

Farming is non-remunerative, he insists with a significant look, his tone that of a tired man. Farmers, particularly the dry-land ones, have actually been losing money in whatever they cultivate and harvest, their debts have grown, their agricultural income is in constant decline.

While we are talking, Bhaskar steps into Ramrao's home. He looks exhausted, his shirt is dirty, his hands look blackened and his pants are wet. As he settles into a plastic chair, he greets me and informs Ramrao that he has come from the cowshed. With Ramrao still in no state to work, Bhaskar tends to Ramrao's cows and goats. He feeds them, bathes them, collects their dung and piles it along the shed—this is to be spread on the farm when monsoon starts.

Ramrao gives Bhaskar water to drink. When he is done, he wipes his mouth and says, 'It is very hot outside.'

Vidarbha summers are gruelling. Temperatures hover around 48 degrees Celsius for days in the summer months. In any case, this region has only two seasons, people joke: one, summer, the other, harsh summer. Winter is a myth and monsoon brief; it is as if the clouds cover the flaming sun only for a moment.

'Tell him to get back to work,' Bhaskar butts in, smiling at me. 'I have to shoulder all of his.'

Ramrao shoots back, 'Did you try killing yourself? I did! And in any case, you rarely worked in the past.'

Chastised, Bhaskar falls quiet, embarrassed at being scolded by Ramrao in front of me. But, he is too thick-skinned to take it to heart. Ramrao asks him the real reason why he has dropped in and Bhaskar begins to nervously shake his legs.

'*Thode paise hayet ka?*' he finally asks Ramrao if he has some money in a low voice.

'*Thye pay beta, mayee ithe jindagee down hay, an tu leka paise mangte,*' Ramrao scolds him for asking him for money when his life is down, but he goes into the kitchen and brings two ₹100 notes and hands them over. Bhaskar is happy with the outcome, never mind the dressing down, which he is used to.

Pocketing the money, he tells me to keep Ramrao in my thoughts—'*Laksha dya mahya mansa kade,*' he says—and looks visibly happy. He is going to buy some ration for his home.

Bhaskar's Gowari community in Vidarbha is traditionally known to look after the village livestock; they call themselves the descendants of Lord Krishna. He considers Ramrao a man with a pure soul, someone who was sent to earth to care for the lesser mortals like him. Much later, one day, Bhaskar tells me Ramrao never got bogged down by loans but was burdened by the struggle of his life. Bhaskar did not go to school, he got married when he was sixteen or seventeen. He has four kids—three daughters and the youngest one, a boy, who is three years old. 'You wanted a boy,' I say to him accusingly once and he blushes.

Bhaskar lives in a shanty opposite Ramrao's cowshed, with a compound built from farm waste—stalks, thorns, bamboo and wood—and has few belongings in it. Still the family looks happy and noisy. His three daughters are ebullient, always playing with each other or with their chickens. His wife, Jyotsna, is a shy woman, doing household chores, and when not home, she is working at someone's farm. Ramrao initially employed Bhaskar on an annual contract, but got tired of his drinking, gambling habits and his stealing from the farm, and fired him.

Bhaskar says his mind is wobbly. He wants to quit drinking and smoking, he unfailingly makes a vow every night. The next morning he breaks his own vow, drinks and smokes with his village friends, fritters away his time, money and energy on his addictions, but quickly feels remorseful as soon as the high wears off.

'Tell that to your heart and not to your mind. Think of your four children,' Ramrao reminds Bhaskar, who smiles ruefully, knowing well that things won't change.

Bhaskar gone, Ramrao returns to his story.

'So, in 2010 I took a hand loan of ₹10,00,000 from a friend, repaid all his loans that year and made a windfall gain of ₹10,00,000.' He produced 200 quintals of cotton, 200 quintals of soybean, 70 quintals of tur, or pigeon pea, 70 quintals of groundnut and 40 quintals of jowar.

'I hired twenty labourers that year to work round the clock. I paid ₹6,00,000–₹7,00,000 in wages alone. That year, I never left the farm. Vimal and I would come to the farm early and go home late. Alakya and Anuja would be home all day managing the domestic chores. Vimal took care of the women labourers and I would go from one farm to another, overseeing operations. All my farmhands too worked very hard.'

Ramrao reaped a bumper harvest and matching returns. That year, cotton, soybean and tur prices had risen high, riding on an impetus and bullish national and global demand. China was importing cotton, Europe needed the soya de-oiled cakes for its dairy, and tur was rallying because India had imported less amounts of it that year and domestic production was good enough to meet local consumption.

As 2011 dawned, Ramrao was flush with cash. Out of nowhere, Alakya received a wedding proposal. She wasn't even seventeen yet but Ramrao and Vimalbai decided to accept it. Vimalbai was ailing, she did not think she would live long enough to see her daughters' weddings. Bending to her mother's wishes, Alakya agreed to tie the knot while she was still officially a minor.

In May 2011, she got married to Rahul Ranganeniwar, ten years older than her and known within family circles in Telangana.

'When she left, my problems started,' he says.

In early 2012, Vimalbai fell seriously sick and passed away.

'That year, I was farming 65 acres. Vimal died in June, and I suffered big losses later that year. I had spent a lot of money settling hospital bills and most of it was borrowed.'

In 2013, Ramrao adds, Anuja married the eldest of the Bolenwar siblings. Munna's elder brother came asking her hand in marriage for his son, Suraj. They did not want any dowry, so he agreed. For the wedding he borrowed more from his aunt and other lenders, including his brother.

With Anuja and Alakya married and his wife no more, Ramrao suddenly found himself all alone.

'I had spent all I had and borrowed even more. I was neck-deep in debt but I was sure I was going to be able to repay it.'

Then, in early 2014, extreme hail and rain partially wrecked his green gram crop sown on 45 acres of land in the winter sowing, after cotton and soybeans had come a cropper earlier in the monsoon of 2013. Ramrao's losses burgeoned.

His daughters' weddings had cost a few lakhs, his wife's medical bills had drained him to the tune of ₹5,00,000 to ₹6,00,00, and the woes on the farm front—prices weren't picking up, the monsoon played truant, yields dropped—did not seem to abate. Continuing losses can be lethal and deeply frustrating.

'Loans, losses, loneliness,' he says in an indignant tone, 'had a terrible impact on me. They brought back all the terrible memories of my childhood struggles, the crushing poverty.' It made him wonder if his life was even worth living. And deep down in his being, the idea of taking his own life was sown.

THREE SLIM BOOKS LIE on Ramrao's iron bed, the only one in his two-room house: *Bhakt Hanuman* by the Gita Press, *Shani Chalisa* and *Shriram Raksha*. He reads these handbooks when he is alone and has some quiet time. He picks up *Shriram Raksha*, flips a page open and reads out a verse; he has to wear his spectacles to read it. His pronunciation is poor but I can follow what he is reciting. He hums the lines, building a rhythm. He perhaps picked up the style of reciting these verses from someone else but didn't manage to learn the language, Sanskrit.

'I get inner peace when I recite it,' he says, putting aside the booklet, removing his glasses and tucking them into his shirt's pocket.

Ramrao has a small library of religious books in a corner of his home. In that space, he also has books on rural life, farming, organic farming, small pamphlets on successful farming models. He has collected them over the years, gifted by friends, relatives or postmen, who come to him and spend hours chatting about their personal lives or trading gossip. On the thatched walls he has pasted a few photos of his daughters and granddaughters.

Ramrao reads the booklets when he feels lonely and finds himself sliding into the abyss of depression and anxiety. 'They bring me relief,' he says.

To see him talk normally and move around is reassuring. He seems better, maybe even finally ready to go back to his farm. But in the coming years he may not lease any land other than farming his own.

I ask him, 'Through the years, how much cotton have you grown? How much of lentils? How much sorghum and the vegetables?'

'*Bappa Bappa ... Hishobach nahi tyaycha!*' He can't make an account of it. Plenty, he says.

Take this: An acre of his irrigated farm yields at least 8 quintals of cotton. A quintal of cotton yields 34 kg of lint, the white pulp from which you make thread. A kilogram of lint yields 8 metres of cloth and, at 2 metres per shirt or pants, you can weave 4 pairs of shirts and pants from a kilogram of lint. That's roughly 1,088 pairs from one acre. A quintal of cotton also yields 64 kg of cottonseed, from which you can get 12 litres of cottonseed oil, and de-oiled cake that is sold as protein-rich cattle feed. From an acre, you get 96 litres of edible oil, several kilograms of de-oiled cakes as export-quality cattle fodder and over a thousand pairs of shirts and pants. Add 8 or 10 quintals of lentils. Plus, sackloads of vegetables, groundnut and sorghum in winter. For a quintal of his cotton, Ramrao gets between ₹5,000 and ₹6,000, but the traders and ginners who buy it make at least three times more after the initial processing. As it passes through the value chain, the raw cotton appreciates at least twenty-four times in value. The primary producers like Ramrao are the only ones who suffer losses, while all other players in the chain make a killing. He puts in a lot of sweat, money and water and yet, every year, ends up a loser.

RAMRAO IS TAKING A walk through his barren farm—a stretch of undulating land that he owns and which is now lush with tall weeds that are swaying in the breeze. Lost in thought, he is quiet. I watch him from the shade of a large fig tree that separates his farmland from his friend Gunwanta Golemwar's 7 acres. It's a contiguous stretch of land.

For many years, Ramrao has been cultivating his friend's farm as if it were his own. Golemwar went to school, then to college and got himself a clerical government job. He is older than Ramrao but the two share a strong bond. The open well on Ramrao's farm also at times irrigates Golemwar's fields. Post retirement, he settled in Yavatmal city, about a 100 kilometres from Hiwara. He invests in his 7 acres and Ramrao cultivates it. The deal is that Golemwar keeps the produce and Ramrao earns the labour and management costs. That farm is also fallow.

In the neighbouring village of Borgaon, Ramrao has been leasing a farmland for more than two decades. It was owned by a tribal farmer, Ghagru Kinnake, who died in an accident a few years earlier. That piece of land has no protective irrigation but is fertile. It lies untilled this year because Ramrao is depressed and unable to find the will to work.

Another 45 acres owned by an agriculture department official in Yavatmal is managed by four people, including Ramrao, but this year he is not in the team. The officer has apparently amassed a lot of wealth over a period of time, including vast stretches of farmland. He gives Ramrao an annual salary of ₹40,000–₹50,000, lower than the going rate because Ramrao owes him a lot of money. The man is in his fifties and a junior officer in the district agriculture office. He is the man Ramrao turns to if he needs cash for a sudden domestic or farm exigency and is never disappointed. In return, Ramrao has been overseeing the cultivation on his vast lands like a trusted lieutenant. Until

2013, he and his friends would lease the land and pay an annual rent. Then the officer began to invest in his crops after the villagers told him they could no longer lease his land and invest in it. He now hires Ramrao and a few others as managers. It will be years before Ramrao and others in the team are able to free themselves from the arrangement.

Ramrao is clearly worried. He is bankrupt. His Central Bank account at Pandharkawda has zero balance—not even a few hundred rupees to his name. He owes a lot of money he would like to repay but he is presently frozen, unable to get going, staring at another season of barrenness which is disastrous for a farmer like him. He needs to gather the courage to go back to his roots, his farm, his brother privately tells me.

But how? In May 2015, he is undecided whether he will cultivate his farm the coming monsoon. His stomach aches, he has no appetite, he looks down and out. He eats frugally, a chapati or two, some subzi, at times dal-rice. He has his meals quickly and does not like spending much time on them. The food his Gond neighbour sends him every morning and evening goes uneaten on occasion. He covers it with a plate and throws it away with a heavy heart after having a couple of bites.

'Even if I want to farm, I can't,' he tells me. He has no cash and is terrified at the thought of borrowing more.

'Tell him to get back to work so that he remains busy,' a worried Ashokrao tells me.

RAMRAO'S ATTEMPTED SUICIDE DID not become a police case. But a talathi, a village revenue officer, did come enquiring about him and his debts when he returned home from the hospital. The talathi collected information about Ramrao—his land size, the extent of his loans, etc. Ramrao and his family did not know why he came or what he did with the information. It was around 2007 that the Government of Maharashtra decided not to register police cases in attempted suicides by farmers. Every farmer suicide, though, is investigated not only by the police but also by the revenue and cooperation department in Maharashtra to find out if it is an outcome of indebtedness or other factors.

After surviving a near-fatal event, Ramrao is going through a lull—he does not know how long it will last. His elder brother and sister-in-law are worried. They reason with him to get him out of his depression and persuade him to start working. Anuja, who gave birth to a baby girl six months earlier, drops in often so he is not lonely, but Ramrao is in such a sullen mood that he won't move. He feels happier when he plays with Anuja's baby. The moment she leaves, he is back in his deep, dark place.

A few months on, the farms should have been awash with green dotted with white—white cotton bolls dangling from the plants almost the height of a six-foot man. By this time, pigeon pea, planted as an inter-crop to cotton, also gets in shape. You see one row of lentils planted after every two rows of cotton. Some peasants sow tur and cotton in alternate rows. All other farms around his fields are on the verge of harvest: cotton, soybean, tur. A kilometre from here is his friend Chinu sheth's chilli farms. They will be ready for harvest by March but the plants look healthy, lush with foliage. The agriculture official's lands too are flush with cotton, soybeans and lentils.

But Ramrao, stuck with his problems, is unable to get going. Physically too, he is still very weak. It could probably be a psychosomatic issue.

We are at the end of October 2015, just ahead of Diwali—a year and a half has passed since the suicide attempt. In his home, he is alone. On his farm, he is lonely. I have met him several times in between but found him deep in his cataclysmic depression. I give him a lot of pep talk but it is futile. I call him often to check on how he is getting along, but his low, slow voice does not inspire confidence.

The summers of 2014 and 2015 were very quiet for him. This is a phase in his life that looks like an endless tunnel without light. He did not celebrate Pola or Dussehra or Diwali for two years. Two rainy seasons went by. India saw a change of governments in New Delhi and in Mumbai. Scores of farmers continued to commit suicide—three a day in Vidarbha, one in thirty minutes in India. Several thousands, as usual, migrated to the towns and cities. About 2,000 farmers quit farming in India every day. Some 7.5 million did so between 1991 and 2011, according to the census reports of 1991, 2001 and 2011. How many more quit farming in 2010–20 we will know in the 2021 census report. The mundane routine of the countryside remains unchanged, though in the cities and across India people feel the 'messiah' in New Delhi is going to catapult the country to dizzying heights of prosperity. 'Achchhe din' is the new mantra among the middle classes and the nouveau riche. Narendra Modi became prime minister in May 2014. The same October, Devendra Fadnavis became Maharashtra chief minister. The BJP is well ensconced in the seat of power, both in the Centre and the state, driven by Modi's unprecedented popularity.

Ramrao, however, is light years away from the euphoria and the rhetoric. This kharif season he did not till or sow crops on his farm nor lease any land. Last year too, he did not farm. In June this year, he thought of planting cotton on at least an acre or two but later abandoned the idea for want of money. He could not borrow more. He stopped seeing a doctor long ago but takes the medicines prescribed by one last year for his stomach problems.

'These days,' Ramrao sighs as we settle down under a tree, his face bearing a painful but significant look, 'I come to my farm every day but don't have the heart to pick up from where I left off.'

This farm, a once-substandard land that he made rich and productive by working round the clock for years, has been his world and yet he is unable to re-immerse himself in it.

'This is the first time I've kept my land fallow.' There is regret in his voice.

He is on a soliloquy again. I observe him up close for the first time—a man done in by the weight of his challenges, his will sucked dry by the turmoils on his farm and at home.

'It is inauspicious to keep it fallow, I know, but what to do!'

Last year he was sick. This year he simply doesn't have the guts. He would need a minimum of ₹1,00,000 to keep his land occupied with crops. Where will that money come from when he has ₹25,00,000 in unpaid debts? And what's the guarantee of recovering his investment? Keeping land barren is to a farmer what keeping a factory idle is to an industrialist. The scales may differ, but the consternation that comes with such a spectre is the same.

Also, families depend on you for wages or must find work on a new farm. Ramrao usually provides work to at least twelve men and women throughout the year. He employs them for planting seeds, removing wild weeds, spraying fertilizers and insecticides, then to harvest the crops and to take them to the markets when they are ready to be sold. He must prepare his land and fix it from time to time, for which he needs labourers. Farm labour is integral to farm operations, so he must look after their financial and family needs ever so often. With all his farmhands, mostly Kolams, Ramrao shares a personal bond.

'I kept it fallow because that is better than losing more money.'

The burden of the loans he has to repay weighs heavily on his mind. This burden is not the same as defaulting on a bank loan. Of his debts, institutional credit is only a tiny fraction. A majority of his loans are from his close and distant relatives, friends and other informal sources that he won't reveal but I can see his anxiety. None of his lenders is pushy, but Ramrao is nervous.

'They helped me when I needed the money,' he reasons. 'How will it look if I don't repay it when they are desperate for it?'

Ramrao's scruples make him suffer. He is aware that if he is unable to repay his loans, there are relations that will turn sour, his social standing will be impacted, and he might lose his community's and his moneylenders' respect.

Banks are beyond him anyway; for them, he is a defaulter.

Ramrao is grateful to his lenders, who have not come knocking. They know what he has been through. In fact, they reassured him and asked him not to worry about the money. Other, less fortunate, farmers in Vidarbha have taken their lives after being hounded and harassed by moneylenders or bank officials. Stories of lenders exploiting farmers in the region abound.

When the Democratic Front government in Maharashtra found itself in the dock over the farmers' suicide issue in December 2005, it needed someone to pin the blame on. The then deputy chief minister, the late R.R. Patil, picked the sahukar, the moneylender. He even went so far as to say that policemen should skin those found to be usurious. Soon, hundreds of so-called sahukars were behind bars, many of them small-time lenders, marginal farmers or petty workers who lent money to farmers instead of keeping it in a bank. They came out of jail as quickly as they were put inside; the police could not build cases against them. It was just a stunt by the government to buy time. But there have been a few instances of vigilante justice against unscrupulous moneylenders.

During my travels, I found innovative ways of borrowing and lending in Hiwara and other parts of the region. I am sure there are several such means in every part of rural India.

Similar to a kitty, there is a rotating financial pool called 'bhisi', where farmers pay a certain sum of money every month and draw lots to decide who among them will get the entire sum. Sometimes they juggle multiple bhisis. At times, the winner of the pot auctions it off to the highest bidder in case he does not need the money immediately but someone else does. So, farmer 'X' can buy a ₹10,000 bhisi for ₹8,000 and suffer a loss of ₹2,000.

Then, there is 'alti-palti', where you basically rotate your loan, borrow more to pay the previous one, and then keep borrowing to pay smaller, older loans. This is usually resorted to for paying back bank loans. Some call it 'khande-palat', meaning switching the burden of a loan from one shoulder to another. Another way to raise money to meet financial exigencies is to borrow someone else's gold and mortgage it with a jeweller, and then pay interest to both.

Micro-finance is also popular. In rural Vidarbha, farmers call it 'Janlaxmi-Dhanlaxmi' after the names of micro-finance companies. At least a dozen such institutions lend small sums to women, who borrow simultaneously from multiple companies.

Of late, rural housing finance has steadily been gaining popularity. Hundreds of farmers who have pawned their farmlands and other assets with multiple sources have begun to mortgage their homes to receive funds under the garb of home renovations, which they then funnel into their farms. Then there are other creditors—teachers, revenue officials, relatives, inputs dealers, traders, doctors—who lend money to farmers at exorbitant rates.

ON 10 DECEMBER 2015, when I drop in to meet Ramrao, he looks like he is in much better shape. But I have just met two families who have lost their men, both farmers, to suicides. Moreshwar Choudhary was thirty-two, Suraj Bhoyar twenty-nine. Two days earlier, on 8 December, distraught over their failed crops and unpaid loans, both of them consumed Monocrotophos. In the dingy mortuary of the government hospital in Ghatanji town, about 45 kilometres from Hiwara, Suraj's body was being taken in for a post-mortem when Moreshwar's was moved out. It became the saddest of meeting places for the two families joined in grief that stemmed from a common thread: cotton.

Moreshwar was uneducated and married; he left behind a one-year-old son and a wife in the middle of her second pregnancy. Suraj had a vocational diploma and was a bachelor. The two never met each other but their short lives ran parallel to each other and ended on the same note. They died in their villages 30 kilometres apart within the span of a few hours. The monsoon that year had arrived after the crops had failed. And when the abysmal yields began to flood the markets in November, cotton and soybean prices fell drastically.

As in the previous two years, owing to a bad monsoon and the resulting crop failure, 2014-15 witnessed negative farm growth, a fact established by the Maharashtra Economic Survey tabled on

17 March 2015 in the legislative assembly. Half of Maharashtra faced drought and crop yields of less than 50 per cent. The 2015-16 financial year is also proving to be bad. What's new is that while the yields are low, commodity prices aren't rallying. That is because China curbed its imports in 2014 as it gave a greater incentive to its growers to improve yield and quality, as a result of which Xinjiang province, where the trial subsidy was implemented, yielded a bigger harvest last season. Though China imported much of India's cotton the last three seasons, it did not do so in 2014 and 2015, affecting demand and therefore prices. With demand not picking up in domestic markets, it resulted in a glut despite the fall in cotton yields in states like Maharashtra.

Suraj and Moreshwar were a casualty of that glut and of the lack of quick intervention by the central and state governments. Ramrao shakes his head in disgust when I narrate their stories to him.

'If I were dead,' he says sardonically, 'there would be a story, but I am of little significance now that I am alive!'

Ramrao is alert to suicides by farmers in and around his village and generally in Vidarbha. He has closely seen two suicides in Hiwara. Nilesh Panchleniwar, Ramrao's nephew, suffered from a mental illness, but Thakur Bais was trapped in a vicious cycle of loans. I remember meeting both the widows long ago. Ramrao has been helping Nilesh's widow to manage her farm after his death. But this year she is on her own since Ramrao is indisposed.

Farmers have been dying in hundreds all over the district—young and old, small and big, women farmers, even children, unmarried men, married men, OBCs, tribals, Dalits. Death has seen no difference. Ramrao personally knew many of them around Hiwara. They succumbed like wilting leaves, Ramrao says like a poet. 'It was wrong of me to try to take my own life,' he says and falls silent.

'THE PROBLEM LIES HERE, there, everywhere.'

Ramrao sees a problem with farming—in its faltering ecology and economics. He didn't have lofty aspirations but even his family's modest ones could not be met from his farm income. Life in the village is hard, so no one wants to stay on any more, but moving out means living in small towns and cities where one will disappear in the swelling crowds, never to be acknowledged or seen again. If left to their volition, no one wants to farm.

He thinks there is no single reason that made living difficult. There are plenty of factors, some old, some new. In a nutshell, he earns a pittance while his expenses are ever burgeoning.

'Whatever I grow, whichever way I grow it, I end up a loser.'

He needs money for his everyday domestic needs, but the farm only yields an income once or twice a year and that is not assured. It fluctuates. And if you are a small farmer with a rain-fed farm but no dairy, no livestock, nor any allied income sources to feed into your finances, you cannot make enough to meet your minimum needs. Vidarbha's farmers are mostly like this—people with only one source of income, their farms.

'The households with somebody in government service or a job where they have an assured income are doing well,' he tells me.

One of his friends has a son working as a forest guard. It is the smallest post in the department but he gets a monthly salary, an assured income, and the family suddenly looks better than the rest of the households in the village.

There are years, exceptional years, when you make profits, the way he did in 2009 and 2010. But the norm is you end up with big losses most years. It's a cycle: it repeats like the seasons, except the period of profits.

Gone are the times when farming was a lucrative occupation. In the twenty-first century, farming has fallen on bad times. Family farming—small, marginal farms of up to 1 or 2 hectares of land—is the only mode of sustenance and livelihood for several families. Those who depend on the monsoon and do not have assured canal or groundwater irrigation and those who grow cash crops are among the most vulnerable farmers in the country. That's over 80 per cent of India's farmers, according to all available records, including the agriculture census of 2015, the annual economic survey reports, or the annual handbooks of Indian agriculture. Indian farms are small, fragmented, non-remunerative, unsustainable and rain-fed—a recipe for farmer distress, a structural cause for a low growth rate and high migration. But small farms produce the bulk of our food, cotton and flowers. Every year India produces more, yet farmers end up with loans and losses.

As P. Sainath succinctly puts it: 'If we superimpose the maps of agrarian distress, rain-fed family farms and poverty in India, they will all match.'

Vijay Jawandhia, a farmer leader in Wardha and one of the founder members of the Shetkari Sanghatna, once defined farming as a profession that has fallen from glory. 'Today farming is like *sau ka saath karna, aur baap ka naam chalana*. You turn a hundred into sixty, only to continue with your parental legacy.' Those who continue farming, he said in one of his speeches, must live on because they can't dare die.

Ramrao failed in his bid to kill himself, so he has to carry on and repay his debts even if he cannot bring himself to resume farming just yet.

By 2000, Ramrao began to lease patches of farms around his village, apart from cultivating his own. He needed to aggregate land to produce more, to earn more. He is not alone in his village or around the country doing that—leasing land in the hope that he will produce more, earn more. Millions of farmer households do exactly this to earn enough to meet their needs and wants.

At the turn of the new century, Ramrao could not afford to buy more land, and the small, impoverished farms mostly owned by the tribals in and around Hiwara were unable to tend to their own lands. The rising costs of energy, seeds, fertilizers and higher wages meant they had to rent their lands and earn their livelihood by working as daily wagers either in the village or in towns. This is a trend not just in Yavatmal or Vidarbha but all over India: farmers cultivating leased lands in official parlance are called as tenant farmers.

In 2000, he tilled his own 5 acres and leased 10 acres from villagers who would otherwise keep their lands fallow. The annual lease rents would typically range from ₹2,000–₹3,000 an acre. Rents were that low. If he made losses, sometimes the land owners would not demand any rent from him. After all, the tenant had tried to grow something but failed. The land owner's idea was not merely to earn rent but to also keep his land occupied and green.

For a decade and a half, the phenomenon of leaving farmlands fallow has been on the rise. A study by the Chennai-based M.S. Swaminathan Research Foundation in 2008-09 found that 17 per cent of cultivable lands in Wardha district were deliberately kept fallow because the owners felt it was better than bearing losses in cultivation. The study was indicative of what's happening across the countryside in many regions of India.

In that sense, Ramrao was not alone in his decision to leave his land fallow that year, though he was made lonely by his crippling depression.

4

SNAPSHOT

I MET RAMRAO SEVERAL YEARS after I first reported on a farmer suicide. For over two decades I have interviewed and tracked the families of several hundred farmers who have cut short their lives, and all of them had one thing in common—they were unable to make ends meet with what they earned from their subsistence farms in the cotton-growing region of Vidarbha. They were unorganized and alone in their struggles. In each case, the trigger was different: a domestic feud, torrential rains destroying and flattening a standing crop, a sudden and expensive health emergency, impending daughters' weddings, or a combination of similar social or economic factors.

That morning in March 2014, Ramrao came close to becoming a grim statistic, another addition to the burgeoning list of farmers who have died by committing suicide—consuming pesticide, hanging themselves from trees on their fields or from the ceilings of their homes, or drowning in a well. Ramrao is emblematic of a problem that plagues India. He survived but others were not as lucky. Many of them died young, leaving behind widows to try and piece together their broken lives. Several women and children have ended their lives too, victims of the farmer distress.

I first came to Pandharkawda in the winter of 1997. I had not even completed a year of my reporting career. The policies of liberalization, privatization and globalization—the LPG triad—had started to unravel since the opening up of the Indian economy in 1991. Regulatory mechanisms were not in place. Banks began to shut their rural branches as they were not profitable. Indian and multinational corporates were slowly tightening their grip on the economy, and the import–export of commodities such as cotton was becoming hassle-free. And information technology was the new rage.

It started with weekly reports of a farmer suicide or two. But by the turn of the century these increased to two or three every day. Farmer suicides spiralled out of control by the middle of the first decade of the 2000s, and have become more widespread today—with a farmer committing suicide every thirty minutes in this country.

When the reports of farmer suicides first started trickling in, authorities would blame them on domestic tussles, jilted lovers, adultery, illnesses and a range of flimsy reasons. But soon the alarming numbers ensured that these deaths became a political issue. When the issue snowballed into a major political and economic concern, the Maharashtra government instituted a door-to-door survey in 2005 in the five districts of Amravati division and Wardha of Nagpur division—Vidarbha's cotton belt—to assess the extent and nature of the prevailing distress. About 5,000 officials went around collecting information. The exercise produced some stunning insights.

Nearly two-thirds of the 1.7 million cotton-growing farm households in the six districts were in crisis. Those in acute crisis were found to have landholdings less than 5 acres or 2 hectares in size. Nearly half a million farm households had some health issue that was compounding their financial woes and a third of the million households had daughters of marriageable age and that was causing concern to the parents—mainly on account of impending wedding costs and dowry demands. Almost all the households were in debt, and with rising production costs and dramatically declining returns, most of them would never be able to break out of this vicious cycle of indebtedness.

The disturbing truths the survey uncovered drove the Congress-led governments in the state and at the Centre to roll out measures to tackle the crisis. The package was limited to the cotton-growing region. In other states too, such as Andhra Pradesh, similar schemes and programmes were being implemented.

Fixing the agrarian crisis was—and remains—a national challenge. But what is it that needs fixing? Suicides or agrarian distress? The former is easier, the latter easier said than done.

In 2005, then Maharashtra chief minister Vilasrao Deshmukh announced a special farm package of ₹1,075 crore. It was for the six worst-affected districts—Amravati, Washim, Buldana, Akola, Yavatmal and Wardha—and was aimed at giving a fillip to irrigation projects, augmenting milk production as a secondary income source, and identifying individual distress-ridden farmers who might take the extreme step and could be counselled and helped in time, among other things. Concurrently, the state decided to pay a compensation of ₹1,00,000 to the immediate family of deceased farmers.

This led to a rather glib division of suicides into two categories: eligible and ineligible. The former applied to the farmers whose cause of death was among the thirty 'agrarian' reasons listed by the government; those whose cause of death was not among the listed reasons were left out of the compensation web.

So, who would determine which suicide was eligible and which was ineligible? The government constituted committees in every district, headed by the collector and officials from the police, agriculture and cooperation departments and farmers' representatives. Over the years, as the issue aggravated, the committees became defunct and the government tended to categorize the majority of farmer suicides as ineligible. In other words, when it was unable to stem the deaths, the state government refused to see them as a fallout of the agrarian crisis. The late Vilasrao Deshmukh even famously brought in saints and seers to help the government deal with mental health problems.

The BJP, which cried hoarse over farmer suicides when it was in the opposition, has downplayed the issue after coming to power in 2014.

ACROSS VIDARBHA, SOCIAL AND political protests mushroomed—for timely credit, compensation for crop losses, remunerative prices for commodities—all aimed at achieving some respite from the continuing pain. One such protest even turned bloodier—one farmer died and several others were injured in police firing at a market yard in Yavatmal's Wani town in 2006. The farmers had been waiting for days for their cotton to be procured at the market yard but an inexplicable, inordinate delay led to the unrest, even as the Maharashtra assembly's winter session was under way in Nagpur.

Simultaneously, several studies were commissioned by the central and state governments. The Indira Gandhi Institute of Development Research (IGIDR), the Tata Institute of Social Sciences (TISS), the now-disbanded Planning Commission-backed study by a fact-finding committee, the Narendra Jadhav Committee, and many subsequent studies elaborately discussed the multiple reasons for the suicides and the agrarian distress. Then Prime Minister Dr Manmohan Singh travelled to Vidarbha and five other states besides Maharashtra for a first-hand understanding of what had gone wrong. He came up with a ₹3,750 crore package for the thirty-six districts—including the six worst-affected in Vidarbha—that the Centre found were most in distress.

He rightly described farmers' suicides as a 'national shame' and went on to underline the need to make farmers bankable again. He promised he would do something about the outstanding loans and help the defaulting farmers again access formal loans. It was an indication that the economist prime minister was aiming to announce a big loan waiver programme. It happened in 2008. The UPA government announced a loan waiver scheme, ratified by the Reserve Bank of India, with a guarantee from the central government. It did away with the outstanding loans of defaulter farmers and helped them get formal bank crop loans again. Wherever the farmers did not qualify, states like Maharashtra pitched in with their own programmes to add to the central scheme.

For a couple of years, it helped augment farm incomes.

The loan waiver scheme was followed with a sumptuous rise in the MSPs for agricultural commodities, including cotton.

India went into a general election in 2009. The measures helped the UPA return to power. But the following five years, the real incomes of farmers dropped and the central measures stalled. By 2014, things were back to square one.

Maharashtra spends more on crop compensation and contingency expenses every year than on its annual farm budget. In 2012, Sudhir Kumar Goel, then principal secretary in the Department of Agriculture and Cooperation in the Maharashtra government, flagged it by saying that there was something very wrong if we spend more on compensation than on a budgeted plan.

In 2007, the National Commission on Farmers (NCF) headed by Professor M.S. Swaminathan, the father of the Green Revolution in India, travelled through Vidarbha's villages and other parts of the country, held extensive consultations with farmers and their leaders, local experts, parliamentarians and state-level legislators and submitted five voluminous reports to the Government of India. The reports focused on a road map to fix the problems plaguing Indian farmers and agriculture, and made comprehensive recommendations to turn the situation around by de-clogging the systemic and structural blockages. But the reports are yet to be comprehensively debated by Parliament.

The NCF suggested measures to fix problems emerging out of soil infertility, climate change, market volatility, and stagnant production and productivity, among other things. It also suggested a new way to measure farm growth by saying that farmers' incomes should be included as one of the factors. It argued that merely measuring the productivity or per-acre yields of a commodity or overall production should not be the sole criteria for determining agri-growth. Among the most important recommendations of the NCF was that the government must calculate the MSP for a crop as 50 per cent higher than the cultivation cost. The recommendation remains unaddressed to date. It is now a major demand of farmers all over India: implement the Swaminathan formula to calculate MSP and make it legally binding.

To address the developmental imbalances within the state—the Vidarbha region lags behind western Maharashtra in growth—then Maharashtra Governor K. Sankaranarayanan constituted a committee of experts, headed by well-known economist Vijay Kelkar. The members studied the factors leading to the imbalance and came up with a voluminous report to carve out measures on how to stem the inequalities within and between the regions. But the 2013 report has since then neither been accepted nor rejected by the state government. That report had confirmed what was known on the ground: agricultural growth in the region of Vidarbha since the turn of the century was in the negative, except for one year, 2009. According to the Kelkar Committee study, almost all other sectors were booming, even in Vidarbha, but rural growth had tanked.

The past two decades have also been a period when rural–urban migrations have increased, short-distance daily migration for work from rural areas to the nearest urban agglomerate has also picked up momentum, there has been increased farm mechanization, more indebtedness, and new technologies and new inputs have been pushed recklessly, apparently to reform the sector but it has all proved to be an exercise in futility.

I remember schemes where the government offered mindless incentives. The Baliraja scheme, for instance, encouraged people to buy two-wheelers, which were supposed to improve transportation and connectivity. And needless to say, it was a failure. It pushed the beneficiaries into debt, and eventually they lost their vehicles while the vehicle dealers made merry.

All along, the financial compensation packages and the various schemes and programmes on offer did not change two fundamental conditions at the root of the region's agrarian distress. One, the primary producer status of Vidarbha's cotton and soybean grower remains unchanged; therefore, his or her ability to intervene and stand up to the market pressures remains negligible; and two, there was no improvement in the per capita income and per-acre return on investment. The diversification of income sources—agriculture and agri-allied sources—and building sustainable and remunerative value chains remain distant dreams. Barring examples that are few and far between, of collective efforts by and with farmers across Maharashtra, nay the country, to improve agricultural practices and income-augmenting value chains, the Indian farmer is getting sucked deeper and deeper into the economic quagmire. The chief minister's and prime minister's packages, loan waivers and the other efforts have momentarily eased the burden of farmers but have done very little to improve farm and allied sector income—neither dairy nor goat rearing, poultry, fisheries and so on.

A rain-dependent, dry-land marginal farmer who solely relies on his farm for income and sustenance earns once a year but has round-the-year, everyday liabilities to be footed by cash. How do you meet your cash needs every day when income flows occur only once or twice in 365 days? The world's best economists should put their minds together to figure that out in a focused conference. Either you increase your returns—which is not in your hands—or you diversify both your sources and farm output—which means a lot of policy-driven interventions of cash and kind.

Apart from the existing market challenges and government apathy, the other big challenge facing farmers is the unfolding water crisis. Farms are failing because of the lack of groundwater brought on by climate change. Also, while we live in an open market economy and most of the problems stem from the markets, the respite is being sought from the state. Governments are spending more on doling out cash compensations rather than drawing up a long-term, multi-pronged mitigation strategy to spur farm growth and curb suicides in rural areas.

Despite several studies, reports and recommendations, the latest being the reports of the NITI Aayog on the doubling of farm incomes, the fact is that rural farm incomes remain poor.

Nothing is more depressing than seeing people end their lives in humiliation, agony and helplessness. Over the years, I have realized that the only difference between those living and those committing suicide is that the former is alive because s/he is not dead. The other parameters—the daily drudgery, the unending cycle of indebtedness, the death of dreams, the lack of resources to meet the bare minimum needs, and the aspirations—are the same.

THE AGRICULTURE LANDSCAPE IS different and varied across Vidarbha—broadly paddy in the eastern parts and cotton and soybeans in the western region. But there are variations within, of agro climatic types, river, forests and grasslands. Over the past century, cotton farming got into trouble. Now, the distress is more uniform and widespread, except in the areas that have protective irrigation and allied sector income and where farmers work in collectives. Small and marginal farmers who sustain themselves on rain-fed farms and nothing else are in great distress. They do not make enough money to meet their needs. They are un-bankable, so to say. They fall back upon informal moneylending systems and eventually get entrapped in their vicious cycle. Agriculture inputs dealers are the new lenders—small revenue officials and school teachers too. The surplus money is circulated in lending, against land mortgage or produce.

Irrespective of your landholding, you are not able to make ends meet. The Vidarbha countryside has been in the shadow of a slowdown for long. The money going out of a village is more than the money coming in. The wealth inequalities are stark within and between a village and a big town and a village and a metro.

A farmer tries everything at his disposal to tackle his financial and social problems. He sells his assets, land, his gold, bullocks, the trees on his farm. But a small trigger—it could be a sudden shock from a crop loss due to a pest attack, drought, price collapse, a torrential or erratic rainfall, a health exigency or any other reason—rips open festering wounds and takes him or her to a point of no return. Some of them leave behind poignant notes, giving us an insight into why they choose death. A farmer's inability to meet his minimum needs results in anger and frustration. This is further fuelled by socio-economic uncertainties, glaring inequalities and the commercialization of life, which often lead to anxiety and depression.

Policy makers in New Delhi and Mumbai are split on the way forward. One group calls for more reforms, further opening up of markets, more privatization, more commercialization, more dependence on high-energy, high-cost and labour-intensive technologies and the removal of subsidies and government support systems. The other calls for increased state intervention at every stage, loan waivers and much more. If there is a lobby pushing for and selling genetically engineered crops, there is another pitching for organic, natural or zero-budget farming.

But if India is to resolve its agrarian crisis, we will need more than a technological or economic correction. We will need a 'New Deal' for rural India, a new holistic approach for infusing money and efforts to resurrect a fledgling rural economy, new institutional structures to make the farmer an equal participant in growth without reducing him to the beneficiary of a dole, and a combination of different strategies for different regions and crops. For a start, we could take a look at the collective and sustainable models that are working well and leverage adaptable lessons from them to be used to restructure schematic interventions. Also, we might need social enterprises that provide services to build sustainable, farmer-friendly integrated value chains from farms to consumers for agriculture and allied sectors. We also need a government that listens, and revamped state agriculture departments that go beyond unveiling a few schemes and programmes and doles here and there.

India has lost twenty years debating and arguing about the best direction to bail out the beleaguered farmers and rural India, but without the desired effect. The state must shoulder this onus because there is no country in the world, including some of the most developed ones like the United States or Japan, which does not provide direct and indirect support to its farmers with subsidies and incentives.

The current situation is like a throwback to the Raj days. In his book *Cotton and Famine in Berar*, Professor Laxman D. Satya writes:

> The British takeover of Berar is a fascinating tale of skillful skullduggery. Historically, Berar was an important subah of the Mughal Empire. After the breakup of the empire in early eighteenth century, Berar was contested between the Marathas and the Nizam of Hyderabad. When the Marathas were defeated (1818), Berar was given to the Nizam for his obedience and loyalty. Constant pressure was maintained on the Government of India by Manchester Chamber of Commerce in response to dramatic political developments in north America. Dalhousie as Governor General was sent to India at the right moment to satisfy Great Britain's appetite for raw cotton. The annexation of Berar was the high point of Dalhousie's administration.

The revenues of the cotton-rich Berar became a bone of contention between the British and the Nizam. The British tied the Nizam down with all kinds of treaties and stipulations before they annexed his kingdom. A dubious military force known as the Hyderabad Contingent was organized under the pretext of providing protection to the Nizam. The revenues of Berar were supposedly primarily assigned to the maintenance of this force. The British resident at Hyderabad made sure that all treaty stipulations regarding Berar were strictly observed. Blatant threats were issued whenever the Nizam raised the issue of Berar's restoration. Factions were created in the Nizam's court to prevent him from consolidating his forces against the British. Angered by the resistance to annexation, Lord Dalhousie in a letter warned the Nizam that the Government of India could crush him under its feet 'so that neither name or trace of him should remain'. The British linked Yavatmal by a feeder railroad to the Bombay–Nagpur–Calcutta route by the 1860s and '70s. This route was built to ferry cotton and teak, mainly to Bombay and Calcutta and from there off to Manchester and Liverpool. Today, these regions produce stuff for sale in the cities but hardly earn enough from what they sell.

To top it off, today's farmer's purchases are expensive chemical inputs. Synthetic pyrethroids—chemical pesticides—came with cotton hybrids in the early 1990s, then came the organophosphates and other compounds. Farmers who could not afford to buy chemicals hanged themselves in their huts or from trees in their farms.

Maharashtra first argued that farmers' suicides were a scourge limited to Andhra Pradesh, then it said the problem was limited to the region of Vidarbha. But by the middle of the first decade of the 2000s, studies suggested that the Indian countryside was in distress and the crisis had assumed volcanic proportions. One thing was found in common: farming, save some exceptional examples, had generally become unremunerative, agricultural incomes had seen a dramatic fall, income sources had shrunk, the informal credit system was thriving, living costs were spiralling and social and economic distress was deepening. Rain-fed small and marginal family farms had become extremely vulnerable to even the smallest market or environmental volatility.

THE FIRST DECADE OF the new century saw urban India speed into the twenty-first century while the countryside stayed where it was, a fact that the Planning Commission's fact-finding committee headed by Adarsh Misra bared in its report.

The new century did not bring any notable change to Ramrao's village other than a cement road and a reverse osmosis machine installed on a borewell for potable water which people had to pay for, but most of the villagers could not even afford to replace the blue tarpaulin sheets on their huts.

Pandharkawda expanded in this period, Hiwara shrank. The raging inequality between a village and its nearest town is starker than the inequality between a metro and a faraway village. Hiwara would expectedly pale in comparison to Mumbai. But it also falls short before Pandharkawda's newly rich, some of whom are migrants from nearby villages. The drudgery of farming, the slow life in a village, the prevalence of diseases and the absence of services that people in Hiwara see available in the nearest town would leave them frustrated every time they travel there for every small need. Munna Bolenwar, for instance, made a move to Pandharkawda some years ago. He wanted his children to go to a good private English-medium school, the most popular reason for small-distance migration.

In two decades, I saw rural Vidarbha go from bad to worse, the same region that was once known for its teeming farms, cotton that fired the mills in Manchester and Liverpool, drew cotton traders from all over the country, triggered central India's industrial revolution and anchored the independence struggle with its handlooms and textiles.

If I painted black dots on the map of Vidarbha representing the multiple deaths by suicide, like the map in the VJAS office in Pandharkawda, some villages and tehsils would be covered entirely. Bothbodan, twenty suicides; Irjhada, a village with barely hundred households, has had forty-two suicides over twenty years; or Bhambraja, seven. These three villages are located in Yavatmal. These are areas where you hear of small sums of debt that the rich in cities would pay in tips while dining at an upscale hotel aggravating the distress of an already beleaguered lot.

The changing financial system is also one of the root causes of the crisis. The financial sector was liberalized in the new economic order. Profitability became the sole concern for banks, so they closed down their rural branches. Consequently, credit supply fell sharply in the 1990s, which led to the resurgence of moneylenders and the informal credit system. In the new century, rural credit volume expanded but was highly skewed in favour of the rural rich and large businesses. A large portion of the increase was due to indirect loans in new areas such as financing commercial export-oriented and capital-intensive agriculture, where loans are given to corporations and partnership groups within the ambit of agricultural credit. This means that agricultural loans moved away from marginal, small or medium farmers towards large agri-business interests. The New Economic Policy brought a drive to privatize, generating new incomes for rich commercial farmers and corporations.

When it comes to profitability, a 2006 Government of India report on Vidarbha calculated that agriculture had the potential to be profitable in Vidarbha too. In reality, however, agriculture is far from being profitable for many farmers—most often earn a gross profit of less than ₹4,000–₹5,000 per hectare. The report compares the MSP for cotton, sorghum and soybean for the year 2004-05 under irrigated conditions. It states that in case of sorghum and cotton, the MSP is higher than all paid costs (including rent and family labour), but lower than the cost of production if interest on owned capital and the rental value of the owned land is included.

A large number of farmers are indebted and marginal farmers are even more likely to be so. In Vidarbha, there is a credit gap of roughly 50 per cent between agricultural credit demand and availability. Earlier, cooperative banks were very important in Maharashtra, but now only a minuscule part of the rural credit demand is covered through institutional credit from banks or rural cooperative societies. The cooperative banks have a high level of outstanding loans as well as high interest rates. Increasingly, the people on the defaulters' list of banks and cooperative societies fall out of the formal credit system and are forced to rely on their social network or moneylenders.

IN 1995, THE NCRB began to keep a record of accidental deaths and suicides in India. Farmer suicides are closing in on 20,000 in Vidarbha, 60,000 in Maharashtra and 4,00,000 in the rest of India. The most recent report available on farmer deaths is for 2018. The NCRB didn't release the subsequent annual reports on time. For 2015 and 2016, the reports were published in November 2019 after the methodology was tweaked to make the figures seem low.

'The government started fiddling with the farmer suicide data in 2013, when the number became absolutely obscene,' P. Sainath said at a lecture in Kerala in 2019. 'In the following years, the methodology was changed, as a result of which farmers' suicides fell by 50 per cent, while the "others" column went up by 128 per cent. In 2016, the government stopped the National Crime Records Bureau from publishing farmer suicide data. In 2017, they shut down NCRB and later merged it with the Bureau of Police Research and Development,' Sainath, who has chronicled the issue for over two decades, explained.

Some researchers studied suicides using the socio-cultural and socio-psychological frame, placing the phenomenon in the context of the post-liberalization changes in society and the individual. Still others located them within the sweeping economic changes that were a consequence of the liberalization of the Indian economy: the changing global trade and the free movement of farm commodities across international borders. Every study captured an important aspect of this complex process but not a single one its entirety.

Ramrao survived the suicide attempt but that has not altered his life or his mental state in any way. One of the most promising mental health action research projects in Vidarbha demonstrated that if mental health consultants are available in rural health facilities, the number of people seeking counselling for their clinical depression goes up and the rate of suicides comes down. With a small investment and a rudimentary intervention, we can reduce the tendency among vulnerable individuals to take their own life. What cannot change in a short span and with piecemeal interventions is the accumulated economic depression sweeping the countryside, the structural complexity stemming from social, cultural, ecological, even political rigidities that create the cause.

Dr Sujay Patil, my friend and a psychiatrist in Akola, reasoned with me way back in 2006 while treating farmers from that district for depression free of cost, 'We can address the symptoms but not the root cause of it.' Even so, having a battery of trained mental health professionals at the cottage hospitals and primary health centres could help reduce the incidence of farmer suicides, if that project is any encouraging indication.

Ramrao has been losing his crop on account of pest attacks, spurious seeds, spurious fertilizers, monsoon failure, monsoon delay, extreme rainfall, the market slump. Not to forget the wild animal menace. Each time, the government has to step in to address the losses. Ironically, while we live in a market economy and want it to flourish, our grievances and demands are directed at the state when we are in deep social and economic mess. Private companies sell spurious seeds, farmers demand compensation from the government. Crop insurance firms walk away with plump profits, farmers seek a loan waiver from the state because the companies won't resolve their problems. Companies are here to make profits, not to guarantee a social and economic safety net. So as long as the agrarian distress remains unmitigated, the state will have to and must provide relief to the beleaguered peasantry.

Until 2014, the Congress and the NCP governments in Maharashtra doused the farmers' anger with doles, even if they were paltry. The BJP government, however, took a different route. It used the same money to finance the crop insurance scheme in which farmers are getting hot air while a few private insurance companies are walking away with profits running into hundreds of crores of rupees in every district. Banks are selling the insurance with the crop loan. Basically, there is privatization of profits and socialization of losses.

Apart from these obvious downsides, one of the biggest shortcomings in Vidarbha's cotton belt is the collapse of farmers' movements, such as the one once steered by the Shetkari Sanghatna, and the regional political leadership's failure and inability to build robust institutions which could lend a hand when farmers are in need. District cooperative banks are badly managed. Primary agriculture cooperative societies that once formed the backbone of the rural farm economy are dead. Regional agriculture universities operate in their silos and have no time to fix on-ground issues. Collectives or cooperatives don't exist and the state machinery is allegedly far too corrupt and inefficient to properly address the problems of farmers.

The state government and its administrative machinery in fact milked this crisis, with cuts in schemes meant for dead farmers' families, or poor and marginal farmers. In 2005, they procured and sold unhealthy and foreign cows that were beyond their productive age, wasting a whopping ₹350 crore on zero returns, as the Maharashtra Pradesh Congress Committee's own report on the chief minister's and prime minister's packages mentioned in 2006. They sold substandard seeds, locally manufactured implements bought under the packages at exorbitant rates, and splurged money on incomplete irrigation projects that are still draining public spending, as the performance audit report of the two special packages by the Comptroller and Auditor General's Maharashtra office, tabled on the last day of the Maharashtra legislature's budget session of April 2008, underlined. Nothing worked because nothing was meant to work.

On the ground, structural social problems continue aggravating: social strife, caste conflicts, the rain-fed nature of agriculture leading to abysmal productivity and extremely poor income standards, and substandard education that is turning village children unemployable. All this is a slow prescription for a systemic subjugation and exclusion from economic progress. Those who can eventually leave their villages and migrate to the cities in pursuit of work, even if that means living in slums in sub-human conditions.

Ramrao, however, must go back to his land. Tilling it is the only way he will make a living, repay his debts and be content.

5

TRAGEDY

AFTER STAYING AWAY FROM active farming for two long years Ramrao is finally itching to get back to his land. On a hot day in May 2016, he tells me that though it would be difficult for him to raise money to cultivate his land, he has to try. That's the only way to repay his piled-up debts. He went to his bank in Pandharkawda to check, but chances are he may not get a loan since he is a defaulter. He must pay back his outstanding dues with interest if he is to apply for fresh loans. What he might do, he says, is pay ₹3,000 to restructure his old loans and bring them back on the ledgers as a current loan, but he doubts if he would get fresh bank loans.

As of today, he says, he has outstanding bank loans worth more than ₹1,00,000. We go check with the bank, and he is right.

Ramrao has made up his mind, though. He is going to farm his 5 acres and Gunwanta Golemwar's adjoining 7 acres because Golemwar will at least shoulder the production costs.

Though not altogether sure about how he will raise the money, Ramrao intends to plant cotton, soybean, tur and jowar in equal measure so that if one fails he has other options to fall back upon. He will ask one of his farmhands to have two tractor-trolleys full of cow dung spread on his farmlands after the weed and wild grass that have grown on his land are removed—this is what he generally does to prepare for the new farming season. He hopes some pre-monsoon showers will bless his land by the end of May so that the soil softens up. Organic manure would better his yield; he has a lot of cow dung piled behind his cattle-shed which he intends to use as manure. He has to do this before the arrival of the monsoon to help get his land in sowing shape.

Ramrao will, of course, also use chemical fertilizers when the seeds are planted. I reckon Ashokrao is by his side this time to give him that much-needed nudge to start working again.

Through the summer we chat, on and off, over the phone. Once again, the rains are delayed and Ramrao hasn't begun sowing.

On the afternoon of 17 June 2016, my cell phone rings. I am travelling in western Maharashtra—Satara, to be precise. It is a cloudy day. It is Ramrao on the other side, sobbing.

'Rahul, Alakya's husband, is dead,' he tells me up-front, his voice cracking as he breaks the tragic news.

Before I can respond, he adds, 'He committed suicide.'

The news is unnerving. I am terrified at the thought of his emotional turmoil, my mind torn between where I am currently headed and where I want to be, Hiwara.

In the same breath, Ramrao, still crying, tells me why this might be the reason he is still alive. 'The almighty had plans.'

Ramrao's reasoning is rooted in his devoutness for the almighty and 'His' grand plans that transcend man's imagination.

Alakya is in her mid-twenties and has a four-year-old daughter, who was born soon after Vimalbai's demise. Alakya has a long, arduous life ahead. I met her once in 2014, but Ramrao would always update me about her and her daughter's life.

After Vimalbai's death, Ramrao had become very lonely. When she was alive, even if she was ailing, Ramrao had solace in her mere presence. They would eat their meals together, take decisions mutually. She managed the household chores and finances, and kept him company. When she was gone, all responsibilities fell on Ramrao's shoulders. When Anuja delivered her first child in 2015, he kept crying in his house, troubled by her memories and the void she left in his life. He thought she was needed to welcome their daughter home, give her post-natal care, play with their granddaughter, sing her lullabies.

'I know her value now,' he told me one day. 'I never appreciated her hard work when she was alive.'

Ramrao is choking as he speaks to me over the phone, his heart breaking under the tremendous weight of his grief. I am worried he may slide back into inertia.

'Stand firm, stand firm,' I try consoling him, knowing fully well how trite the words sound.

Rahul's suicide brings with it a sense of déjà vu—Ramrao is aware of it. He is shattered. If only his son-in-law had someone around him in his final moments... He knows Rahul's death could have been averted if he or someone else knew about his tensions. He, after all, knows better than most the razor-thin difference between death and life.

Just a week ago, Alakya had gone back to Adilabad after spending three days with Ramrao in Hiwara on the occasion of Vimalbai's fourth death anniversary. She had made no mention of anything being wrong with Rahul or their family.

Alakya had no inkling that Rahul had suicidal thoughts. That was why at first she thought that someone had killed him, Ramrao tells me.

Of all deaths, suicide is the hardest to deal with. Due to its gory suddenness, it leaves families in turmoil, particularly when the deceased is young and dear. You ask the widow of a farmer who committed suicide if he ever showed signs of having suicidal thoughts and almost every one of them would answer in the negative.

Ramrao's frustration stems from his helplessness. He could do nothing that could have prevented Rahul from taking that extreme step, and that the young man did not think twice before killing himself, didn't think about his wife, daughter and family members.

The irony is not lost on Ramrao. Two years ago, it was he who had chosen death over life, but survived. Now it is his son-in-law, who hasn't.

He recounts to me how Rahul had come rushing with Alakya on his bike from Adilabad the day Ramrao had consumed poison. Still sobbing, he says, 'He had consoled me saying that I should not worry about my problems, but he himself forgot that advice today. He was a very loving man. How will Alakya deal with this now?'

'What happened exactly?' I ask him, mustering courage.

He reveals what happened. Early morning, Rahul's body was found in a playground in Adilabad. A year ago, he and Alakya had moved to that town in Telangana from their village in Kamtala,

Maharashtra. He would pick up small jobs and help his father on the farm, though the two had major differences. He had left home the previous morning to apply for a job, spoken with Alakya in the evening but hadn't returned home the whole night. Before he left home, he had bought a packet of milk and a chocolate bar for their daughter, Varshini. When he did not return till late at night, Alakya thought he may have gone to the village or got stuck at work. She had a faint inkling that Rahul may be in trouble, as he had looked worried the past few days. But he had refused to share his problems with her.

When she was in Hiwara, Rahul had gone back to Kamtala to start the sowing operations on their family land; his father had asked him to do the sowing on 3 acres, so he must have borrowed some money from private lenders, but the land still belonged to his father. In addition to this, he was searching for a job in Adilabad that would sustain him, Alakya and their toddler.

Rahul never consumed alcohol or had any vices. He was a well-behaved young man who loved his wife and kid. He had a quarrel with his parents and a brother-in-law over the ancestral land. They did not want him to take to farming or seek his share in the farm, but permanently shift to Adilabad and take up a job instead.

Ramrao loved his son-in-law. Rahul was thirty-three at the time of his death, ten years older than Alakya. Varshini is four, and has just begun to talk in Telugu.

Ramrao had found Rahul modest, honest, hardworking. He was a self-made man with small needs. He wanted to be a farmer, which was why Ramrao had chosen him over the other suitors from affluent and big, landed families. Vimalbai, who was then alive but ailing, had liked him too. The Ranganeniwars, Rahul's parents, came across as well-meaning individuals with the values of a family rooted in the agrarian economy. Ramrao's distant relatives knew of them as warm people who were doing well. Rahul's two elder sisters were married and happy. He was the only son of his parents. The concerned parents in Ramrao and Vimalbai felt Rahul was a perfect match for Alakya, seventeen at the time of her marriage, because Rahul came across as a sensitive human being. They got married in mid-2011 at a big wedding hall in Kelapur village, situated on the highway to Adilabad, 20 kilometres from Hiwara, with villagers standing witness to the rituals to bless the newlyweds. Ramrao threw a big feast. Vimalbai was happy that she could witness her elder daughter's wedding. She did not live to see Anuja's.

Ramrao had money that year from the previous years' profits, so he gifted his daughter plenty of household goods—a refrigerator, a double bed, a grinder-mixer, a fan and a lot more. Ramrao and his wife also gave her gold—or 'streedhan', as it is called in these parts.

'*Bhay changla porga hota ji.* He was such a good boy,' Ramrao says quietly.

A person out on a morning walk noticed Rahul's body and informed the Adilabad police, who confirmed his identity and informed his family in Kamtala. Alakya came to know about his death later in the morning, because the family did not inform her immediately, thinking she might not be able to stand the terrible shock.

The young man, in all probability, consumed the pesticide he had bought the previous evening. He didn't leave a suicide note behind. Alakya discovered later that her husband had spoken with his friend the previous evening. He had been angry—not with his wife but with his other family members who didn't want him to enter farming. He had not found a job to eke out a living, he was not being allowed to take to farming, he thought he was being ousted from his property at the insistence of one of his relatives.

Rahul was barely matriculate and could only find low-paying, temporary work and wanted to stick to farming. He had been pushing his unwilling father to give him an equivalent share in the family farmland, but his father was not yet ready to bequeath a part to him.

Whatever the reason, Ramrao laments, Rahul is dead and Alakya is all alone with a young daughter to fend for.

'If her mother were alive, Alakya would not have had to worry,' Ramrao says, sounding like a broken man. He adds: '*Me ase paryant tila me kahi tras hou denar nahi*. She will not face any trouble till I'm alive.' Then, he hangs up after I tell him we'll soon meet.

Ramrao rushed to Adilabad to be by the side of his daughter and help her tide over the tragedy. His sister, Suman, is already with Alakya, who is inconsolable. The incident has shaken Ramrao's confidence at a time when he is desperately trying to return to farming.

'I CAN'T DIE UNTIL my child turns eighteen and society won't allow me to live peacefully that long.'

That was Nanda Bhandare, a twenty-four-year-old female farmer whose husband committed suicide in the winter of 2004 in a village in Yavatmal. Her son was two. Nandabai is a Kunbi, a predominantly landed OBC in Vidarbha, a politically dominant caste in the region. She told me during our first meeting, 'I have a difficult journey,' summing up her life ahead.

Nandabai, now touching forty, has grown older, bereft of happiness or joy, heavily weighed down by her daunting everyday routine—raising a child, fighting with her in-laws for her land rights, and working on the village farms to earn a wage.

A bereaved Nandabai was angry with her departed husband when I first met her at her home days after his suicide. She would often fight with her husband—and why shouldn't a wife do so, she had said, if things go astray. But she loved him and wanted him to quit his bad habits—he was an alcoholic. After he did so, they were blessed with their first child.

Thousands of farm widows lead lives of struggle, filled with pain and suffering, all alone. I fear Alakya's journey may be the same now, though she is lucky to have Ramrao firmly by her side. Not many farm widows are as fortunate. They have to single-handedly raise their children, earn a living from the farm or otherwise, repay the unpaid debts and confront society with all its good, bad and ugly.

In October 1997, I met the widow of 18-acre cotton grower Ramdas Amberwar, a Beldar by caste, who had swallowed pesticide to end his life. He had left behind a detailed note chronicling the reasons he had chosen to end his life. He was in his early forties and neck-deep in loans. He had five daughters, their weddings and old parents with health problems to take care of. When he was gone, all his responsibilities—loans, raising daughters, and their eventual weddings—befell his wife, Saraswati, a gutsy woman who refused to crumble under the weight of her challenges.

In the twenty-three years I have known her, Saraswatibai has endured situations most of us can't even fathom. She lost one of her daughters to a kidney ailment for the want of money. She could not afford good healthcare. She has not been able to forgive herself for it. Her youngest daughter, Manjusha, barely three years old when her father died, wanted to become a journalist. She went on to do her graduation and then a postgraduate degree in mass communication and journalism from the journalism school in Nagpur, but she could not withstand the mighty competition and the pressures of urban media. She went back to her village of Telang Takli to help her mother with the farm. Saraswatibai has married off her three elder daughters, and for each wedding she had to sell an acre or two, or her cows, to throw wedding feasts for the village and pay hefty dowries so that her daughters are safe and happy in their marital homes.

She paid off her husband's loans, borrowed more, farmed with astonishing alacrity, braved weather uncertainties, learned to tackle choppy markets, convince bankers to lend her more, participated in women's gatherings, and grew tired and older.

'I had dreams too,' she once told me. But, somewhere through the years, she stopped dreaming.

When I first met her, she looked older than she actually was—a glaring similarity among farm widows—her hair grey, her forehead lined with wrinkles, and she was introverted.

'I never found time for myself,' she told me once during an interview at her modest concrete house situated in the middle of her congested village, amidst small, dilapidated mud-huts. She had to take up farming after her husband's death. She was stuck with never-ending family responsibilities: her daughters' weddings, then their deliveries, health issues, grandchildren. I once asked her about her likes and dislikes and her modest dreams, and she had stared at me blank, her face wearing an expression as if to ask me what kind of a question that was!

'I've never had the time to think about myself. Not when I got married, not when I was a child, not when I got older. Maybe when I am alone and all these girls are gone to their homes, I will think about myself.'

SINCE THEN, EVERY WEEK, every day, for more than two decades, many more Ramdases have killed themselves in the dusty countryside of Vidarbha, leaving behind loans, children and wives, their families burdened with responsibilities and trauma. Some of them managed to rekindle their lives with the support of in-laws, or parents, brothers or good Samaritans, but most of them struggled. A lot of them were driven out of homes, children in tow, their properties annexed. Most of them had to fall back on labour work to earn a living.

Through the years, I have noted an appalling social reality: widow remarriages are still taboo.

Left with little choice, farm widows who do take up farming after their husbands display outstanding grit. They plough their lands with astonishing alacrity and dogged perseverance. That is not to say that men don't exhibit grit and determination. But the same attributes in the widows take on a different colour.

Aparna Malikar, a widow who went to the game show *Kaun Banega Crorepati* and sat across the Bollywood icon Amitabh Bachchan to win a jackpot in a special show, still farms by herself. Annapoorna Suroshe, whose husband committed suicide in a village in Umarkhed tehsil in Yavatmal, raised three young children, married her daughter off, stabilized her land and repaid debts by taking up multiple jobs. Another widow from Washim left farming and started plying a six-seater auto in the rural parts of the district to make her living, her mother by her side to support her and her young children. Ujjwala Pethkar was barely twenty-five years old when her husband committed suicide in Kurjhadi village of Wardha, but she farmed all by herself, raised her children, repaid her debts, tried innovations on her farm, and survived.

These are but a few examples of the countless farm widows who are the resolute faces of women farmers in India, rebuilding their broken lives in spite of mounting social and economic pressures. There have been women farmers too who have committed suicide, and their suicides don't get acknowledged as farmers' suicides because most of them don't have farmland in their names.

Agricultural distress in Vidarbha has affected rural women in several ways—increased work, debt repayment, reduced consumption and a lower spending on healthcare.

The unsustainable nature of agriculture questions the belief held by gender development scholars that the ownership of agricultural land will automatically reduce poverty and ensure food security. It was assumed that since agriculture is increasingly becoming 'feminized', the improvement of women's endowment through land will increase production, decrease poverty and ensure food security. But there is no proof that land ownership reduces poverty, since that land is fragmented and farming increasingly unremunerative.

Agriculture is undergoing a number of changes and these severely impact women, especially the farm widows who are forced to face daunting tasks. Met with the challenge of securing and maintaining livelihoods within precarious structures, widow farmers develop and nurture negotiation mechanisms through which they deal with the structural inequalities of everyday living. In a study conducted by scholar Anurekha Chari-Wagh (2012–14) on the coping strategies of the farm widows in Wardha district, three important measures to cope with extreme vulnerability and marginality were observed.

One, engaging in multiple paid labour jobs. Farm widows not only work in their own fields, which entails hard labour with uncertain economic returns, but also as daily agricultural paid labourers in the fields of other farmers. To make up for the lack of paid work in agriculture, they undertake non-farm paid work such as tailoring, working as domestic help, cooking and cleaning either as part of school mid-day meal programmes or in hotels, making rotis or cleaning vessels, thereby stretching their working hours to almost sixteen hours a day, balancing multiple paid and non-paid jobs, all of which is time-consuming, backbreaking, insecure and lowly paid.

Two, austerity measures such as reducing and prioritizing needs. In order to manage life within limited resources, widow farmers live severely austere lives. They cut their spending, especially on themselves. All members of the household are continuously engaged in the process of reevaluating their needs to bring down expenses. Not only are small pleasures (such as books, good food, festivals) sacrificed but also essentials (healthcare, medicines), thereby impacting the children quite severely.

Three, investing in creating a future that does not depend on agriculture. An important mechanism is investing in dreaming of a livelihood future that does not depend on agriculture. Widow farmers believe that the only way to deal with economic insecurity is to ensure that their children do not have to depend on agriculture to secure their livelihoods. They try extremely hard to motivate their children to focus on education so that they get a formal job that grants healthcare, employment and pension security and they can escape the drudgery and uncertainties of agriculture.

Beyond the social challenges the farm widows face, the centrality of women in Indian agriculture is often unacknowledged and neglected.

The Economic Survey of India, 2017-18, for the first time explicitly mentions: 'With growing rural to urban migration by men, there is "feminization" of agriculture sector, with increasing number of women in multiple roles as cultivators, entrepreneurs and labourers.'

In 2007, the Planning Commission said an estimated 20 per cent of rural households are de-facto female-headed due to widowhood, male desertion or migration. These women thus not only manage land and livestock but also provide subsistence to the family without any male assistance. The Planning Commission also noted that agricultural productivity was increasingly dependent on the ability of women to function effectively as farmers. Women play a crucial role in agricultural development and allied fields, including crop and livestock production, horticulture, post-harvest operations, agro/social forestry, fisheries, and so on, said the National Commission for Women in 2001.

The National Sample Survey Office data for 2011 showed two trends with regard to women's role in agriculture:

1. Women who were classified as agricultural workers were predominantly found in the non-productive agricultural sector rather than the more productive non-farm sector.
2. A trend of increased feminization of agriculture, where women's share in the total number of agricultural workers is increasing.

Globally, there is empirical evidence that women have a decisive role in ensuring food security and preserving local agro-biodiversity. Rural women are responsible for the integrated management and use of diverse natural resources to meet the daily household needs, stated the Food and Agriculture Organization of the United Nations in 2011. This requires that women farmers should have enhanced access to resources such as land, water, credit, technology and training. In addition, the entitlements given to women farmers would be key in improving farm productivity. The differential access of women to resources such as land, credit, water, seeds and markets also needs to be addressed.

The 2011 Census report stated that of the total female workers, 55 per cent were agricultural labourers and 24 per cent were cultivators. However, only 12.8 per cent of the operational holdings were owned by women, which reflects the massive gender disparity in the ownership of landholdings in agriculture, pointed out the Economic Survey, 2017-18. There was a concentration of operational holdings (25.7 per cent) by women in the marginal and small holdings categories. In India, it is also estimated that only 12.7 per cent of land holdings are in the names of women, even as 77 per cent women rely on agriculture as their primary source of income, said the United Nations Development Programme in 2015.

The lack of titled land prevents women from accessing a number of benefits that they should otherwise be able to lay claim to, such as institutional credit, bank loans and federal agricultural benefits.

❧

Ramrao has returned to his farm in full zeal.

'There is no other way but to pick up my plough,' he tells me as we sit chatting at his home a month after we last spoke.

Rahul's death, Alakya's loss of faith in life, a young Varshini to look after—it is overwhelming for him. On top of it, he has old loans to repay. The weight of his responsibilities is crushing, he rues with teary eyes. These days, Ramrao does not fight back his tears whenever he is in a pensive mood—a sign of a sensitive and empathetic man.

'Alakya has decided to live with her in-laws and they are okay with it,' Ramrao informs me. 'That is good of them.'

Alakya feels Varshini's schooling must not be affected, and she is right, he says, because her focus now is her daughter.

'And for me too, it's my daughter.'

Ramrao shows me Rahul's post-mortem documents which confirm that he had consumed Monocrotophos to kill himself.

Ramrao considered his situation and arrived at the conclusion that he must redouble his efforts, cultivate his lands and repay every bit of his loans while supporting Alakya and Varshini. Tough times lie ahead for them—and him—and when faced with such a situation, the best he can do is focus on his farm.

A few days earlier, he went back to two of his trusted sources for money: Golemwar and the Yavatmal agriculture officer, and they did not disappoint him. They were aware of his predicament. Munna Bolenwar too has promised to pitch in.

The problem is that the banks aren't lending him any money unless he clears his old dues, and the talk of loan waiver is still just political rhetoric. No one is sure if they will get their loans waived off this year. So, Ramrao must borrow from private sources, even if that capital comes at high interest rates.

Banks lend about ₹15,000 an acre for cotton. Ramrao needs ₹40,000 for an acre. 'Even if the banks lend me money, it is not sufficient,' he says. In any case, he would need to take private loans. It is just that this year he would need to take all of it from informal lending sources.

Days pass, Ramrao manages to finish his sowing and bring his farm back on track—he has planted cotton, soybeans and tur in the monsoon, which has been average so far.

As the October heat abates and winter is about to set in, one day Ramrao calls me with an update.

'I will need to stand by Alakya,' he tells me, dejected.

He noticed Alakya's in-laws were behaving distant when he recently visited them. He senses bad times are in store for his daughter. The father in him stands guard, the farmer in him wonders how he is going to manage, where the money will come from.

THE GOOD THING ABOUT note-bandi, chuckles Pramod Metkar, a forty-year-old 12-acre cotton farmer, is that it does not hurt those with no money. 'Like me!' He is, truly, cashless. 'Jokes apart, isn't this a good decision?' Metkar asks me. A lot of cash hoarded by rich people will tumble out of the closet, he says buoyantly, and it will be good for the country.

Why does he think a lot of cash will be unearthed by Prime Minister Narendra Modi's demonetization decision of 8 November 2016, I ask him over a cup of tea at a roadside stall in Malegaon village, about 40 kilometres from Wardha city on the edge of a teak forest that is part of the newly carved out Bor tiger reserve. The

Government of India through this decision ended the use of the existing ₹500 and ₹1,000 denomination notes as legal currency. Modi claimed the action would stem the tide of black money, push a cashless economy and end counterfeit currency.

'I heard about it. Everyone's saying that. I hope the government collects black money and spends on us,' Metkar quips. An old villager sitting on the opposite bench listens intently.

It has been about fifty days since the 'surgical strike on black money' was unleashed. How is it affecting the villagers, I ask him.

Metkar enlists their hardships: 'People here have no cash, even to pay wages to the women picking cotton on farms. Prices have been hit, but we are used to distress.'

The old villager butts in. 'I don't have money to go see a doctor.' He says he has postponed going to Wardha town to seek medical help for his joint pains.

'I am running my stall on credit,' adds the woman owner of the tea stall, who is keenly listening to our discussion and wants to join in. 'My daily business has been affected,' she says, a tad angry.

Malegaon is a village with a population of about a thousand people, mostly small land owners cultivating cotton on un-irrigated soil. It is pretty similar to Ramrao's village. The nearest bank branch is 33 kilometres away in Sukali village, beyond the forest patch. The village has a one-room post office, where a young Ashwini Lende is the manager. Old people and extremely poor families deposited their old notes with the post office since the bank is far away: ₹3,00,000 from sixty-three members, she informs. But the post office has no new notes for remittances. So far, Ashwini has given ₹10,000 in cash to her members—fives notes of the ₹2,000 denomination. Two days earlier, when she got the notes from the central office in Wardha town, she first called five old women who could not go to the bank but needed money and gave one ₹2,000 note to each of them.

I am on my way to Ramrao's village but I have taken a detour to the villages in Wardha to see how demonetization continues to affect the rural areas. Across the country, stories of hardships abound. People are queuing up outside banks to exchange their money in a staggered manner. Confusion prevails, the unorganized sector has been hit hard, labourers are scampering for work, fresh arrivals of farm produce have suffered due to a major slump in prices. It emerges that several old people and bank employees suffered heart attacks and reportedly died as a consequence of an ill-thought-out government policy.

Cut to Babhulgaon, a village about 60 kilometres from Malegaon.

'It's a good decision,' says Suresh Wankhede, a farmer who has brought in female cotton labourers from Bhidi village a few kilometres away. They are all set to board a tempo bound for home after the day's work when I decide to stop and have a chat with them.

Why does he think it's a good decision?

His answer resonates with Metkar's. 'A lot of rich men's black money will be caught and put into our development,' he says nervously, gauging whether the female labourers in the group agree with what he has said. They clearly don't. Wankhede hasn't been able to pay them. He has no cash to pay for their wages. And unless the women get cash in hand, they can't buy stuff to meet their daily needs.

Wankhede's cotton remains unsold since the markets have remained subdued since Modi's announcement. What's more, he tells us, the loaning of small sums of money by people in the countryside to each other to meet everyday exigencies has completely stopped.

How much does he owe the women? A few thousand rupees, he says. 'I owe a lot of money to a lot of people,' he adds. 'I won't break even.'

An old woman in the group blurts out, 'How does it help me?' 'How do we run our homes?' one of them asks loudly. In the first week of demonetization, she says, women accepted wages in the old notes of ₹500 and ₹1,000, but they stopped soon thereafter. 'Who has the time to stand in bank queues every day to deposit the money or withdraw it? Do we work and feed our families or stand in long queues?'

When Modi announced demonetization, the immediate losers were the poor landless women—like the group I am talking to. Is the decision good or bad, I ask them.

'How do we tell? Everyone's saying it is good, but how does it improve my life?' the old woman says. The women board the tempo and leave. Wankhede says that his economic situation may not improve but those who have made big, black money in a short time will suffer.

Throughout the day, the men and women I speak to betray their realities for the perception that some rich men's hoarded money will now be caught and funnelled to them.

VIDARBHA'S BELEAGUERED COTTON AND soybean farmers—facing recession for over two decades—have never stopped believing that some magic spell will lift them out of their circumstances. Their misplaced optimism—that someone's big cash pot is about to be caught and spent on them—is a symptom of the unending economic inequality they have been subjected to. On the ground, the landed have gone bankrupt, the landless have turned poorer and are left with no choice but to desert the village for a new urban nest.

That's why, when people saw the prime minister make claims of supposedly punishing rich men, in yet another televised speech, they fell for a scenario meticulously built by him and his supporters.

'A lot of people have made a lot of money in the last few years,' says one farmer standing in the crowd at a Bank of India branch in Sukali village about 30 kilometres from Wardha town. 'It's good to have a crack at them.'

This man, whose daughter's wedding is slated for January 2017, is facing a cash crunch and says the move has affected him too. But, he adds, hardships and anxieties are not new to him.

When I reach Hiwara, Ramrao tells me the joke doing the rounds these days is 'line up if you want relief'. Clearly, he is irritated with the joke. He says demonetization has come at a time when he was trying to rebuild his life and his farm. Diwali had just got over and Ramrao, like the other farmers in Hiwara, was planning to take his cotton and soybean to the market for sale, hoping he would get a good price for the produce. That was not to be. Note-bandi dragged him and many others back to square one.

'*Ata hee ek navin dokedukhi aali.* This is a new headache now,' he tells me and adds, 'as if I did not have enough problems already.'

This is turning out to be another bad year for Ramrao, and for most small and marginal farmers in Vidarbha. Traders are refusing to pay cash. In the event that they agree, they are not willing to pay the market price for the produce.

'If I want cash, I must sell my cotton at a lower price. If I want the market price, I have to wait for months before they pay me,' he says. 'I can't wait, I have to pay wages and repay debts.'

Farmers in this part prefer cash payments because they are quicker and they need the money in hand for further transactions. Going to banks means shelling out money on travel, standing in long queues, and losing the time they would rather spend on their farms.

Ramrao accepted a few hundred rupees less on every quintal of cotton he sold because he desperately needed cash. He sends money to Alakya every month so that she has some cash on hand for her needs.

The announcement of demonetization is followed by a prolonged cash shortage for months, significantly disrupting the Indian, particularly the rural, economy. Hiwara is no exception. In December 2016, when I meet Ramrao, both the rooms of his house are stacked with cotton as he is not sure whether to sell it now or wait a while. When he sells the cotton, he will have to pay wages to his labourers, pay the money he owes to input dealers and clear some of his old loans. But money supply has shrunk, cotton and soybean prices are at a low, and Ramrao is anxious.

6

MARIGOLD

On the rainy morning of 7 August 2017, Ramrao calls me and expresses an eagerness to meet. We haven't met or spoken in a while.

The first half of the year has been tumultuous for me. A sudden job loss brought financial problems in its wake. In a bit of a disarray myself, I have not been able to visit him. We last met in April for a few hours. He had seemed raring to go. His son-in-law's death was behind him, the aftereffects of the note ban were still playing out in Hiwara and his income had taken a beating in the kharif and rabi seasons of the previous year. But he looked like he was slowly regaining his confidence.

Demonetization devastated the informal economy of Hiwara and dented farmers' incomes right when their fresh produce was making its way to the market. Ramrao's tur, worth about ₹75,000, was procured by traders at the Pandharkawda farm market, but they had not yet made the payment because he desired it in cash to settle his labourers' wages. The traders instead wanted to transfer the money to his bank account, or give him a cheque. Ramrao decided to wait for his money because he trusted the traders.

In May 2017, Ramrao told me over the phone he would cultivate his farm, tend to the agriculture officer's 45 acres with three of his friends, cultivate his friend Golemwar's 7 acres in partnership and lease 10 acres of the Borgaon land from his Gond tribal acquaintance. He was confident of raising money for inputs for all this. He wouldn't divulge how.

Borrow more? Or maybe Ashokrao would pitch in. He wasn't forthcoming with the information and I did not pursue it further. Institutional credit was out of question since he had not been able to pay back his old dues. There was talk that the state government may finally announce a waiver, given that angry protests by farmers were sprouting all over Maharashtra and beyond.

No formal loans also meant he wouldn't be able to subscribe to the Pradhan Mantri Fasal Beema Yojana, a crop insurance scheme, which the government says is a farmer's protection against going broke.

In July, the Maharashtra government led by the BJP and the Shiv Sena announced a crop loan waiver scheme, which I reckoned would greatly help indebted farmers like Ramrao, but it would be months before the peasants actually began to receive the benefits. There is a cumbersome procedure they have to follow. They have to queue up at state-appointed service centres to make online applications and submit documents such as land records and bank statements. It would take months to complete the formalities, after which the state, via an outsourced agency, would scrutinize the applications. Once approved, farmers would finally be eligible for the loan waiver benefit.

Ramrao hasn't applied yet. The queues are long and time-consuming. He will apply once he readies all the necessary documents. But he tells me long queues have become symbolic of this government. Last November, post notebandi, villagers had to stand in long queues outside banks.

As I am chatting with Ramrao, I am reminded of an old man I had met in Hiwara. He was irritated by the note ban and didn't understand the government's digital push; unaware of what it meant, he had asked me, '*Hye kay online online chi ding ding laun thevli hay sarkarne.*' For half the population, particularly the elderly who were illiterate and had never stepped out of their villages, the increasing digitization of everyday services was akin to a bomb dropped out of the blue by the government.

Long serpentine queues in rural Vidarbha, nay, much of India, outside government-approved service centres and banks were a post-notebandi feature that marked the Modi government's push for the digitization of all government schemes and subsidy programmes. It resulted in hardships and trouble for villagers everywhere.

During our chat, I interrupt Ramrao and let him know that things have been a trifle difficult at my end too.

'I know,' he says, 'I called to check how you are doing. *Tumcha kahi phone bin nahi, male kalji vatli an bhetaychi iccha jhali.*' He says he was worried as he had not heard from me in a long time and wanted to meet.

With this, Ramrao has broken the professional wall that I had built between us—the interviewer and the interviewee. I don't know what to say or do, but I am moved by his words. He reminds me that empathy exists.

He even tries giving me a pep talk.

'*Kadhi himmat nay haraychi bhau,*' he says, asking me never to get bogged down by the challenges in life.

He sounds buoyant and turns my counsel on me. I sense he is on his field surrounded by his labourers. Ramrao has this habit of speaking aloud so that the people around him can hear him talk. He does not boast but likes to flaunt his friendships, so his unlettered farmhands know he has friends all over.

'I once forgot this lesson and I nearly died,' he says, reminding me of how close he came to death in 2014, an event that he constantly jokes about today. 'My son-in-law forgot it,' he adds, suddenly sombre.

'What's up? What's happening on your farm?' I ask him, expecting he will tell me the reason why he has called.

'Bhau, you have to come over as soon as possible. I need to bring you to the farm,' he insists. 'There's something that I want to give you, and there is something that I want to show you.'

Must be something important, otherwise he would not prod me to visit him. He never does. I tell him I shall visit him soon. He reiterates that even a few hours would be enough but I must come. 'Okay,' I promise him and end our conversation.

A WEEK LATER, MID-AUGUST, I am on the road to Hiwara.

The rains have taken a break. It did not rain much in June but thankfully it did in July, and across the countryside people have finished their sowing operations. The weather is awfully sultry. I have driven on this highway several times, a slender one-way road now transformed into a broad four-lane highway. It came up over fifteen years. Around 2000, then Prime Minister Atal Bihari Vajpayee announced the construction of the Golden Quadrilateral, an ambitious new highway network for India. This was part of the north–south corridor project. Dr Manmohan Singh expanded and expedited it. Machines came to work as the highway rolled out in stretches. Roads were increasingly churned out using humongous machines of all sorts by private companies on a build–operate–transfer basis. A new India took shape, roads no longer needed men and women in hordes for construction work. Very few labourers worked on the highway at any given time. I never saw too many of them working on-site. Toll nakas, or toll collection centres, came up. I have had to suffer potholes during all my trips in this part of the world, but in the past three years the journeys have become smoother and faster.

The new infrastructure came at a cost, though. Thousands of neem and mango trees that once lined the highway and formed a dense canopy that had served as a cover during the harsh summers for decades were felled. New trees were planted but they never took root. The several flyovers built on the broadened highway anatomically divided the villages on its route. There were stories of families splitting up as they fought amongst themselves for shares in the cash compensation received from the government. The big vehicles that sped past on these flyovers threatened the small bicycles or carts on the road. What remained a constant through all these changes were the blue or yellow tarpaulin sheets covering the frail and dilapidated huts along the highway, making these villages and hamlets look like second-class citizens against the newly affluent burgeoning cities. In a sense, the broad new highways further distanced cities from villages, people from people, and carved out new nations even within a backward region such as Vidarbha.

People driving their cars between Nagpur and Hyderabad on that highway aren't bothered about the rains being on time. They will still be able to afford food, even if it is expensive—lentils at ₹100 a kg, vegetables at ₹120. But the farmers who live along that road would struggle if the rains fail, or are erratic, or a heavy downpour wrecks the soil and the standing crops—as is the case this year. Farmers are worried by the dry spell. However, surprisingly, the cotton plants have grown stunningly tall. In stark contrast, the soybean crops stand wilting, awaiting rain.

Travelling from Nagpur to Hiwara, the highway to Hyderabad turns ninety degrees at what used to be Jam, a small village, during my childhood in Wardha district, now a popular stop for passenger buses and travellers. Twelve kilometres from there is Hinganghat, the erstwhile textile town that suffered a major economic downturn when its mills fell silent like most others across Vidarbha, from Nagpur to Khamgaon, decades ago.

Historically, the railways linked these towns. Or maybe it was the other way round. The towns came up along the Bombay–Nagpur, Bengal–Nagpur and later the southern routes: Hinganghat and Pulgaon in Wardha district; Badnera, Daryapur and Achalpur in Amravati; and Khamgaon in Buldana, among other centres. The national highways to Hyderabad and Bombay that meet in Nagpur were, in a way, roads that interlinked the central, western and southern worlds of cotton and textile.

The region had 163 integrated textile mills until the 1980s, all of which collapsed and finally shut down by the mid or the late 1990s. Vidarbha had already lost its handloom industry in the 1980s, when India got a new textile policy that crushed the traditional textiles and pushed out the old players of the once-booming business—lock, stock and barrel. Powerlooms dislodged the handlooms first and then knocked down the integrated mills.

Some big names went broke and exited the sector. In my home town, the Empress Mills—the torchbearer of the Tata empire—taken over by the Maharashtra State Textile Corporation in the mid-1980s, finally came to a grinding halt in 2004. Before that, the Model Mills crumbled and the Cooperative Spinning Mills of Nagpur bowed out of competition, all unable to make a profitable transition to the ways of the new globalizing world.

The shutting down of handlooms and the textile mills, and the tragic collapse of Vidarbha's roaring textile economy, which had lasted a hundred years or more, proved to be precursors to the cotton farmers' suicides in later years. The cotton growers lost their major buyers. They had given them long staple cotton if they wanted, short staple cotton when they needed and the famous Oomra, which performed very well in the foreign markets. Farmer suicides and distress followed the crisis in the cotton processing industry of the 1980s and '90s. First, Telangana shot to the news for farmers' suicides, then Vidarbha. The region lost the cotton-to-cloth process it was home to. Historically, Berar farmers had been the primary producers and the local textile industry had kept demand alive, stabilized the cotton trade and passed on to the farmers in some degree the profits they made from their cloth and beautiful apparel.

The famous Morarji Mills of Hinganghat are rubble today. The Pulgaon cotton mills are history. The Khamgaon mills are in a shambles. And the Empress, which once employed hundreds of people and was Nagpur's emblem for a century, has been replaced with a mall.

When I reach Hiwara, Ramrao informs me he is on his farm. Over the phone, he tells me to go to his home, he is heading back. I sit on the swing in the front porch of Ashokrao's modest home and wait. Ashokrao's daughter-in-law Nalini brings me tea. Here, tea is always sugary and strong. Nalini tells me the weather has been abnormally sultry this year and rains are playing truant. Two days ago, she continues, it poured like cats and dogs and destroyed the roofs of some shanties. The downpour only took place in Hiwara. There was not a drop in the surrounding villages.

Nalini is a young woman eager to get out of the agrarian system. The daughter of a farmer herself, she wants her husband, Ramrao's nephew Pravin, to continue with his job—a commission-based sales position—and support his father financially but not take to farming himself. Ashokrao has also not been pushy; he knows it is better to be on a monthly salary than repay a monthly debt. He once explained to me how a farmer's life is a life in debt. Unlike the other girls or women in the village, or her mother-in-law, Nalini stays home, working her leg-peddled Usha sewing machine, and earns small sums of money from villagers. She does patchwork, fall-pico, embroidery, stitching baby clothes and children's pants and shirts. She is happy with whatever little cash she is able to earn from it. Her daughter is two years old and needs attention, she tells me in Marathi with a heavy Telugu accent. At home, the Panchleniwars usually speak in Telugu, but outside they converse in Marathi.

Ramrao hugs me the moment he is home, a warm, friendly embrace. This is new. He holds my hand and reminds me of a Marathi saying which translates into the old English adage: tough times don't last, tough people do.

'This roof got damaged two days ago,' he says, showing me the damage before we step into his home. 'Minor ones I can fix, but some families suffered big damages and will need to spend money to rebuild their homes.' He says one of his labourers would need to rebuild his old, fragile hut that caved in due to the storm. 'I'll need to help him with that,' he says.

Ramrao takes a breather, wipes the sweat off his forehead with a cotton cloth and offers me a glass of water. The water tastes surprisingly clean. He informs me that the village panchayat has recently installed an RO machine—a reverse osmosis unit—on a borewell. Villagers can buy purified drinking water now. It's not exactly bottled mineral water, but Hiwara's households can buy a container of 50 litres for ₹3; a women's self-help group operates the RO on behalf of the panchayat. Hiwara falls under the Fifth Schedule of the Constitution, where the Panchayats Extension to the Scheduled Areas Act (PESA) is applicable. The RO machine was installed from the funds given by the tribal welfare department. Across Maharashtra, RO machines are mushrooming in towns and villages and private water sales are a booming business.

After lunch, we walk to his farm. Both of us are sweating and panting due to the crushing humidity. The village's main alley—a cement road—smells bad, there's human excreta everywhere. Hiwara is not yet open-defecation free, and in the monsoons the children sit on the road to relieve themselves because they fear going into the farms where snakes, frogs and crabs abound. Stagnant water and dirt all around become breeding grounds for mosquitoes. Soon, Hiwara can be expected to report a spate of viral fever, diarrhoea and diseases. The weather this month is conducive for such outbreaks.

On the way to the farm, Ramrao briefs me about Alakya's problems with her in-laws, his financial woes—the Central Bank did not give him crop loan again this year—and the massive challenges he faces every day to balance his spending.

When we reach his farm, he says to me, 'Come this way,' leading me through the rows of tall cotton plants with unusually thick foliage. The soil on the farm is muddy, which makes it awfully difficult to walk on. My boots are soiled and I am getting sucked into the moist pits. Ramrao is walking briskly despite his torn rubber floaters. He is not worried about his legs. He is more concerned about his cotton crop which he thinks is in serious trouble. Small bolls hang from the branches of the cotton plants on his field. They will, when they mature, burst into white cotton.

I ask Ramrao if the growth of the plants points to a potentially robust crop and he responds, 'Not necessarily.' The height of the plants is, however, exceptional this year, he tells me. I follow him, drenched in sweat, wading through the plants to the middle of his farm, near the well, when I smell marigolds. There is a patch of land where small flowers are blooming on knee-high plants. These are local varieties. There are hybrid plants too—lovely yellow, saffron and ochre. Marigold usually comes in full bloom in October, so it is a few weeks before the fields are dotted with colourful flowers.

'This is early flowering,' Ramrao tells me buoyantly. He plucks some flowers, uproots a few saplings and collects them in a bag for me to take home and plant in my garden.

And then he picks a few cotton bolls with his fingers to show me small bores beneath them that look like pin-pricks. I spot many bolls that bear similar marks. Ramrao cracks open a green, hard boll that is yet to mature to show me what lies inside. And a small, centimetre-long pink worm twirls up, as if to say hello. It's alive and has perhaps laid eggs inside. The white lint, still under formation, has already been devoured by the worm. This will soon multiply into thousands of worms, who will devour this farm in a matter of days. By harvest season, the pink bollworm, as it is called, will turn the entire produce into poor-quality cotton not fit for any use unless Ramrao physically finds the infested bolls and destroys them. They multiply fast.

Presumably of Indo-Pak origin, the pink bollworm feeds only on a few crops such as cotton, okra, hibiscus and jute. It lays eggs on flowers, young bolls, axils of petioles and on the underside of young leaves. After hatching, the young larvae penetrate the ovaries of flowers or young bolls within two days of hatching.

The larvae turn pink in three to four days and the degree of pink depends on the food that the larvae eat. Dark pink results from eating mature seeds. Larvae prefer feeding on developing seeds and generally pupate inside the seeds and bolls. Affected bolls either open prematurely or rot. Fibre qualities such as length and strength are lowered and the cotton lint in the infested bolls gets damaged by a secondary fungal infection.

Pink bollworm generally arrives with the onset of winter and continues to thrive on the crop as long as flowers and bolls are available. Long-duration cotton allows the pest to survive for a longer period in multiple cycles, thereby affecting the subsequent crop. The pink bollworm is genetically predisposed to undergoing hibernation or diapause, allowing it to be dormant for six to eight months, until the next season.

Bolls after bolls of Ramrao's cotton crop are threatened by this small pest. It is the same case on every field. He thinks it is a bad omen. This worm has come back after decades.

'Now what do you do?' Ramrao wonders. 'I did everything to make sure my plants grow well. What can you do if there are unexpected threats?'

He walks slowly through the rows of cotton plants, carefully observing each stalk. In between he turns back to show me an infested boll. From across Vidarbha, reports of a massive pink bollworm attack are pouring in. The cotton scientists at the Central Institute of Cotton Research (CICR) in Nagpur had expressed fears about this infestation for some time. This is a new factor aggravating the problems of the beleaguered peasantry.

For two decades, every year, an insidious new factor is added to the list of old reasons compounding the problems of the peasantry. Pink bollworm is the new factor in 2017, like note-bandi was the previous year. The old structural problems remain: small and fragmented lands, rain-dependent dry- and arid-land agriculture, liquidity crunch, lack of access to institutional credit, problems with access to high-quality seeds and inputs, the volatile nature of markets, social discrimination, the lack of alternative income sources, and so on.

'Farming is the most difficult profession,' Ramrao says loudly as he hands me the bag of marigold saplings and flowers. 'Take these flowers and shower them on the deity you love. Plant these saplings at home. They will bring happiness and fragrance to your home, they will brighten your life!'

Once a proclaimed non-believer, Ramrao is goading me to take the flowers to a temple. 'What is so special about this marigold?' I ask him. He merely smiles but parries the question. We walk back to his house. It is Alakya who, in December, will give me the answer.

TONSURED HEAD, A LARGE dark vermillion mark on his forehead—it's his large bloodshot eyes which reveal he is nervous, maybe even frightened.

It is swelteringly hot outside and the house is packed, adding physical discomfort to the prevailing air of unease. His old mother and an amputee father, who lost both his legs long back, sit behind him. Their breathing is laboured as though it's a burden. They look older than they perhaps are. Guests, mostly relatives and villagers, are finished with their lunch. There is an eerie silence enveloping the house.

Namdev Soyam, the young man in his mid-twenties with the tonsured head and vermillion mark, is clearly disoriented. His movements are slow. He stammers while responding to my questions and stares at me as if lost. His wife looks on in silence from a distance, worried about her husband's pitiable condition.

'He is in shock,' one of his relatives tells me, finally noticing the young man's state.

On a plastic chair next to him under the thatched porch of their home rests a freshly garlanded, newly framed photo of a young man. Rose petals and marigold flowers lie strewn around it and burning incense sticks lie in front of it. The photo announces the tragedy that has befallen this family. They are a 15-acre, rain-dependent farming household of Pardhan adivasis. It has been forty-eight hours since twenty-three-year-old Pravin Soyam died, when I arrive a day before Dussehra, on 29 September 2017, at the household.

Tembhi village is about 40 kilometres south of Pandharkawda—not far from Ramrao's village—on the highway to Hyderabad. Pravin was Namdev's younger brother. Namdev was unwell, so their father, Bhaurao, had sent Pravin to the farm to spray pesticides. 'That was on 25 September,' Bhaurao tells me, his eyes glued to the garlanded photo. Pravin was healthier, taller and ten times more hardworking than Namdev is, he says softly.

'What did he spray?'

My question prompts Namdev to get up. He goes inside the house and reappears with bags and cans of a range of insecticides: Asataf, Ruby, Polo, Profex Super and Monocrotophos. He places them on the mud floor of the verandah, next to the plastic chair on which Pravin's A-4 sized photo rests.

When cotton hybrids were introduced in the early 1990s, they came with synthetic pyrethroids to tackle new pests. After that, new-generation, highly complex toxic chemicals have been unleashed onto farmers to manage pests over the past two decades. The farmers spray absurd quantities of these on their farms without adequate knowledge of their application. Proscribed weedicides such as Roundup Ready can be found freely in the market.

'What are these for?' I check with Namdev and he stares back at me in stony silence. 'Who told you to use this?'

He does not answer but stares intently at me.

'The inputs dealer from where we bought the chemicals told us to spray these on the fields,' his father says.

Neither Namdev nor his father can read or write, or even pronounce the name of any chemical they have bought. There is no way they will ever know the compounds in those chemicals, if they are fit to be sprayed on the farms, and in what quantities.

The cocktail of pesticides, mixed in a big blue drum full of water, that he sprayed and inhaled on that muggy, hot day proved fatal. Pravin's death was not due to pesticide consumption but caused by accidental inhalation. The accident happened after an unprecedented pest attack on the fields—something Ramrao had intimated me about the last time we met.

Like Ramrao, and most farmers in the district, the Soyams mainly grow cotton, soybeans and lentils on their farm. As the family mourns the sudden loss of Pravin to an unexpected cause, Vidarbha is waking up to a pesticide disaster.

Spurred by reports of widespread pesticide poisoning across western Vidarbha, a phenomenon new to these parts on such a large scale, I am travelling in the cotton country to learn more. I call Ramrao over the phone and he informs me that he has halted spraying pesticides out of fear for his labourers' health in the wake of reports, from all over Yavatmal and Amravati, of tens of farmers falling sick due to inhalation or dying from contact poisoning while spraying. 'My men's lives are more important than cotton,' he tells me.

Dussehra and Diwali are marred by the dance of death.

'*Tumhale sangitlo hoto!* I had told you,' he says, boasting about his foresight. '*Yanda bhay garmi aahe ani bond ali ne mamla pura bhaskavun takla aahe.*' He blames the exceptional heat and the pink bollworm for the state of affairs.

I continue my journeys into the ravaged hinterland, promising Ramrao that I will see him soon. In the following two months, I visit tens of villages, check in with patients at the Yavatmal district general hospital, and meet several farmers to understand the extent and gravity of the accidental pesticide poisoning. Cotton fields all along the roads seem taller than average. The thick vegetative growth makes it suffocating for anybody to enter the rows of cotton plants which are planted in the high-density system.

From July through November, there is a flood of farmers in hospitals, both government and private, with complaints ranging from vision loss to nervous breakdown and respiratory problems.

I MEET DR ASHOK Rathod, the dean of Vasantrao Naik Government Medical College and Hospital (GMCH) in Yavatmal, for an interview in the first week of October. He tells me, 'This is a very unusual phenomenon and something I have never witnessed.' His hospital is in the middle of a full-blown public health crisis and clearly short on ideas on how to tackle it, something that sadly results in aggravating the situation.

'We first noticed a sudden spike in such patients in the last week of July,' he says. 'They all came in distress, with complaints of vomiting, dizziness, nervousness, respiratory problems, a sudden visual impairment and disorientation.'

For five months, three wards of the hospital—numbers 12, 18 and 19—were chock-a-block with farmers and farm labourers ailing from heavy toxic poisoning.

In July, forty-one patients came to the hospital. The figure rose to 111 in August, and September saw more than 300 patients pour in, all of them with similar complaints. The crisis continues to unfold in October and November, with more than a thousand farmers getting admitted to different hospitals in Yavatmal. Similar complaints are reported from Akola, Washim, Amravati, Wardha and Nagpur—the other districts of Vidarbha. The agriculture officials are perplexed. So are the health officials.

The cases taper off by the end of November, with winter setting in and farmers completely stalling the spraying of pesticides out of fear. But by then, the damage is done: to humans and the cotton crop that is under an unprecedented pest attack.

Every village had someone falling sick. As Narayan Kotrange of Manoli village did when he felt dizzy one day after spraying a combination of profenofos and a synthetic pyrethroid on his 10-acre leased land. 'I had done nine sprayings already, but on the tenth occasion I decided to stop. I could not work for the following entire week, I was ill,' he tells me.

On the seventh day of spraying pesticides on a farm where he worked on an annual contract, twenty-one-year-old Nikesh Kathane collapsed around noon in the first week of October. 'My head felt very heavy,' he says in mid-October, recuperating on a bed in the ICU of the Yavatmal hospital, the same ward where Ramrao was admitted in 2014. 'I could not see anything. I was losing my vision. I was terrified.'

His modest farmer parents were tense. 'We rushed him to the hospital the same evening,' his brother Laxman says. That helped. Any delay could have proved fatal. Nikesh, who has vowed never to spray pesticides ever again, had muscular spasms. He is out of danger but petrified being surrounded by nine other patients in the ICU battling for their lives. He has been in the ICU for a week when I meet him. He used a China-made, battery-operated spray pump—it makes spraying easier, faster and thus more dangerous. 'You spray more in less time with this pump. I now know it is bad.'

Nikesh is from Dahegaon village, 30 kilometres from Yavatmal city. I discover five more patients from his village recuperating in the other wards of the hospital; they are safe but suffering from the aftereffects of poisoning. In ward 18, Indal Rathod, twenty-nine, a 4-acre farmer from Wadgaon village, is still disoriented. He has been in the hospital for about ten days.

Fear and panic reign in the crowded hospital wards and in the dusty cotton hinterland. Cotton farmers, for long tormented by a cycle of indebtedness, lowering of income, nature's eccentricities, and erosion in their social and economic status, are faced with a new and unanticipated problem.

'The blood tests of these patients show that the poisoning hit their nervous system,' a junior resident doctor, who is attending to Nikhil and others in the ICU, tells me. The impact, he says, was the same as consumption but its treatment was difficult as one could not perform a stomach wash to remove the traces of poison. Inhaling fumes directly affected the respiratory system. There was more, but the reasons would only be discovered over the course of the investigation.

Hundreds of farmers continue to suffer from the aftereffects of the tragedy. Some of them lose their eyesight and would never be able to get back their vision. Many others would never be able to go back to farms, shattered and rattled by the poisoning to pick up spraying pumps again, which affects farmer–labour relations.

The testimonies of farmers who are hospitalized, and of the kith and kin of those who die in the tragic accidents, indicate two broad trends: one particular insecticide formulation in powder form caused visual impairment among those who used it, and those who used a specific liquid formulation suffered from nervous system breakdown. These formulations contained a mix of profenofos (an organophosphate), cypermethrin (a synthetic pyrethroid) and diafenthiuron, prescribed to be used on multiple crops. Combined together, they formed a deadly toxic composition, as the literature suggests, potent enough to kill a man.

Pravin Soyam's health deteriorated gradually. At first, he complained of chest pain, then vomiting and nausea and, towards the end, nervousness. Within twenty-four hours, he had slipped into a coma.

The day after he fell sick, he died within three hours of reaching the cottage hospital of Pandharkawda. Doctors attending to him suspected that he died of contact poisoning—he and the others who died or fell sick did not take adequate safety precautions that ought to have been followed while spraying. No farmer in this part follows the measures: like wearing hand gloves, a mask or body-protection apparel. Bare-bodied, in a tearing hurry to finish their work, spraying more to earn more, the farmers and farm labourers put their lives on the line every day through the spraying season. Pravin complained of weakness on the day he went to spray the farm, but refused to see a doctor.

As I sit talking to his father, something strangely reminds me of Ramrao. A garland of marigold hangs by the framed photo of Pravin, whose life was yet to start when it got snapped. He did not take his own life, but was felled by a process of the industrialization of agriculture that went beyond his or his family's comprehension.

'We thought it was due to the heat. It was hot and humid, and fever is common during this period,' Bhaurao says. When Pravin's condition deteriorated the following evening, Namdev and his mother took him to the primary health centre in the next village, where an attendant, sensing that his was an emergency case, referred him to the Pandharkawda hospital. They reached the hospital around 7 p.m. Pravin died in his old mother's lap around 10 p.m. His post-mortem report simply said: 'Death due to organophosphate poisoning.'

AFTER FINISHING MY FIELD trip mid-October, I stop by Ramrao's home. He is as usual on his field.

Ramrao knows there has been mayhem in Yavatmal and much of western Vidarbha's cotton-growing villages. 'This thing, the deaths due to inhalation,' he tells me on the phone, 'tragic!' And then he hangs up, saying he will be with me in five minutes.

'*Me don batlya peun melo nahi, lok vasana marat hay*,' he announces loudly as he enters his compound, as if he had been waiting all this while to make the wisecrack. He finds it odd that he did not die after consuming two bottles of insecticides, while people were now dying just from inhalation. '*Ajab nyay aahe*!' Fate is strange indeed.

I smile at him. It is another example of Vidarbha's dark humour. People crack jokes over their problems, see humour in death and laugh at themselves. Ramrao freshens up and returns wiping his face with a towel. He then urges Nalini to make us tea.

'This year, pests have come in hordes,' Ramrao cites as the reason behind the spurt in the intense spraying of a mix of pesticides. 'See, this is all ignorance,' he says of the deaths that have stirred the administration and spread panic among villages. 'Most farmers don't think, don't ask, don't know what to spray for what pests.'

He blames the government but also his own kind for being ignorant. He too is ignorant about new chemicals, he says.

Ramrao expects at least 30 per cent losses due to the pink bollworm infestation, or maybe more. He has managed to physically destroy a lot of such infested bolls. That's what he has been doing all through the previous month or so. It will also affect the quality of his cotton, which in turn will fetch him lower prices. He will suffer losses on account of a decline in his productivity and the substandard quality of his cotton. It's the same story with other farmers in Hiwara, who complain to me of the unforeseen losses this year.

The new-generation chemical pesticides and farm inputs involve a complex world of biology and chemistry that has taken farming to a whole new, incomprehensible plane for farmers. And they are expensive. Ramrao spends a minimum of a lakh or two on pesticides, insecticides, weedicides, growth promoters, fertilizers and much more, and so do other farmers. Collectively, Hiwara's farmers spend large amounts of money on farm inputs (seeds, fertilizers, chemicals), on energy (diesel for a tractor, power for the pumps) and labour wages (which fluctuate depending on demand and availability).

One day, at my request, he tabulates how much he has to spend per acre to grow cotton. In the 1990s, it was ₹4,000 to ₹5,000. In 2017, his per-acre production cost is over ten times that amount. He spends more money today than he did two or three decades ago to grow a quintal of cotton, tur, chilli or any other produce, but his income from it remains more or less stagnant. His production costs have multiplied—he uses more units of fertilizers, more chemicals, even more organic manure to grow the same amount he did ten years ago. He had to stop using a tractor because it was too expensive.

Ramrao was fortunate, though. He was ignorant about what he was consuming to kill himself. The insecticide he consumed, Coragen, is not an organophosphate, unlike Monocrotophos, a poisonous chemical that cotton farmers in this region use to tame the colonies of pests of all kinds. Had he taken 'Mono' or Endosulphan, the pesticide thousands of farmers have consumed to kill themselves, the poison would have choked him to death. For many years, Endosulphan was the number one killer—of pests and of farmers. It was readily available, easily accessible, and cheap.

Manufactured by Dupont, Coragen is chlorantraniliprole, an insect control compound from a new class of chemicals—the Anthralinic Diamides, normally used to contain sugarcane pests. Ramrao had bought it for his green gram and vegetables. Water-soluble, it is to be sprayed on crops with utmost care as per the guidelines that come with the insecticide bottle. That is true of handling any chemical in agriculture. Doctors say this particular compound can affect the kidneys, setting in motion a reaction that can cripple the functioning of vital organs, which in turn may lead to death. In Ramrao's case, it had not yet got into the veins and seeped into the blood.

Chemical pesticides impact the parasympathetic nervous system, which controls our metabolism too.

Any poisonous chemical used as a pest-control measure generally increases the acetylcholinesterase level in blood. Acetylcholinesterase, also known as AChE or acetylhydrolase, is the primary cholinesterase in the body, an enzyme that catalyses the breakdown of acetylcholine and of some other choline esters that function as neurotransmitters.

Atropine injections—one of the immediate interventions—reverses that action and helps drop the acetylcholine level, mitigating the impact of pesticide poisoning and steadily cleansing the blood to restore the functioning of the nervous system and metabolism. Atropine acts antagonistically to the organophosphate poison by stimulating acetylcholine. Organophosphate molecules get absorbed via the skin, through inhalation or in the gastrointestinal tract through deliberate consumption. Once absorbed, the molecule binds to an acetylcholinesterase molecule in the red blood cells and makes the enzyme inactive. This leads to an overabundance of acetylcholine within synapses and neuromuscular junctions. Over-stimulation of nicotinic receptors found at neuromuscular junctions can lead to fasciculations and myoclonic jerks. This eventually leads to flaccid paralysis. Nicotinic receptors are also found in the adrenal glands which may cause hypertension, sweating, tachycardia and leukocytosis. Organophosphate poisoning also produces symptoms based on its action on muscarinic receptors. Muscarinic receptors are found in the parasympathetic and sympathetic nervous system. Sweat glands within the sympathetic nervous system get overstimulated and cause large amounts of sweating. The parasympathetic effects of organophosphate poisoning can be seen in multiple systems including the heart, exocrine glands and smooth muscles. At some point, which is different for each specific compound, the acetylcholinesterase-organophosphate compound undergoes a process called ageing. This renders the enzyme resistant to reactivation, making some treatment options useless.

On the other hand, although chlorantraniliprole is widely claimed to be nontoxic to humans, doctors say it may cause conduction defects. It has a different mode of action compared to other common insecticides and acts as a ryanodine receptor modulator. Here's how it works: chlorantraniliprole activates ryanodine receptors through stimulation of the release of calcium stores from the sarcoplasmic reticulum of muscle cells, causing impaired regulation, paralysis and ultimately the death of sensitive species. The differential selectivity of this compound towards insect ryanodine receptors explains its low mammalian toxicity. It is active on chewing pests, primarily by ingestion and secondarily by contact, and shows good ovi-larvicidal and larvicidal activity.

RAMRAO BURSTS INTO A loud laugh. 'In any case,' he says in a sarcastic tone that is natural to him, 'there is no need to consume poison. Farmers will die standing in queues for every damn thing.' There have indeed been some deaths due to exhaustion and fatigue as several old farmers suffered heart attacks all over India while standing in queues to apply for various schemes and during demonetization.

Ramrao and I are joined by his old maternal uncle, Vitthalrao Shankaneniwar, his elder brother Ashokrao, his cousin and other farmers from the neighbourhood who are back home after a hard day's work. They share stories of pesticide poisoning from around the vicinity and talk about their desperation resulting from the pest attacks on their crops. I see Ashokrao annoyed for the first time.

All of them have stopped their spraying operations out of fear, despite the pest attacks and impending losses. Winter is about to set in. The soybean crop, they say, has bombed. Prices of all the commodities—tur, cotton, soybean, chillies, vegetables and perishables are down. The cotton crop holds no promise because of the pest attack, and the productivity of the Bt cotton hybrids has plateaued.

A month later, by the end of November, the Special Investigation Team (SIT) formed by the state government to probe the Yavatmal deaths submitted its report. It acknowledged that about fifty farmers lost their lives between July and November 2017 in Yavatmal and other parts of eastern Vidarbha and over a thousand fell ill, some lost their eyesight but survived the contact or inhalation of a cocktail of pesticides. It stated that a few lives could have been saved if the Yavatmal hospital had means to perform the crucial blood test required to detect the presence of organophosphate compounds in the farmers. In the absence of the cholinesterase test and the antidote, doctors continued to treat the patients symptomatically. Also, there was no communication between the district and the state administrations regarding the gravity and scale of the health emergency.

Under the Insecticides Act, 1968, it is mandatory to constitute a district-level interdepartmental committee which would then institute a monitoring mechanism to keep a tab on whether farmers, agencies and companies were complying with the provisions of this law. Neither such a committee existed nor any monitoring mechanism was in vogue.

The state government constituted the SIT on 10 October 2017, following a report by a fact-finding team headed by the divisional commissioner of Amravati, Piyush Singh. It comprised six other members, including Dr Vijay Waghmare, director of the Central Institute of Cotton Research (CICR), Nagpur, and Kiran Deshkar from the Directorate of Plant Protection, Faridabad.

The report submitted by the SIT was not made public by the Maharashtra cabinet until the Bombay High Court asked it to release it to the public in January 2018 while hearing a public interest litigation.

In exceptionally humid conditions, the SIT report stated, working on the farms was like walking through mist into a toxic chamber, inhaling fumes. 'The concentration of new formulations of pesticides and other chemicals increased the toxicity and possibility of inhalation and contact poisoning in extremely humid conditions,' it said.

While the report did not mention the complete breakdown of the agriculture extension system, or the responsibility of training farmers in the dos and don'ts of handling highly toxic chemicals on their farms, it did indicate that the farmers were attempting things on their own, desperately trying to contain pest attacks and pushing plant growth in the hope of better crop yields and returns on the advice of inputs dealers.

In that four-month period, western Vidarbha's cotton farmers made a cocktail of synthetic pyrethroids, organophosphates and other new-generation chemicals in addition to plant growth promoters such as gibbralic acid (to increase plant girth), indol acitic acid (to increase plant length), and indol butyric acid (for better roots) and some unapproved chemicals such as humid acid, nitrobenzine and amino acids. The farmers used a combination of Fipronil and Imidacloprid pesticides that have not been approved for use—the local markets are flush with such imported, ready-to-use, liquids. There are no checks whatsoever or a system to keep a tab on the unabated use of unapproved chemicals. For instance, there are sixteen talukas in Yavatmal, but the district has only one quality-control inspector assigned to it and even that post was vacant for two years.

In view of the farmers' unabated use of chemicals to control pests on cotton, soybean and other crops, the SIT recommended that the Vasantrao Naik Memorial GMCH in Yavatmal should be equipped with the facility to perform the cholinesterase test, which helps understand what is inhibiting the neurotransmitters, and given access to the organophosphate poisoning antidote. The GMCH in Amravati, the divisional headquarters in western Vidarbha, could better manage the poisoning epidemic as it had the facility to perform the cholinesterase test and the antidotes to treat such poisoning.

The SIT team also recommended setting up separate ICUs at the sub-district hospitals at Wani and Pusad, the tehsil headquarters in Yavatmal, in addition to setting up a separate thirty-bed ICU at the Yavatmal GMCH and a twenty-bed ICU in the Akola district government hospital to deal with pesticide poisoning cases. It recommended the setting up of a state-of-the-art toxicology lab at Yavatmal GMCH, given the district's long history of such cases. In 2017 too, the health authorities had not sent blood samples for toxicology tests immediately, which proved to be a key gap in the management of the mass poisoning incidents.

But the SIT report largely pinned the blame on farmers and farm labourers for such a massive outbreak of contact poisoning as they had failed to adhere to the rules and protection measures prescribed for spraying chemicals on robust, dense and tall cotton plants in humid conditions.

The SIT recommended a complete ban on Monocrotophos, the organophosphate banned in many countries due to its toxic effects on humans and birds. Though the Maharashtra government complied with a limited-period ban in November prohibiting its sale and marketing for sixty days, it did not enforce a complete ban on its use. The Union government has the power to ban Monocrotophos countrywide under the Insecticides Act, 1968. The states too can suspend licences or stop renewing or issuing fresh licences the way Punjab did in 2017 with twenty pesticides, including Monocrotophos, which the Food and Agriculture Organization classifies as 'acutely or highly hazardous'. Kerala is another state that has banned Monocrotophos, and Sikkim, a fully organic state, does not allow any chemical use at all.

The SIT in its other major recommendation stated that the government should not approve the use of an insecticide unless there is an antidote available in case of poisoning. It also indicated a spurt in the use of plant growth regulators and recommended that the government ensure there is scientific scrutiny of the long-term use of such chemicals before they are approved for use.

As of January 2021, though, no SIT recommendation has been implemented.

Hidden in the report, however, was another major observation that forms the crux of the problem in Vidarbha and beyond, something that Ramrao and some other farmers of Hiwara had told me about. The cotton fields were ravaged by an unprecedented attack of pests that turned the farmers desperate. Of all the pests, though, the return of the pink bollworm was particularly worrisome.

THE BLACK SCARS DOTTING the green bolls of a wilting cotton plant on forty-two-year-old Ganesh Wadandre's farm carries a message for the scientists working on white gold: find a new antidote.

'Those are the entry points,' Wadandre tells me. He has a 5-acre farm and is well regarded by his fellow villagers in Wardha's Amgaon-Khadki village. The village falls between Nagpur and Wardha, a place famous for a Hanuman temple where travellers stop to take darshan. Wadandre is an ardent devotee of the deity, and I am reminded of Ramrao. The worm, he tells me in the language of an expert, drilled into the boll from where the black scars appear.

This is exactly what Ramrao had showed me in August.

'If we crack it open, you'll see a pink worm devouring it from within,' he says, exuding nervousness and anger. I know it by now, having seen it on farms all over the region during the past few months. As he cracks it open, a pink worm less than a centimetre long indeed wakes up. It has devoured the cotton boll before the formation of white lint, leaving it worthless.

Wadandre's account, similar to Ramrao's, typifies the emotions of cotton growers across Maharashtra. At the peak of the cotton season, hectares and hectares of cotton fields were left devastated by swarming armies of pink bollworm, causing unprecedented damages not seen in thirty years.

Fields around Wadandre's farm too show telltale signs of pink bollworm attack: black, wilting, scarred bolls sprouting into blackened lint, which is of no use.

'No pesticide is useful for this,' he says. 'It is that lethal. What's the use of Bt cotton now?'

Amgaon-Khadki is about 150 kilometres from Hiwara but the two are bound by the same problems—from the financial crunch to the pest exigency. Villages in Vidarbha's cotton belt are truly identical in their troubles.

Some official estimates based on surveys done by the agriculture and the revenue departments peg the pink bollworm infestation at over 80 per cent of the 42 lakh hectares under cotton cultivation in Maharashtra, and the damage ranging from a modest 33 per cent to over 50 per cent. In January 2018, Maharashtra predicts a dip in the cotton production by 40 per cent—an admission of large-scale pest destruction. When you are already anemic, any more blood loss is fatal. It's like that right now—farmers running thin on their finances jolted by another major loss on top of an ongoing agrarian crisis.

Such is the scale of infestation that hundreds of small and rain-fed cotton farmers like Wadandre abandon their fields in December 2017. The picking costs, he tells me the next month, overshot the amount he would recover by selling the battered cotton. 'It's cheaper to leave it than to harvest it.'

That's what cotton farmers in Maharashtra did in 2017 and early 2018. Ramrao did not. He picked all that he could so that he could at least bear the labour wages. Some ran bulldozers on the standing crop, others mauled it, still others did not pick cotton in sheer disgust as the worm swarmed large swathes of snowy white cotton fields. I stood witness to the devastation by the pink bollworm and to the fact that the governments in the state and at the Centre did nothing more than promise a better crop insurance scheme and support for organic farming.

A pitiful harvest followed the fatal fallout of accidental pesticide inhalation in western Vidarbha. As winter peaked—a time the pink bollworm relishes—the cotton peasantry stood shattered by the impending losses, a new reason adding to their pile of woes.

When I first met Wadandre, he had no hope for his farm. The rate at which the pest was multiplying every day, he said, made him nervous. 'I might flatten my farm soon.'

No amount of pesticides or insecticides would help. The worm bores into the bolls and protects itself from chemical sprays.

The crisis is an indicator of the storm brewing in the Indian cotton fields. The much-touted Bt cotton, which had controversially entered the Indian scene fifteen years earlier, has cracked. What's more, there is no new technology on the anvil. The desperation in the farmers and within the establishment is mounting.

I think of Ramrao and call him to share my observations, and he reminds me of what he had told me: This pest has come back with a vengeance and would leave farmers devastated this year.

THE RETURN OF THE pink bollworm first sent alarm bells ringing in the country's agriculture establishment in 2015. The initial estimate of the destruction, as per the state farm commissioner's office in Pune, was then pegged at 20 lakh hectares—that is, half the total sown area under cotton in Maharashtra. India had about 130 lakh hectares under cotton in 2017-18, and the pink bollworm menace was widespread in Gujarat, Maharashtra, Madhya Pradesh and Telangana.

The Union agriculture ministry acknowledged the problem but rejected the demand from Maharashtra and other states to de-notify Bt cotton. Instead, the Centre asked all cotton-producing states to deal with the menace on their own 'by involving various stakeholders'.

The Indian cotton research establishment was mighty worried over the 'breakdown' of the genetically modified (GM) Bt cotton following field reports in 2015 and 2016 of the return of pink bollworm on standing crops in all major cotton-growing states. Their anxiety was on display at the two high-level meetings held in May 2017 in New Delhi by the Indian Council of Agriculture Research (ICAR) and the Indian Council of Scientific Research (ICSR). The two bodies specifically discussed public sector initiatives on GM crops in the wake of reports from the apex cotton institute in Nagpur, the CICR, and the intensity of the pink bollworm's outbreak. The CICR feared that American bollworms were also set to return as a major cotton pest sooner rather than later.

Monsanto, the American agricultural biotechnology multinational now bought by the European behemoth Bayer, currently has a monopoly over India's Bt cotton seed market, with two of its popular technologies to control the virulent bollworm pests. The Indian public sector has no presence in the GM seed markets. A few institutions are now beginning to wake up to the possibilities of GM crop research and have begun work on research for a limited number of crops.

'There's no doubt that the bollworms are back,' CICR director Dr Keshav Kranthi wrote in an article in *Cotton Statistics and News*, a weekly publication of the Cotton Association of India. 'How best we can sustain the bollworm control efficacy of Bt cotton is a major concern.'

In both the high-level meetings, scientists pondered over the best available options to control the bollworms but did not go beyond two or three measures.

'The best long-term strategy for India is to grow short-duration Bt cotton hybrids or varieties that don't last beyond January,' Kranthi, who has since moved to the International Cotton Advisory Committee (ICAC) in Washington DC, told me in mid-2017. That would negate the bollworms, for they attack the cotton bolls mainly in winter season, he reasoned.

The problem is that most Indian seed companies produce long-duration Bt cotton hybrids. Moreover, the 2017 bollworm infestation actually started early, in the monsoon, and for some inexplicable reason continued well after the winter season the following year.

Bt cotton contains cry (crystal) genes derived from a soil-dwelling bacterium, bacillus thuringiensis, inserted into the cotton plant genome (genetic material of the cell) to provide protection against the bollworm.

The CICR studies had feared that the irrigated cotton areas in Gujarat, Karnataka and Maharashtra would be in the grip of pink bollworm attacks. North India would not see the pests immediately but in a couple of years, the studies had predicted in 2016. They were right.

Though the pink pest showed up sporadically on Bt cotton first in 2010, the signs of a major worry emerged in November 2015, when Gujarat farmers reported a massive pink bollworm infestation on their standing cotton crop. An inch-long worm chewing the boll from inside looked in the pink of health, signalling the breakdown of this expensive, genetically modified cotton meant to combat its infestation.

In the last week of November 2015, a woman farmer in Gujarat's Bhavnagar district randomly plucked a few cotton bolls from a plant on her field and cracked them open for the team of visiting cotton experts to see what lay inside.

'She was very angry,' Kranthi, the principal scientist who led that team, recalled during that conversation with me in mid-2017.

The scientists were aghast to see that pink-coloured worms had devoured the green cotton bolls from inside. The woman farmer's anger was triggered by her imminent losses—the small but menacing pest had dented both her cotton yields and its quality. But the scientists' worry went beyond it. The Pectinophora Gossypiella (Saunders), popularly known as pink bollworm, had made a comeback in India after three decades. It was a hint that American bollworms could return too. The two pests were among the most lethal insects that troubled cotton farmers in India in the 1970s and '80s. Bt cotton was supposed to be a fix to both.

The CICR studies showed that, in the 2015-16 season, acres and acres of cotton crop were affected by pink bollworm, reducing the yields by an estimated 7–8 per cent.

'Pinkworm has developed resistance to the much-touted Bt cotton technology,' Kranthi said. 'Over a period of time bollworms will also develop resistance.' It means farmers would now have to adjust to a less-potent Bt and BG-II cotton technology and go back to using insecticides to control bollworms.

The problem with the pink bollworm is that farmers can't find out the damage before the bolls burst, leading to shocks during harvest and also at market yards where the bollworm-damaged cotton fetches much lower prices.

Unfortunately, there is no new technology in sight now or in the near future, whether GM or insecticides, that promises to replace BG-II. So, India is back to square one, with regard to cotton, which occupies nearly 120 lakh hectares, next to wheat and rice, and creates crores of man-days of employment in rural India.

The BG-II technology, which involves the introduction of Cry1Ac and Cry2Ab genes from bacillus thuringiensis into cotton plants, was claimed to build resistance against three insect pests: American bollworm (Helicoverpa armigera), pink bollworm and spotted bollworm (Earias vittella). The first-generation hybrids, or Bt cotton, contained only one Cry1Ac gene in the seeds.

The return of the pink bollworm and the serious damage it caused to the crop in 2016 pit around fifty Indian cotton-seed companies against Monsanto. Monsanto had introduced Bt cotton in India around 2002-03 by transferring the technology to Indian seed companies at about 20 per cent royalty on every seed bag sold. At least forty-six companies refused to pay royalty to Monsanto but that is a different battle—and another story.

That year, in Vidarbha, a bag of 400 gm of Bt cotton hybrid seeds cost ₹1,000, and Monsanto would get a royalty of ₹200 per bag. According to seed market observers, while the cost of Bt cotton and BG-II hovered around ₹800 per 400 gm bag over the next thirteen years, Monsanto's royalty remained at 20 per cent of the price.

In 2006-07, Monsanto released BG-II hybrids that slowly replaced Bt cotton as the companies phased out the first-generation Bt hybrids, saying the new technology was more durable. The real reason, however, was this: by then, Monsanto no longer had patent rights over BG-I, and could not claim royalty as it did in the initial years. In fact, the company, or its Indian entity, the Mahyco Monsanto Biotech India Limited (MMBL), never had a patent for BG-I in India, as farmers' leader Vijay Jawandhia discovered through a series of Right to Information (RTI) queries later. But farmers continued to pay hefty royalties to the company.

Its patent for BG-II was in effect, so it pushed those hybrids in the Indian market as it would fetch them royalties from the companies and, in turn, from the cotton growers. BG-II, therefore, became the golden goose it claimed would improve yields and incomes and reduce pesticide consumption, thereby saving on costs big time.

The BG-II hybrids now occupy nearly 95 per cent of the land under cotton cultivation in India, according to government estimates.

All along, Kranthi wrote in an article, there was no road map for the sustainable use of Bt technology in India in consonance with ecology and the environment. At least six different Bt events were approved without any event-specific plans devised for their sustainability. Science and scientists were never taken seriously, especially when resistance issues were pointed out. More than a thousand Bt cotton hybrids were approved within just four to five years, creating chaos for agronomy and pest management. The result: Indian cotton farmers faced serious uncertainties of pest management starting 2018.

While the first reports of pink bollworm infestation surfaced in Gujarat in 2010, it was on a very small area and on the first generation of Bt cotton. Between 2012 and 2014, it spread to a much larger area. In the 2015-16 season, surveys conducted by CICR showed that pink bollworm larval survival on BG-II was significantly higher across Gujarat, and the pest had developed resistance to Cry1Ac, Cry2Ab and Cry1Ac+Cry2Ab, particularly in Amreli and Bhavnagar districts. Farmers were already using insecticides to contain pink bollworm in addition to other insects, mainly the sucking pests.

The damage, according to the CICR's extensive field surveys in December 2015, was more especially in the green bolls during second and third pickings—cotton is picked by farmers from bolls as they come to flower in stages spanning four, sometimes five, months, from October through March.

The CICR's studies came up with several factors for the resurgence of pink bollworm and the failure of BG-II. Among others: the cultivation of long-duration hybrids that serve as continuous hosts of the pink bollworm.

Kranthi said that Bt cotton in India should have been released in open pollinated varieties (or straight-line desi cotton), not in hybrids. India is the only country to have permitted Bt genes to be impregnated in the hybrid varieties instead of straight-line—farmers need not buy seeds from the market again if they plant straight-line varieties, but with hybrids they have to buy seeds every year—which was a costly proposition. The BG-II should not have been approved in long-duration hybrids but we, as a nation, did exactly the opposite.

INDIA INTRODUCED BT COTTON around 2000 and Vidarbha started to see the proliferation of its cultivation from 2002. As Bt seeds crowded the inputs dealers' shops, the non-Bt hybrid seeds or even local varieties vanished in a few years. By 2004, I could see no old seed varieties at any shop in Vidarbha, not even at MahaBeej, the state government-run seeds corporation.

In the initial period, the marketing campaign run by Indian seed companies for Bt cotton seeds was so intense that it resembled the fervour and mood of electioneering. After all, there was money to be made.

Monsanto was the first company in the world to develop and commercialize Bt cotton technology, namely, Bollgard-I (BG-I) in 1992, a single-gene technology consisting of Cry1Ac, which targets the bollworm. Subsequently, it released a second-generation cotton technology consisting of two genes of Bt, namely, Cry1Ac and Cry2Ab, called Bollgard-II (BG-II), as pink bollworm became resistant to BG-I. In 1998, Monsanto licensed its Bt cotton technology to MMBL, a joint venture of the Maharashtra-based seed company Mahyco and Monsanto, for further sub-licensing in India.

About fifty domestic seed companies first entered into an agreement with MMBL for procuring its Bt cotton traits for a one-time, non-refundable fee of ₹5,00,000 and a recurring fee called trait value (royalty), or the estimated value for the trait of insect resistance conferred by the Bt gene technology.

A significant portion of Bt cotton seed prices forms trait value, and fixing it has been a matter of contention since 2005, since that determines the selling price of the seeds. A 450 gm Bt cotton seed packet cost ₹1,700–1,800 in 2005, compared to the non-Bt cotton seeds, which cost ₹300.

Problems arose within the industry when in 2017 cotton farmers reported widespread infestation of pink bollworms on BG-I and BG-II cotton plants in most parts, except north India. Domestic companies began to raise questions about trait value. Why should they pay royalties to Monsanto when the trait supposed to combat the pests had clearly failed?

When the matter landed on the government's table, the ministry, responding to demands from sections of the seed manufacturing sector and the farming community, in late 2016 scrapped the royalties on BG-I and reduced the royalty for each 450 gm packet of BG-II seeds from ₹184 to ₹49, much to Monsanto's chagrin.

The GM-cotton sector in India is entirely occupied by Monsanto-owned technologies. India approved six GM-cotton technologies for commercial cultivation, but the Monsanto-owned varieties occupy over 90 per cent of the area, marketed by nearly fifty seed companies, under licence agreements from Monsanto.

In February 2016, the Competition Commission of India (CCI) prima facie found evidence of the contravention of some sections of the Competition Act by Monsanto and its Indian arms, including MMBL, on a complaint lodged by some domestic companies led by the Hyderabad-based Nuziveedu Seeds Limited (NSL) and agitated farmers' groups. This triggered a corporate war within the industry, ultimately splitting it—with some companies siding with the multinational giant while others went on a warpath, wanting to wriggle out of agreements.

For twenty years, the Bt cotton controversy dominated the cotton landscape in India and shaped debates around genetic engineering in agriculture, even as farmers' suicides and the cotton crisis unfolded on a massive scale. Bt cotton technology was supposed to increase production and per-acre yields while addressing the agrarian crisis. It did so only marginally, for a brief period of time. Both production and productivity rose in the first few years but have dropped over the past decade—Indian cotton productivity is among the lowest in the world despite a near-total conversion to Bt cotton. Trouble-torn Vidarbha's cotton yields, which have always been very low, stagnated even further.

Between 2002 and 2005, Vidarbha saw a steep rise in the land acreage under Bt cotton at the cost of the last remaining traditional and hybrid varieties of seeds. Desperate farmers, deep in debt, believed the Bt seeds would increase their yield manifold and help reduce their pesticide costs. But it did not happen. For one, the companies' claims were tall and, two, Bt was—and still is—disastrous for un-irrigated Vidarbha farms. Besides, the onset of such sophisticated technology coincided with the collapse of the valuable extension network of government and agriculture universities. As several studies recommend, for agrarian reform the government should prioritize the resurrection and reinvigoration of the agriculture extension machinery.

THE COTTON SEED IS what determines the key parameters of the output—staple length, strength and productivity. The use of American cotton and its hybrid varieties has increased from a mere 3 per cent at the time of Partition to 70 per cent of the cultivated area in India today. Only 20 to 30 per cent of the area is under Indian cotton, Gossypium herbaceum and Gossypium arboreum—species limited to India and commonly called desi varieties. There is another species that grows in India—G. barbadense, that is, a tetraploid like G. hirsutum. Roughly 50 per cent of the cotton-growing area in India is under hybrid cotton (mostly inter-species hirsutum hybrid), and the rest is under 'open' pollinated varieties.

India is one of the very few countries growing hybrid cotton, the others being Vietnam and China. The latter recently entered into hybrid research on a limited scale. The United States does not grow hybrid cotton.

In India, seed research has largely concentrated on developing hybrid varieties of the naturally long-staple American cotton. As a result, India has been at the forefront of hybrid cotton research in the world. It has produced the first ever tetraploid cotton hybrid H4 (in 1970), the first ever budded cotton G.Cot.101 (1974), the first ever released diploid cotton hybrid G.Cot.DH7 (1985) and first ever long-staple desi cotton hybrid G.Cot.DH9 (1988). India is also the first and only country to use hybrid Bt cotton. However, despite many firsts, India's productivity is among the lowest in the world. This indicates there is something wrong in the direction of its research.

Many experts argue that a key concern is India's over-dependence on American cotton as a source of varietal research. Though American varieties have higher productivity, it has increasingly been established that their cultivation is not sustainable in India. Vidarbha is a great example. Since American cotton is not suitable for India due to agro-climatic incompatibility, it leads to frequent crop failures. It also requires more water, more inputs, and its yields plummet after three years. Although unsuitable for Indian conditions, the long-staple American cotton is popular because machines to gin and spin desi cotton are not readily available.

The second issue is the concentration of research on hybrids. The problem is that hybrids do not give consistent yields after one year. In the US, Australia and China—the three top cotton-producing countries in the world—the focus of research has been to develop seeds of improved varieties and largely shun hybrids.

In recent years, there has been new and promising research on desi cotton varieties. Scientists in India have found that these varieties outperform the hirsutum varieties by a margin of 35 to 50 per cent and are particularly suited to water-scarce conditions, but this research faces resource constraints.

According to a report of the NCF, these varieties have good fibre quality, which is comparable in all respects to a leading hybrid variety. The farmers using them have registered huge savings on the cost of cultivation and have been able to do multi-cropping. But the report points out: 'In spite of the outstanding performance

Ramrao Panchleniwar freshens up at his home in Hiwara village, Yavatmal, in Maharashtra's Vidarbha region, after a day's work in November 2018.

Cotton plants sprout out of the seeds sown in Ramrao's farm a few days earlier in August 2019. Vidarbha is known for its black soil.

Ramrao in January 2021 with his saviour Pramod Nellawar, to whom he is eternally grateful. Pramod is the auto driver who took Ramrao to hospital on the fateful day in March 2014 when he consumed poison to end his life.

Two family photos hang on a thatched wall in Ramrao's home, March 2018: (*above*) Ramrao's elder daughter Alakya with her husband Rahul Rangeneniwar, who committed suicide in June 2016; and (*below*) Ramrao with his wife, Vimalbai, who passed away in 2012.

Ramrao's daughters, Anuja (*left*) and Alakya (*right*), at their father's home while he is away in the fields, December 2017.

Ramrao poses for a family photo with Alakya, her daughter Varshini and Anuja's daughter Lavya at his home in January 2021.

Ramrao oversees the second sowing operation after the partial failure of the first sowing of cotton on a farm he leases in his neighbouring village of Borgaon , July 2019.

Ramrao performs a ritual called Sitadevi on his farm before the start of the cotton-picking season, October 2018.

Ramrao's elder brother Ashokrao (*third from left*) with some other residents of Hiwara, most of whom belong to the Kolam tribal community, after finishing the gruelling farm work on a day in November 2018.

Dry and wilting cotton bolls on Ramrao's fields that have been hit hard by a pink bollworm infestation, January 2021.

One of Ramrao's trusted lieutenants, a farm labourer called Istari, and two women from Hiwara in the midst of sowing cotton seeds in July 2019 in the traditional way: with a plough tied to a bullock to furrow the land.

Bhimrao Atram, a farm labourer who works for Ramrao, and two women farmhands during the sowing operations on Ramrao's farm in July 2018.

Ramrao scans his turmeric plantation, which will come to harvest in a couple of months, in January 2021. He has switched to turmeric on a part of his land as it is safer to grow than some of the other crops he is used to.

of new desi varieties, their commercial popularization has been extremely poor.'

The Indian cotton seed industry is built on selling hybrids. So, while the seed industry can meet the demand for hybrid seeds, it is not able to supply farmers with desi cotton varieties. The NCF report says that the gap is substantial and that the availability of desi cotton varieties is limited to about 80,000 to 90,000 quintals against the requirement of 0.42 million quintals. Today, about fifty companies market more than 3,000 Bt cotton hybrids with catchy and popular names across the country. It is estimated that cotton seed is largely marketed by the private sector with a negligible share of the public sector seed companies.

A report submitted to the Government of India in 2008 by Maharashtra's commissioner of agriculture regarding the performance of Bt cotton stated that the yield was on the decline in the preceding three years, and that there was not much of a difference between the productivity of Bt and non-Bt hybrid seeds in rain-fed conditions. But the cost of production was double that of non-Bt seeds.

Moreover, as Kranthi put it in 2017, India is back to square one with the breakdown of Bt cotton and no new seed in sight.

In twenty years, Vidarbha has seen a massive upsurge in Bt cotton use amidst the bitter confrontation between those who favour it and those who oppose it and the organic-versus-inorganic divide. The large-scale Bt cotton use has meant that India has lost its indigenous cotton diversity and germplasm, leading to a monoculture of one type of hybrid.

The one thing I can vouch for: it did not alter farm incomes. If the yields rose marginally, the production costs grew manifold and so did the indebtedness. And it did not bring back farm and crop diversity. Instead, it further reinforced cotton monoculture.

Ramrao started using BG-I in 2003. He saw his yields rise and then plummet. Then he switched to BG-II in 2009. His yields rose, but soon his life took a tumultuous turn. He tells me one day that he was better off being poor than buried in debt.

As a pauper, he could at least get sound sleep.

RAMRAO DID NOT GIVE up on his crop. He did whatever he could to tackle the pink worm attack and reduce his losses. This is the first time since his suicide attempt that he properly focused on his farm. Some of his lenders desperately needed their money back to meet their own exigencies.

I am back in Hiwara on a cold, wintry morning in December, on the eve of Christmas, because I am eager to meet Alakya, who is visiting her father after a long time. Varshini, her daughter, has Christmas vacations. It has been a year and a half since she lost her husband. Ramrao is always worried for her.

This is the best time of the year to visit Hiwara: things are dry, clean and people are a tad relaxed. Much of the work is done. Winter sowing is through. Those who farm a single crop are about to migrate in the new year. Woollens are out. Old people sit in the sun, chewing tobacco. Young men gossip and play cards round the year, but during this period they do it round the day because they have more money in their pockets.

Ramrao is away on his farm, planting his winter crop, tending to his cotton and lentils. Alakya and Anuja are home. They have drawn a beautiful rangoli at the door, painted the tulsi-vrindavan and decorated the door with a marigold garland.

The two sisters have several similarities with their late mother, Vimalbai. They are, as Ramrao described his late wife, slim, bony-faced, tall, with curly long hair, big eyes and they walk with a spring in their step. I had never seen the two sisters and their toddlers together. Nalini is with them too. The three women look happy. Anuja knows that her elder sister has a hard life ahead. But they thank God that Ramrao survived in 2014, or they would be orphans.

'Did you plant the marigold that my father gave you some time back?' Alakya enquires with a smile, expecting an affirmative answer.

I say yes and ask her what the story behind the marigold is. I sense this story holds some importance for the family.

'My father did not want to marry early,' Alakya says and dives into the story of her parents.

Anuja and Nalini are all ears. Ramrao was not even eighteen years old when Vimal's proposal first came for him. He didn't have the guts to tell that to Ashokrao, whom he respected but also feared. He was so shy and nervous, he shaved his head thinking if he looked ugly, he would be rejected by Vimal when he went to see her. The prospective bride was sixteen.

Ramrao finally managed to convince his brother that he did not want build a family at such a young age. He reasoned that the family should first marry off Suman before his wedding.

It so happened that Vimal's elder brother, Suresh Ukerlawar, too, like Ramrao, did not wish to marry because he wanted his younger sister to be married first. The Ukerlawar family hailed from Nipani in Telangana.

A year later, Vimal's family—her father actually—came back to the Panchleniwars with a new proposal. Vimal's brother would marry Suman if Ramrao married Vimal, he told Ashokrao, who liked the idea. There would be no exchange of dowry and the two weddings could be held simultaneously to save expenses.

The only trouble was Vimal's health. She had asthma, because of which she needed to regularly see a doctor. But Suresh was a great prospect for Suman, who had remained unmarried because the family could not afford her dowry. Suresh was a good, hardworking farmer and he liked Suman. Reluctant at first, Ramrao finally accepted the proposal for Suman's sake.

'Is that why Suman and Ramrao are close?' I ask Alakya.

'Yes, the two grew up like friends. And they both feared Ashokrao and our grandfather, who was also very strict.'

Ramrao agreed to the proposal, knowing well that he was marrying a woman with health problems. The two families came together and hosted the weddings in Hiwara in a modest way. Vimal's farmer father had a soft corner for Ramrao, who remained the old man's favourite son-in-law for life.

Vimal was deeply introverted and an austere but affectionate woman. She managed her family well within the available means, but loved splurging on her children and food. She was a good cook and made very tasty laddoos.

'I always secretly thought someone should write my parents' story,' a teary-eyed Alakya tells me rather emotionally.

'Why?'

'It is just that their struggle deserves a story!'

The only image she has of her parents is one of always being on the farm, toiling hard in the summers, winters, or rains. Her mother was physically weaker than most women but would pick 80 kg to a quintal of cotton every day in the picking season. That was way more than what is considered good.

'It was like saving ₹500 a day on labour,' Alakya says.

Ramrao spent a lot of money after 2012 on Vimal's health. She would be in hospital on and off due to her asthma, which had begun to affect her other vital organs with every attack. He kept borrowing for her treatment—thousands of rupees that he spent on multiple hospital trips.

In 2012, just before her death, Ramrao spent two months in the Yavatmal hospitals trying to bring her some relief. Alakya had been married off, Anuja would take care of their home and Ramrao shuttled between Hiwara and Yavatmal, attending to Vimalbai. From time to time, other family members, including Ashokrao and his wife, the villagers, and their close and distant relatives in Telangana, would chip in to relieve Ramrao of his hospital duties and help him with the financial burden. But Vimalbai was sinking.

In her last days, Ramrao brought her home and cared for her. That was when Ramrao turned to the god Hanuman and prayed for her life and health. And pledged to give up meat.

Even when they lost their first child, Manjula, to a severe chest infection when she was barely a year old, Ramrao did not go to the temple. It was the first major tragedy in his personal life. He remained an atheist until Vimal's health worsened. He went to the temple and sat there, quietly praying for her life, fearing losing her and a long, lonely life that awaited him. He loved her. She was his companion. No one could fill her void. The day she died, in fact, while she was breathing her last, a completely shattered Ramrao sat in the temple, surrounded by his farmhands, praying fervently. He was not home when she passed away.

'My mother loved marigolds. They were her favourite flowers.' Alakya remembers her mother would pluck a marigold flower and wear it in her hair every evening, when it was in season, after finishing work on the farm. She would, in fact, plant marigold between the cotton plants to ward away pests and, as she would say, evil. For her, marigolds were a good force.

After her death, though, for some reason, marigolds no longer smiled on Ramrao's field. In 2014, he tried planting the flower. In 2015 too, when he was still depressed, he tried planting marigolds, but the flowers would not bloom. This year, five years after Vimal's death in June 2012, Ramrao finally has marigold flowers in full bloom on his fields. The family thinks Vimal is smiling on them once again. They think she has attained nirvana.

All through the season, Ramrao offers a marigold flower every day to Vimal's photo. For him, marigolds flowering on his farm is an indication that his departed wife is happy. Vimalbai, he philosophizes, is by his side.

7

BHAGAVATA

'*Nand Patlale mulga jhala, an sagla bramhand anandi jhala*!'
(Nanda was blessed with a boy, the entire universe was jubilant)

THE MIDDLE-AGED MAHARAJ IS beaming from a small wooden stage on one side of the hall, delivering punches after punches in chaste Varhadi, narrating the mythical tales of Krishna's birth and his antics as the maverick god. Villagers of all ages lap up the stories of his heroics.

Today is the fifth day of the Bhagavata Saptah. It is late February 2018, and Holi is around the corner.

Hiwara's kids—most of them unkempt and unbathed, but a few, just a few, in clean, decent clothes—are in attendance: twenty or thirty of them, lean, dark, some of them with white spots on their bony faces, indicative of calcium or some other micro-nutrient deficiencies. The girls are shy but they sit in rapt attention. One particular girl, six or seven years old, who lives across Ramrao's home and goes to the zilla parishad school, has come dressed as Radha. They are all here to listen to the stories about Krishna, not so much for the devotional songs, or the mystical–spiritual analysis, or the teachings from the Gita. Their mothers have brought plates full of sweets, homemade or bought from the town, to be offered as today's prasad. Flowers and rice grain drenched in vermillion and turmeric powder fill up their puja thalis.

Most farmers in the gathering seem relaxed. Their cotton season is over. This has been a strange agriculture year, when the pink bollworm made a comeback, the expenditure on chemicals went up, and several fellow farmers died of contact poisoning while spraying their fields.

Of all the enigmatic tales about Krishna, Ramrao loves the one about his friendship with Sudama. Born into a poor Brahmin family, Sudama is one of the most ardent devotees of his friend, who has become the leader of Dwarka while he himself has stayed a poor Brahmin. Krishna tests Sudama's devotion to him from time to time. One day, when Sudama comes to meet him at his palace, Krishna seeks what Sudama has brought in his small cloth bag. Sudama is meeting Krishna to ask for his help to come out of poverty, but the god instead wants the pounded rice that his poor friend has brought with him.

Ramrao loves the story because he is able to relate to Sudama—a devotee who is tested by god despite the former's unwavering love for the latter.

'Tho paha itka mayalu manus, pan tyale pohe dyayle lavte Krishna. An majhya shetatle vange-dal, male khau det nahi tho.' Despite Sudama's unconditional love for him, Krishna makes him give him his rice flakes, Ramrao goes on, and the same is true of me. 'God does not allow me to have brinjals and millets from my own farm. He takes away everything and leaves me with nothing, year after year.'

Ramrao's explanation is like a terrified child's self-soothing; he is reassuring himself that his losses were God's wish.

Who does not love Krishna's tales, particularly his childhood miracles? They invoke the classical bhakti traditions of this land. I have been enamoured by the Gita, fascinated by 'Gitai', a treatise on the quintessential Gita teachings by the venerable Acharya Vinoba Bhave, Mahatma Gandhi's staunch volunteer—the 'first individual satyagrahi', as Bapu would call him, who spent his life at his commune on the banks of the Dham river in Wardha district.

Today, the maharaj is narrating the mystical anecdotes of baby Krishna lifting the Govardhan hill, fighting Kaliya, the multi-headed demon-snake, and killing his mighty maternal uncle Kans. 'And thus Krishna lifts the hillock to give shelter to the Yadavas,' he says and goes on to regale his audience with a bhajan in praise of Krishna. The children are thrilled, the gathering is relaxed, and presently spellbound.

'Kans is worried,' says the narrator, halting the bhajan. 'But Gokul and Mathura are celebrating.' He weaves devotional songs aided by an orchestra into his narrative, making the entire rendition riveting. He explains the purpose of Krishna's avatar and intricately expands on the different characters: Yashoda, Radha, Krishna's naughty friends, and the Yadavas. Whenever the world's problems pile up, Vishnu assumes an avatar and comes to the mortal world to free the troubled people of their woes. He goes on and on with a certain air of authority on the subject and the audience is enraptured.

'God is in all of us,' he notes at one point. Ramrao looks at me approvingly and nods in agreement.

The middle-aged maharaj, one Prashant Bhoyar from Ghatanji, another cotton-trading town in Yavatmal some 40 kilometres away, is an astute storyteller and a consummate performer. There is a vast tribe of such kirtankars who entertain rural people all across India around this time, just before the onset of summer.

In Vidarbha, the trend of the Bhagavata Saptah is on the rise. There was a time when bhajans and kirtans were part of the religious and spiritual life of the countryside. Many a modern reformer took it upon himself to educate the farmers not only on social and moral values but also on sustainable farming methods. In the past twenty years, some of the spiritual traditions have been lost. The new ones are driven by commercial compulsions and business-like considerations. For many, this has turned into their bread and butter now, and villages host such religious functions out of a spirit of competition: 'The neighbouring village did it, why can't we? We must host a bigger celebration so that we outshine them.'

I know some villages that bucked these trends when the agrarian distress grew extreme. They called for '*Ek Gaon, Ek Ganpati*' (one village, one Ganpati pandal) to prevent the lavish spending on unnecessary religious programmes. Some social reformers in the region—the most notable among them being Satyapal Maharaj, the player of a local popular hand-held drum called khanjari—strive to instil some sense in the villagers amidst the growing chatter for expensive, DJ-driven celebrations. Yet, most villages are spending more and more on social, religious, cultural and family events from borrowed money, inspired by urban trends which they try to emulate.

WHEN FARMERS' SUICIDES WENT up, the Maharashtra government tried to fund bhajans and kirtans as a way of reinventing the idea of such community assemblies to rekindle broken bonds, but that did not cut much ice with the farmers, troubled by dramatically rising costs of production and life amid falling incomes.

One particular programme that the Maharashtra government promoted and which was popular for some time was mass weddings. The state funded voluntary organizations to hold weddings on a mass scale to cut down on costs and save farming families from being forced to splurge big amounts of money on the actual event and also dowries.

Several villages in Vidarbha benefited from this programme before it got hijacked by local political leaders, causing these weddings to be discontinued. The leaders floated NGOs which started hosting lavish weddings, defeating the very purpose of mass weddings. However, there are still a few good organizations that host modest functions for the poorest of the poor, small farmers or the landless, and push for social reforms. There are some villages in Vidarbha that have adopted mass weddings for their communities. They host five, sometimes ten, weddings and arrange a lavish meal for the entire village. The Bhagavata Saptah and the 'one village, one Ganesh pandal' are part of those reforms—they help reduce social tensions and save on unnecessary expenditure.

Bhoyar Maharaj has built an entire enterprise—a costly sound system, lavish costumes, a team of musicians and actors sourced mostly from Yavatmal villages. The maharaj also puts up a range of devotional books for sale at his venues. A teenager accompanies him just for that. In his performance, he also enquires about the farmers' well-being, their crops, and shares anecdotes and gossip from other parts of the district. He is a travelling alert, bringing news from the neighbouring villages and districts.

When the maharaj starts narrating the story of baby Krishna sucking milk and blood out of Putana, the demoness who comes in the avatar of a beautiful woman wanting to breastfeed and poison Krishna, the kids are edgy. There is a performer dressed as 'Putana Maushi' in black attire, wearing a mask to frighten the children running helter-skelter in the temple hall, making loud heheheheeehahahaa sounds on the microphone. His theatrics enliven the gathering, particularly the young ones. Putana is holding a doll that is not letting go of her; the maharaj has fallen silent as the performer takes the stage and captures the attention of his audience. This high-decibel drama goes on for ten minutes, until the demoness drops dead and the musicians play celebratory tunes on the tabla and the dholak. The maharaj starts chanting 'Hare Krishna, Hare Hare' on his microphone, and the audience follows in unison. The auditorium rings with the collective chants.

In that heady ambience, a smiling, young Krishna—a village girl aged ten, wearing a crown with the god's signature peacock feather stuck to it and with a flute in her hands—climbs on to the stage. The claps ring louder, the chants become wilder, the tabla and dholak beats grow faster. The flute player is as if lost in a trance as he plays a breathtaking and mellifluous tune, and then the maharaj stands up, his eyes closed, both hands in the air. He slowly bows to the Krishna seated on a plastic chair next to him on the stage and joins his hands in obeisance. The gathering too is up on its feet, bowing to the lord. Finally, the crescendo dies. The spell is broken. The music stops and the hall is immediately filled with chatter. Children laugh and giggle. It is time for the afternoon break.

The katha will begin at 4 p.m., an aide of the maharaj announces. Women waiting with their thalis get up and walk one by one to the child playing Krishna, touch her feet and then take the blessings of the maharaj. Then they distribute sweets, coconut and sugar to the devotees in the gathering.

Ramrao and I sit relaxed, eating the prasad, our backs to the wall of the hall, still under the spell of the bhajans. Finally, he gestures to me to follow him out.

'Thank god for the stories,' I say to Ramrao as we walk back to his home. 'What would people do if there were no stories?'

He smiles and says there would be no meaning to their lives. 'We feel dead most days. This helps remind us that we are alive.'

Hiwara's families host the maharaj and his team. Some of them take care of the lodging and food; others deal with their demands pertaining to their performance. The maharaj, who looks younger than he is, has been put up at Ramrao's cousin's home. This way, Hiwara shares the costs. Together, the village raises money to pay their fees.

Bhoyar, the maharaj, has now made this his livelihood, but he is a farmer too. He tells me, when I meet him during the lunch break, it is difficult to make a living from farming alone. Rain-fed farming is not lucrative any more. Gone are those days when the village landlord was respected and enjoyed a social standing. Cotton brings you only losses, he goes on. A person in a regular job, even a petty clerk, makes more money these days than a farmer of 10 acres does. Children don't want to join their parents in farming because they see them working hard every day but ending up with losses, worries and frustration. Finding labour has become a problem. Rains have become moody.

'I took to bhajans and kirtans because I love doing this,' he says, removing his headgear, a beautiful cotton bandana. 'It is also a way to make farmers happy and spiritually inclined.'

Bhoyar learnt the kirtan and devotional storytelling skills from a senior singer and kirtankar in Ghatanji. Since he could sing and act, and had a deep interest in spiritual traditions and mythological stories, it became his calling.

'It is profoundly philosophical,' he says.

The Bhagvata is one of the eighteen mythical treatises called the Puranas, composed originally in Sanskrit but adapted in multiple languages, integrating the themes of dvaita (dualism) and the advaita (monoism), and weaving it with the philosophy of devotion.

There's a reason why Hiwara organizes Bhagavata Saptah every year leading up to Holi. Ramrao tells me about it.

'There used to be a lot of feuds, quarrels and disputes as people would consume alcohol and fight with each other,' he says. One year, Bhaskar came back drunk and beat up his neighbour over money. Another year, there was an ugly quarrel between the Kolams and the Yelmis over a trivial issue—it turned bloody. Men would come home heavily drunk and beat up their wives. Then one day in January 2008, Gajanan Chandurkar, a landless man in his late sixties, came up with the idea of the Bhagavata Saptah and took the lead in organizing it. 'Now, through the week, no one plays the card game of teenpatti, people try to stay away from alcohol, and families from different castes come together.'

Even today, Chandurkar, a hefty old man with a limp, leads an informal organizing committee in Hiwara to host the Bhagavata Saptah. He takes it upon himself to raise donations for the celebrations and maintains complete transparency in the expenses. Everyone trusts him to never pocket any money from the collections. He wears a rudraksha chain and a white Nehru cap whenever he leaves his home. Villagers never defy him.

'We already have so many worries, we don't need more feuds,' Chandurkar tells me when I drop by his small hovel where he lives with his wife. It is just two small rooms covered by mud and thatch, and he has a couple of wooden cots inside them. 'We have enough problems without adding unnecessary quarrels to them. Alcohol is the root cause. But when we hold a religious function, villagers stay away from it for a week. Holi passes peacefully unless...'

'Unless, what?' I ask.

'Unless someone like Ramrao consumes poison,' he says, cracking up at his own joke and patting Ramrao on the back, who smiles nervously.

Chandurkar is compassionate and likes Ramrao. In turn, Ramrao cares for the old couple who have no children of their own. The husband and wife live off the meagre amount of ₹600 a month they get from the state government under the Niradhar Pension Yojana. He used to get ₹1,000 earlier, but for some reason the government has deducted ₹400 from the dole. In times of need, once in a while, he relies on Ramrao's generosity.

RAMRAO IS SHOUTING AND pelting stones at the trees that line his cotton farm and separate it from the shrub forest towards the eastern side. The village is to the west. He is livid.

'What's happening?' I ask him when I reach his farm.

'Bastards! Monkeys. They are eating into my crops.' He looks irritated and exhausted.

On a huge tree, I spot a monkey herd, staring back at him from a distance, Ramrao on this side and another farmer on the other. The monkeys seem to be enjoying teasing Ramrao and his folks after having raided his farm a while ago.

I am visiting Ramrao a month after Holi, March 2018.

'This is like living in a zoo,' he says. 'Monkeys, nilgais, tigers, boars, deer—I get all of them here. Late last night, a pack of foxes came here. Boars are all over. These bastards ruin my crops even when they are not hungry.'

Ramrao's neighbours are harassed too. There is little a farmer can do to shoo away wild animals. It is a problem of mammoth proportions. You can't kill them. You can't drive them away. You can't protect your farm. You are helpless. You bear the losses and convince yourself that such is your fate.

The cotton season is over although some bolls remain unpicked on the plants. Ramrao says some pink bollworms could survive the summer. The pigeon pea and green gram he planted on 2 acres have been harvested. The groundnut he has grown on an acre of land is ready to be reaped. He is worried about a particular virus that has infected the groundnut crop all around Hiwara this year. Apart from the virus, the wild boars and blue bulls who raid his farms for water and food, destroying the crop more than devouring it, are plaguing his mind.

Groundnut is grown all over Vidarbha, wherever farmers have a source of water, as a winter crop, then harvested in April. It's a good, sturdy cash crop. But across Vidarbha farmers have weaned away from it because of the growing menace of wild animals.

One can hardly do anything about it, he notes wryly as we walk past the first farm facing the road and step on to the one owned by his friend Gunwanta Golamwar where cotton seems to have been fully plucked. Even now, whoever has a good source of water grows groundnut, if not green gram, as a second crop. On the acre of land alongside the seasonal rivulet that dissects his farm—deepened this year with an earth mover by Munna Bolenwar, who is entrenched in government contracts—Ramrao has planted jowar, the sweet sorghum that would serve two purposes: food for himself and fodder for his cows.

'It's going to be of super quality—white, big grain.' Look how tall it has grown, he remarks with the glee of a child. It indeed has. I gauge it to be around 8 or 9 feet. The sorghum grains would fetch him ₹1,500 to ₹2,000 a quintal, and the green, wet foliage will provide fodder for his cows.

There is so much pride when a farmer sees his crop standing robust. It is the culmination of all his hard work and nurturing. Ramrao rolls his pants up to his knees and takes careful steps to enter into the dense thicket of sorghum to inspect the tillers. He looks very, very happy.

In half an acre he has planted sesame seeds and moong dal, which will come to harvest in a fortnight. He will sell the produce in the Pandharkawda market and earn about ₹50,000—not much, but enough to see him through his summer needs and allow him to pay wages.

Once these crops are collected, another season would be over. In the meantime, Ramrao is nowhere near repaying all his debts. He may not repay his aunt's hand loans. Some of his relations are not seeking money from him any more.

OVER THE NEXT TWO months, while most of India has been battling drought and distress, I visit Ramrao twice and call him often to find out how he has been doing. He is invariably on his farm, working and driving away monkeys who seem to be frequenting his farm more often this year.

By the end of March, he has harvested moong and jowar and sold them to raise money as expected. The entire groundnut crop—he was hoping to harvest at least 20 quintals of it—goes bust, wrecked by the viral infection and by wild boars. Though he makes money from jowar and moong, he incurs losses on the groundnut.

Late March, he calls to inform me that Damu Atram, a villager, miraculously survived a tiger attack. There has been a spurt in tiger attacks all over Vidarbha. Damu, a sixty-year-old Kolam tribal, was working on his field one evening when the striped wild cat attacked him from behind, then ran away when he screamed for help. He suffered grievous wounds on his neck and his head. He is safe but scared, Ramrao tells me. But there's an adolescent tiger roaming around Hiwara, he informs me.

'We will meet him when I am in the village next,' I suggest.

'Yes, of course.'

Late April, with temperatures soaring, he calls me, concerned about the trouble brewing in Alakya's life. Her in-laws have refused to give Rahul's share in the property to her after initially promising to give 3 acres. To me the story sounds typical. I am not surprised but angry. Alakya will now have to fight for her rights, and chances are she will be driven out of her in-laws' home and back to Ramrao. Very few women get their share of land post their husbands' deaths. The Yelmi community mediated on two or three occasions but failed to convince her in-laws to give her a share.

Ramrao and Munna Bolenwar also went to broker peace with the Rangeneniwars, who were instead incensed by their presence and refused to budge. In December 2017, the in-laws had agreed to write 3 acres in Varshini's name but asked Alakya not to stay with them. It is a typical ploy in such cases—you own the land, we keep it.

For almost two years after her husband's death, Alakya lived with the Rangeneniwars at their ancestral village under much pain and stress—for a few months, with her sister-in-law in another village like a caged parrot—but now Ramrao can't allow her to bear it, he tells me some time in May. Alakya is virtually homeless, he says with much sadness. For a year or so, Varshini has been out of the school. She is staying with her maternal uncle now, a kind-hearted man to whom Suman is married.

'I am getting her back,' Ramrao tells me during my visit to him late May. That's when we also drop in at Damu Atram's home. He has recovered but is still fearful of going back to his farm. He still gets nightmares.

Strangely, Ramrao looks relieved and happy. He is sad about Alakya's struggles but happy that she has agreed to return home with her daughter. He will take good care of them, he says.

If this isn't enough, Ramrao must deal with another problem he confronts every summer: raising money to buy inputs for the next season and pay labour wages to prepare his farm.

Summers make him nervous. It is the time when he has to go back to the same lenders, same inputs dealers and the same relations to whom he owes money. He needs to borrow more and assure them that he will return their money once the new crop comes in.

You have to live through the despair and helplessness, also the embarrassment of going back to your lenders. But you must if you want to till your land. That's the first thing you learn as a farmer. You must learn to swallow your self-respect and suppress your anger.

Ramrao is agitated that the Central Bank, where he has a crop and savings account, won't give him fresh loans unless he settles his old dues—that's about ₹1,50,000. For some inexplicable reason, he has not got the benefit of the loan waiver scheme the Government of Maharashtra announced in June 2017. He should have got ₹1,00,000 waived off. Some of Hiwara's farmers have got it, but most haven't. The government deposited the waiver money in the banks in spurts and tranches. And while the old loans remain unpaid, new ones have piled up.

Since the loan waiver programme was announced, it has spent ₹19,000 crore until October 2019 but failed to grant respite to a struggling peasantry across Maharashtra. On the contrary, it has choked the banks and crippled the formal crop loan system.

Ramrao went to his bank branch on several occasions to check if his crop loan had been waived off but came back disappointed. Once when I accompanied him to the bank while I was visiting him, the branch manager politely told him that there was some problem with the data—Ramrao has two bank accounts and neither got the relief. He was not alone. A majority in Hiwara did not get it. This means he has to settle his old bills, which in turn means he needs more money. He will do it as he always has. He tells me he will sell a flock of his goats, maybe a bull too, and seek out advance funds from the agriculture officer in Yavatmal. All put together, he needs ₹1,00,000 or so in May.

Ramrao gets up and makes a list of people he is going to tap for a quick loan—people he must contact one by one in the hope that someone will honour the call. He knows it won't be easy to get a loan. In 2014, the motivation to till the farm had deserted

Ramrao. This year, he is more than upbeat. He has a new goal, new meaning to life. He has to support his daughter, and her daughter. Though the season has ended with losses for Ramrao, he is happy that Alakya and Varshini are returning to him for good.

'Ramrao,' I ask him as we sit at his home, 'where are you with your loan repayment?'

'I gave a couple of lakh rupees to an inputs dealer and ₹50,000 to a cousin.'

To his lenders he gave all that he earned from the farmland he leases in the neighbouring village of Borgaon Katli from a Gond tribal farmer, and the money he made from his sorghum and moong. He couldn't keep anything for himself.

8

FARM

Rains are on the cards, the kharif season is on its way. On 6 June 2018, I call Ramrao. He is feeding his cows in his cattle shed.

The pre-monsoon showers accompanied by stormy winds, he tells me, ripped off flimsy tin roofs of many hovels in Hiwara over two days. He counts at least half a dozen kuchcha homes—mainly of the Kolams in the Kolam-Pada—that would have to be rebuilt. That means more expenses on the heels of a bad season that saw a small worm tear into the farms and people.

Houses are a great indicator of the inequalities that exist within any village. In Hiwara, only a few poor households have small one-room cement houses constructed alongside their old kuchcha huts under the government housing scheme. Big farmers live in cement houses, but half the village still lives in thatched or mud-brick homes, which suffer damages or cave in, every time there are heavy showers or hailstorms. Some of them on the right hand side, along the road that turns into the village, Ramrao informs me, got badly damaged. His house suffered minor cracks too and those will need to be fixed, otherwise rainwater will trickle inside through small gaps.

A month earlier, the harsh summer made it difficult for people to do anything. There is no work for men and women during the summers, so they stay home to keep safe from the heat and exhaustion, or migrate to the city to do menial work for cash. Ramrao tends to his cows and goats during this time.

A little while ago I met a village herdsman who had an unusually high number of goats in his herd. When I asked him about it, he said that a trader from Telangana had brought him goats to tend to for a few days, after which he would take them back to Telangana. It appeared that the trader was rotating the goats gifted to the farmers there under a scheme. The Telangana government buys goats to be given to the farmers from the trader, then the same trader buys back the same goats from the beneficiary farmers at a depleted price and sends them to this herdsman in Hiwara. Before long, the Telangana government again will need more goats to be distributed to the new beneficiaries.

What if the herdsman sold a few of those goats and made extra money? He said the trader won't mind!

'It's a scam anyway,' he said and laughed.

Ramrao informs me that Alakya has returned to him with Varshini in the meantime. She brought home all her belongings, including the refrigerator he had gifted her. She couldn't get back her gold ornaments—her in-laws won't part with them.

His granddaughter got admitted to a convent school on the outskirts of Pandharkawda, right opposite the cottage hospital. He paid ₹60,000 to the school for her admission. He gives me a detailed update about his daughter before our conversation veers back to the issue of farming.

'Did you buy seeds and other inputs?' I ask.

'No, not yet,' he says, 'but I will.'

'When?'

'Let me first arrange for the money.'

Ramrao, I'm sure, must have spoken to his regular lenders and gone to the bank to enquire if he could get a crop loan.

The rural bank branches are slowly dying—or they are allowed to shut shop as they are not viable. And for the cotton farmers, particularly those in the dry-land area with small and marginal holdings, getting a crop loan is like leaping into the night sky and fetching the moon.

In Vidarbha, for two decades, the number of farmers getting a crop loan from the banks never crossed 40 per cent. According to several government reports, including that of the Planning Commission's fact-finding team on Vidarbha led by principal secretary Adarsh Misra, around the middle of the first decade of the 2000s, the figure was around 25 per cent.

As bank loans are hard to come by, farmers are forced to rely on private, sometimes usurious, lenders for their crop and domestic finance. Over the past decade, therefore, Vidarbha and particularly Yavatmal have seen a massive penetration of the rural micro-finance and rural housing finance companies that lend money to women self-help groups at an annual interest rate of anything between 20 and 36 per cent. They lend small sums of money round the year. Formal banking and non-banking finance companies have also seen a robust growth of gold loans—loans advanced to farmers against the collateral of their gold. Tonnes of gold are in their custody against the loans they have advanced.

Earlier, there used to be middlemen in this region who would pay farmers for their expenses round the year, in return of which the farmers would sell their produce to them. Some lenders were actually aggregators, who would buy farm produce from small and marginal farmers and sell it to the big traders. Very few of them still do brisk business but largely that system has collapsed. New lenders have emerged—the inputs dealers, government employees or unauthorized private lenders who do short-duration, high-interest lending for hefty returns. It is illegal and exploitative, farmers know it, but they are desperate for the money.

We conclude our conversation with Ramrao promising me that he will inform me in advance when he starts his sowing.

Two days later, he calls me to say: '*Udya ya. Perni karto.*' He asks me to come the next day.

Ramrao is about to commence sowing for the 2018 kharif season. It is the first year since his suicide attempt that he is back to being his old hardworking self, fully focused on his own and leased farms—in all, about 20 acres or so. He is taking up the management of the Yavatmal agriculture officer's 45-acre farm in Hiwara with two others. When I wonder about how he managed everything within a day, he explains he bought seeds and inputs on credit from a friendly dealer who owns Tanmay Krishi Kendra, a friend of his nephew Pravin. He will do the sowing in a staggered way so that he can space out his spending. Pravin advised Ramrao, and his father Ashokrao, to buy a new cotton hybrid of BG-II variety—there are close to 3,000 Bt cotton hybrids in the market. Ramrao got twenty 450 gm packets of cotton seeds of four different Bt cotton hybrids, eight packets of pigeon pea, two of sweet sorghum and a few bags of fertilizers.

A small trader who had purchased a few quintals of his tur in May paid him the dues, which he will use for paying the wages. His soil is moist enough to receive the seeds. Even if there is a big gap in the rains ahead, Ramrao can irrigate his farm from his ground well, a luxury not many farmers in Vidarbha enjoy. Most farmers who depend only on rains for watering their crops will have to wait until mid-July to finish sowing the seeds. June has been seeing dry spells after initial rain, though it is the best month for sowing—the earlier you do the sowing, the better it is for yields and overall crop growth.

When I arrive at Ramrao's home on the morning of 9 June, there's amazing chatter.

For the first time, I see a single-door refrigerator, a spacious king-size double bed and the addition of a few steel utensils to his belongings. Ramrao's house is flush with the material possessions that came back with Alakya.

Ramrao is elated to offer me chilled refrigerated water.

Alakya is home. She is making chapatis, rice and sabzi in large quantities for themselves and the farmhands. Two women are by her side, helping her with the cooking.

A dozen young men and women are squatting in the front yard. I am surprised there are so many youths in the village because I have not seen most of them in Hiwara before. The only time I have seen a few of them is during the annual Ganesh festival or Durga Puja. Two of them are buried in their cheap smart phones, others are talking among themselves in their native Gondi language, while a couple of others are merely listening to the chit-chat around them.

Ramrao is giving instructions to a middle-aged, tall man with broad shoulders, who is listening to him while preparing tobacco on his palm, nodding and intervening to correct his employer.

The two are engaged in hectic conversation. The man then taps the tobacco, picks it up with two fingers and tucks it in his mouth beneath his lower lip—it's the way people consume tobacco here.

That's Deepak Kochade, Ramrao's old farmhand and an expert in sowing. It is always Kochade and his tribe leading the sowing.

'Start from the nullah end,' Ramrao tells him, 'and maintain proper distance between the two rows. Last time around we did not maintain enough distance and it affected the yield and brought in pests.'

'*Hou ji,*' Kochade notes. The man himself owns 3 acres on which he plants cotton and pigeon pea, and doubles as a labourer as his land is rain-fed with shallow soil and has a lot of boulders. The land isn't enough to sustain his family. He and his wife, Rekha, work on others' farms. From their wages, they till their own.

'Take those along,' Ramrao tells Kochade, pointing towards five or six iron stands on which hang yellowish sticky papers. 'Put them in the cart along with the seeds and fertilizers.'

'These are pheromone traps,' Ramrao informs me.

Pheromone traps are the easiest, most inexpensive and organic way of controlling pests, including the pink bollworms. The worms are drawn by the lustre and smell of paper, get sucked into the dome-shaped trap and die. If you put these all over the farm, between the rows, they help prevent the pests from laying eggs and growing. The 2017 pink worm menace prompted Ramrao and other farmers to go for this technique to check the pests early on.

Kochade says he wants them too, and Ramrao informs him that he can find them in the Pandharkawda market for cheap. A trap costs ₹200. The iron rods are Ramrao's. One can instal the pheromone traps also on wooden sticks.

'Follow what I told you,' insists Ramrao and Kochade nods. Clear old stalks, run the bullock-dragged plough in straight lines, burn off the stalks, plough again and make the women, boys and girls sow one or two seeds each at a distance of 2 feet.

Majid Khan of Kadu Borgaon will bring a tractor fitted with a rotavator, Kochade tells Ramrao. 'He will charge ₹500,' he says.

Ramrao angrily retorts: 'Are these rates from some other planet?'

'Okay, I will ask him to make some adjustment,' Kochade smiles.

Rotavators help save time and effort. With their rotating blades, they effectively turn the farmland over and break it down, crushing dry stalks that are then easy to collect and burn. Cultivators, tillers and rotavators assist farmers with aerating, which improves soil drainage and allows plants and vegetables to grow quicker.

Kochade leaves the house with the labourers. They are headed to Ramrao's farm. They will follow his instructions but not to the letter—they will do some things from their own experience—but they will make his farm ready for sowing.

Once upon a time, Ramrao and his family did much of this work and did not need labourers. These days, he can't physically do all the work by himself.

Alakya is going to join the labourers in the sowing of seeds. Very early in the morning, she and Ramrao performed a small puja, cracked open a coconut and prayed for a good season. Theirs is the first farm in Hiwara to start sowing this season because of the well it has. Sowing on the leased farmlands will have to wait till the rains arrive and drench the soil enough for the seeds to be planted.

'What's the puja about?' I ask.

'We do it to please ourselves.' Ramrao laughs heartily and adds, 'I know it won't be any different this year.'

Soon, I join him and Alakya, who is wearing a shirt over her sari, on the farm, where the group of women, boys and men gathered at their home earlier is now all set to plant seeds. They all have their hair covered by cotton cloths. The land has been cleaned of all the stalks while Kochade is driving his cart with a plough tied behind the bullocks to dredge rows on the moist soil in which the labourers will plant seeds.

I once asked Ramrao why the plants grew in straight rows and he shot back, 'Because that's how bullocks walk.' If you develop a circular machine in the future, the plants may grow in that fashion, but when they grow in rows, it is easier to tend to them, remove weeds, put fertilizers and water them. Bullocks walk straight and make a slow U-turn at the end of the farm, and then walk back straight again, making parallel rows for sowing. The width of the plough is adjustable. If he is planting cotton, the width is kept maximum—4 to 5 feet. But if it is soybeans, you have to narrow it down to just one foot or so.

RAMRAO HAS NOT MECHANIZED his farm. He thinks it is important for him to give work to the bullock owners. Investing in big machines is a risk in the countryside anyway. They are energy- and cost-intensive. Unless you are a big landholder with bigger yields, or you can rent your machines to other farmers round the year, that investment does not make any sense. And this year, he tells me with a firm belief, most farmers will hire bullocks and not tractors for farm operations because diesel and petrol prices are surging and the previous year's pest attack left the farmers reeling under losses.

The labourers have tied pouches, fashioned out of thin cotton cloths, around their waists to hold the seeds. It seems symbolic that women do the sowing. Handling seeds and sowing them is a delicate affair, tied closely with the concepts of germination and fertility. Thirty to forty years ago, women farmers would coat the home seeds—the ones they kept for the next season—with cow dung before planting them. There was no need to buy seeds every year when they used their own, but the farm output was not much. Then came the hybrids in the late '80s and early '90s, and growers began to shop for high-yield varieties from the markets. In the early 2000s, the Bt cotton hybrids took the markets by storm, promising pest protection and high yields. What hasn't changed is the handling and planting of seeds by women.

At this moment, Meerabai, one of Ramrao's long-time labourers, and six other women and four girls around ten to twelve years of age are getting ready to plant the seeds. A young boy, who says he is in the eleventh class, joins them too.

It will be a painful first day.

'By the evening, my legs and back will hurt. Tomorrow morning it will be all right,' the young boy says shyly with a smile. Most labourers take a painkiller or an analgesic at night throughout the sowing season to deal with the aches. To plant seeds in a humid environment is back-breaking work.

Ramrao and Alakya give one last but important instruction to the labourers as they remove seeds from the glossy packets.

'Basant variety in the extreme left corner—that side.'

'Then sow these, Rasi-659, two or three rows.'

After that, in the middle, right in front of where we stand, he wants them to sow 70-67, a BG-II hybrid of US Agriseeds, a variety Pravin wants him to try out this year.

'Moksha—the tested KCH-15-K39 variety—after the 70-67, and towards the extreme right end plant KCH-100 of the Kaveri seeds.'

Ramrao registers it in his mind and Alakya splits the seeds between the teams, each of them tasked to sow only one variety. Alakya is leading two other women to plant 70-67, the young boy and two girls walk to the extreme left side of the farm to sow Basant. Ramrao asks the others to fan out and commence sowing so that the 5-acre farm, or at least half of it, is sown by the evening.

Throughout the year, he will keep a close watch on how each of these varieties performs under the same conditions.

In between, they will leave a row to plant tur, of which he has got eight bags of seeds, and sorghum in one corner for his domestic needs. Tur as an inter-crop to cotton is an old practice in Vidarbha: two by two, two by one, or some farmers sow two by three, the first denoting the number of rows of cotton, the latter tur.

In the '60s and '70s, cotton never occupied more than 40 per cent of the land area, while food crops—sorghum, lentils, sunflower, safflower, maize—covered the remaining part. All through the '80s and post the '90s, the region saw the cotton monocultures emerge, decimating food crops and oilseeds.

Once sowing is done, they will sprinkle urea and fertilizers for nourishment and better germination. For two days of sowing, Ramrao needs hard cash—about ₹15,000 to ₹20,000—because the labourers must be paid immediately, and if he needs more seeds, he must have enough money to pay quickly.

'It is like pouring money in a bottomless pit,' he tells me, sounding a bit exhausted. '*Kiti bi taka, sampat nahi.*' However much you add, it's never enough.

From this day on, Ramrao will need a constant flow of money to be spent on the farm and he will need to juggle his domestic needs with the demands of his farm and his ability to raise money. To be able to do so, he will continue to knock on people's doors, he will dip into his savings if he has any, or sell his assets if he has no other option.

As the men and women quietly do their work, Ramrao walks me to the shade of a fig tree, where he uproots dry stalks and lays a small carpet for me to settle on. Our lunch is arranged here. We will eat whatever Alakya and the other women have brought, wrapped in paper. It will be a community meal.

Through the day, I witness the brisk, painstaking but steady way in which the men and women sow seeds as the plough dredges the soil in straight rows. They stand up, pick seeds from their pockets, bend down and release them through their fingers at two, three, sometimes four spots in quick succession—two seeds in one spot just in case one fails to germinate. Each packet of 450 gm has a germination rate of 65 per cent. For an acre, Ramrao will use at least about three packets of seeds. He has to wait till October for his yields.

Man's audacity to convert what once were wild weeds or perennials into annual crops and turn the forest ecosystem into agriculture is at the heart of modern civilization. It is astonishing to plant a seed and see it come to life and grow, slowly but surely, every day—flowers first, then bolls and then the bursting of bolls into natural fibre. From one cotton seed, multiple flowers, then lint and seeds. From one grain of jowar, multiple grains. From a soybean, several beans.

Life on a farm is slow. Only in recent history have we made artificial plant growth-promoting hormones that farmers are increasingly using to accelerate the process.

If you leave aside the commerce and economics and focus only on the seed, its growth, life and nature, the farm cycle is bewitching. But throw in the questions of economics and you are in a soup. The uncertainties of the market, nature's vagaries, the price fluctuations and the isolated, lonely life on a farm can sound the death knell for anyone.

EARLY NEXT MORNING, RAMRAO decides to take me around the village to introduce to me his labourers at their homes.

For a long time now, the Indian countryside has faced this weird irony. The rate of rural farm and off-farm employment has been stagnant, declining or virtually non-existent. You confront labour scarcity at the peak of sowing, weeding or picking of cotton. At times the villagers bring labourers from the cities by paying higher wages and arranging for their transportation. You see angry farmers competing among themselves for farmhands.

It is indeed rare that a farmer and his labourers share personal warmth and generations-old relations the way Ramrao does with his men and women. Without them, he knows, farming is impossible.

We first meet Bhimrao Devrao Atram and his wife Parvatibai, an old couple that has now stopped working but they were once part of Ramrao's labour force. Parvatibai has a wrinkled but smiling face, she sports a large round bindi on her forehead and constantly chews betel leaf with tobacco in it that paints her mouth red. The couple once worked round the year on others' farms and lived off the paltry wages. They married their children off with the small sums they saved over years. They live with their elder son, but it is Ramrao they turn to for small sums of cash.

The old man tells me of a time when labourers also got a small share of the crop at the end of the harvest. It was called sarva, an incentive for working with a landlord. The system died down with modern farming; people wanted money that was more certain instead of burning their hands in the volatile and uncertain nature of commodity prices. No labourer would want a share in risks, the old man jokes—it is all Ramrao's headache!

We drop in next at Deepak Kochade's house. He is out in his field, where he is planning to plant sorghum for his domestic use and cotton on an acre of land for cash. His wife, Rekha, serves us black tea, which turns to be sweeter than sugarcane juice. Theirs is a small two-room cement house that was built under the Indira Awas Yojana, she tells us. The couple, in their mid-forties, has bare minimum needs and sometimes it is Ramrao who takes care of their exigencies. They have a teenage son, the smart and shy young boy who was at the sowing operation on Ramrao's farm, and two elder daughters, who are happily married and live in distant villages.

We meet Bhaurao, among the oldest hands. He is poor but he never begs for money. He is a slim and tall man in dhoti-kurta who rarely speaks. I always find him smoking a rolled bidi.

Then we catch up with Istari, a tall man in his mid-fifties with broad shoulders and unkempt hair. He has been one of Ramrao's most trusted lieutenants for years. A Gond adivasi with a modest home, he, his wife and two children all work as labourers. Istari is the man for all seasons. He sows, he removes weeds, he runs the bullocks-driven plough, he sprays pesticides—he does everything, and Ramrao takes care of his home as if it were his own. When he smiles, Istari bares his yellow teeth. He loves his old mother, who is fragile and has cataract in both eyes. Istari has no land. From his life savings he married off his two girls but could never afford to send his four children to school. He himself never went to one.

We then walk down to Bhaskar's house. He is nowhere to be seen. We meet his kids and wife, who tells us that he migrated for work. Bhaskar's wife is an ever-smiling woman who knows her husband is an alcoholic but can't do much to change his ways.

Ramrao explains with a smile: 'Bhaskar must have taken a lot of money from people, so he left the village.' His wife blushes, as if it were an acknowledgement.

This is what Bhaskar does: he runs away from the village for days, sometime months, to evade his lenders. He will return when people would have forgotten about the money they lent him.

Ramrao keeps reminding me that barring only a handful of homes belonging to the Yelmis, most of the Kolam and Gond homes are actually shanties. And he is right. These small wards throw up stories of starvation, penury, struggle and poverty. Yet, they also show up astonishing ways of human bonding. The villagers have their small animosities, feuds between castes and creeds, but they also bond with each other to face hardships.

As we stroll down the village alley, Ramrao rues about how the rich are becoming richer and the poor poorer. He tells me about a few individuals in Pandharkawda—the government employees, the forest rangers—who make a lot of money by taking bribes.

We catch up with his old friend Dadarao Buche, who owns 21 acres and is a diligent farmer. Despite his relatively large land, he remains a modest man, and that is because he makes just enough to make ends meet, fund his son's education and keep his lands going without shouldering much liability. He is a symbol of a once-big landlord family losing its sheen because it failed to diversify its income sources and remained full-time farmers.

Dadarao has an old house, seemingly untended for many years, with teak doors and windows that haven't been oiled or cleaned for ages, and a big cattle shed where a tractor stands parked instead of cows. He tells me he can't tend to cows any more, so he has kept only two or three animals and has switched to machines for farm work. He buys organic manure for his land whenever he needs it.

Buche's son lives in Nagpur and is preparing for competitive exams. Ramrao's friend is uneducated but proud of his son; he is unaware of the charade that he has built around his studies and preparation in his village, far removed from city life. Most probably the boy will end up doing nothing. He may return to his village and reluctantly take to farming or pick up a small daily job and live off that.

A lot of youngsters from the villages move every year to the bigger towns, trying to make it big, prepare for some competitive examination or get a good job, wilfully aware that they are fooling themselves. They can't compete with the urban, convent-educated, English-speaking, suave millennials. It is not their fault but it's an unequal world. Thousands of young boys and girls from across the Vidarbha countryside migrate to the cities for study and work. Some of them do well. Most don't. They bide their time while their peasant parents support them with money and material.

A majority of the Ola and Uber drivers in Nagpur are young boys who came to the city from villages across Vidarbha. Waiters in hotels too. Many of them study in colleges during the day and work at night to foot their room rents and bills. Farmers feel it is better that their children live in cities because they know that in the villages they have no future.

We meet some others who are waiting for the rains to come in bursts so that they too can sow seeds. Most of them talk about lack of money, delay in getting bank loans, or difficulty in arranging informal loans this year. They speak of massive losses they suffered on account of the pink bollworm attack; they speak of health hazards farmers and farm labourers suffered due to pesticides and how it would have an impact on people's mindset this year.

Buche also says bluntly, 'If things don't improve greatly, this year will see more farmers' suicides.'

Most haven't got the benefit of the loan waiver scheme that the Devendra Fadnavis government announced the previous year. No one got the cash compensation the government announced for the crop loss due to the pink bollworm either. They remain bank loan defaulters, a reason why most of them won't get fresh credit. Like Ramrao, most farmers are deeply anxious about bank loans, the monsoon and prices.

A GOOD CROP.

A good year.

A good monsoon.

A good price.

These are rural myths. In a peasant's lexis, there is nothing like a good year. It's always an average or a better year.

Ramrao says farmers around him invariably end up losers. When they begin sowing, they usually start the season with a lot of anxieties: Will we get loans? Will it rain on time? What should we sow? Will it grow well? Will we get good prices?

Unfailingly, for most peasants, a year ends with heartbreak. For the region, it brings more challenges, more migration, more suicides. Some farmers do well. They are exceptions. Ever since I began my journey into the cotton hinterland, I have seen few things work, some go bad, but most remain constant or get worse.

Cities have grown exponentially. New investments have adorned them. A lot of new buildings have mushroomed. Hiwara has seen no substantial change. The huts with blue or yellow tarpaulin sheets to stave off rain—they remain the same. Torn and worn out.

Compensation for the failure, loss or destruction of crops due to natural exigencies or raids by wild animals and packages have become a constant political demand. A sort of inferiority complex has crept in among the peasantry after years of distress. The inequality and difference in living standards come to the fore when a brother, even if he and his family are engaged in menial jobs in a city, comes visiting during festivals. A family member with a small but regular salary in the city looks richer than the ones back in the village who are cultivating 10 acres of land—leave aside the government employees or the nouveau riche, with whom there can't be any comparison in the rural world.

I never see young boys and girls in Hiwara play any sport, though the zilla parishad primary school has a small playground marked by newly planted Ashoka trees along its compound wall. A couple of teachers shuttle between Pandharkawda and Hiwara to teach and they appear committed to do their job and to the children. But most youths dream of permanently stepping out of their village.

A month after Ramrao's first sowing, I visit Hiwara. He is worried. It must rain in a day or two, he tells me, exasperated. Otherwise, the seeds on his leased rain-fed lands won't germinate. An extended dry spell has plunged all the villagers into tension. Ramrao and most others have had to sow seeds again, thrice at times, in the spots where previously sown seeds failed to germinate and died. Each time they buy new packets and throw in fertilizers.

Vidarbha has been witnessing weird rainfall patterns—extreme rain events on the one hand and extended dry spells on the other—over the past couple of decades. Scientists say this pattern is part of the climate change impacting the planet.

All around Ramrao's farm and as far as you can see, men and women are on their fields under overcast skies, eager to finish the first step of a new season, hoping it rains. They are sowing the seeds manually and, as he had predicted the previous month, working with pairs of bullocks. I don't see many tractors on the fields.

Ramrao has raised money from multiple sources—he sold a bull, sought some money from Ashokrao, Munna lent him some, he bought inputs on credit, and he got some money from his friend Peddineni Srinivasulu, aka Chinusheth, a farmer from Telangana who leases tens of acres of land around Hiwara and invests heavily to grow chillies, which he later sells in his home state. When he earns, he earns in truckloads. When he loses, he loses badly. Chinusheth in turn borrows money from the sahukars in Andhra Pradesh and Telangana and at times helps farmers like Ramrao.

Hundreds of Andhra farmers once leased lands in this part in the '90s but, when the agrarian crisis aggravated and deepened financial woes, they stopped coming. I saw several of them commit suicide in the early years of the next decade, when chilli and cotton prices dipped sharply and markets turned volatile.

Ramrao also sold last year's tur stocks to a private trader to raise ₹70,000, from which he paid for some inputs. He prays for seeds to at least germinate this time. On one of his farm plots in Borgaon he had to sow seeds all over again. Not one of them had germinated due to an extended dry monsoon spell. Re-sowing is a regular feature in the lives of the farmers. In the past decade or so, this has become a constant. The rains take a break. Moisture loss in the soil results in non-germination. The heavy use of chemicals has degraded the soil quality too.

Re-sowing means some more burden. You have to spend again on seeds, fertilizers and urea and pay extra wages to the labourers, demand for whom shoots up in July and August when rains pick up and rain-fed farmers—a majority of all farmers—scamper to finish sowing. More demand means their wages go up relatively, but they still remain lower than what they would earn in cities.

By MID-AUGUST ALL INDICATORS point to a deficient monsoon in the state—Yavatmal is no exception. All over, there is clamour for water. In the last week of August, Ramrao phones to tell me the bank is yet to give him a crop loan. He hasn't received a waiver either and, to top it off, the cotton and soybean yield isn't going to be great this time around.

'The bank manager says go ask the tehsildar, the tehsildar says go ask the collector, the minister says go ask the chief minister. Do I farm or go question these people about the waiver?'

In mid-September, when I am headed to Hiwara to meet Ramrao, all along the road I see fields of cotton plants left stunted by the lack of rain. It has been a drought. There are exceptions—the few plants that look robust and healthy are the ones being watered from wells. Some farmers are working on their fields, looking disconcerted, plucking weeds, tending to their plants, observing their growth. Pink bollworms and other pests are back. I spot labourers spraying pesticides, wearing colourful Chinese and India-made pumps on their backs. Farmers are deploying bullocks more than tractors to till their land because diesel prices are soaring and they have no cash. They are buying weedicides on credit to rid their farms of weeds because labour is hard to find. It is a saving to spray chemicals than hire labour, but there is flip side. It is ecologically suicidal. In all this, there is only one solace: the heat is not as bad as it was the previous year.

There is a big problem, Ramrao tells me during the visit. Farmers don't have cash, which had led to a labour crunch—the landless are migrating for work to cities because farmers have no money to pay their wages. A lot of farmers are not recruiting farm labour because banks haven't lent money to raise crops and borrowing from private lenders is expensive. Last year's loan waiver seems to have crippled the crop loan cycle.

In 2009, when the UPA government announced a loan waiver scheme, it paid the banks over three installments the loans waived off farmers from across the country. In short, the Centre shouldered that burden and not the banks. In the subsequent loan waivers announced by the state governments, the Centre gave no counter-guarantee. So, the states promised the banks they would pay for the loans waived off but the nationalized banks that come under the purview of the Reserve Bank of India would not restructure the loans until the states paid them the loan installments. Thus, while the waivers remained a political announcement, in reality the banks were coaxed or forced to waive off the farmers' dues without getting the money from the state governments. This led to a financial squeeze, and the farmers' crop loan accounts continued to be described with terms such as 'defaulters' or 'outstanding loans' in the banks' ledgers. As a result, thousands of farmers were deprived of fresh formal credit in a new season.

Banks are bleeding with the swelling non-performing assets. Because the farmers are hoping that their outstanding loans would be waived off, they are obviously not repaying their dues. Most of them, like Ramrao, have no money to repay in any case.

With little or no work, nothing much happens in Hiwara. People are trapped in their daily chores, stuck in a routine. On the surface it is a simple life, but at its core there are unseen processes that upend their existence, turning it into an insurmountable challenge.

In the last two decades, metros have exploded, cities have expanded, some villages on the highways have grown into big towns, but villages like Hiwara remain stuck in the past, as if fossilized in time. Kolam families keep to themselves and hardly ever mix with others. The youth while away time, gambling in secret. Ten years earlier, the villages on the road from Pandharkawda to Jhari town were racked by the scourge of 'matka', a vicious gambling game in which poor farmers and labourers lost their hard-earned money. It took one police officer and a strict superintendent of police in Yavatmal to crack down on the local gangsters running the show and end the menace. The women were happy. They want the police to crack down on the liquor shops as well. Though the organized gambling scene is gone, gambling in the village persists. You will always find men of all ages huddled together, engrossed in it. When Ramrao walks past them, he often scolds them for wasting their precious time.

'*Salyaho, kamale laga be.*' You morons, do some work, he tells them. And they laugh at him almost every time, or simply disperse and reassemble once he has left the scene.

Everything is tied to the crop cycle here.

Cultivating a farm is not easy. In May, when Ramrao must prepare the land for the sowing season, he has to work an early and a late shift, taking a break from 11 a.m. to 5 p.m. when the skin simply cannot bear the harsh sun. June through October, the hot weather turns the farm into a natural sauna. But it's no relaxing, five-star experience. It's hell.

I once tried my hand at running the plough clamped to a pair of huge humped bullocks. This was soon after the first rains, when the fields were muddy and humid. Ramrao hesitated. He didn't want me to do it. I would fall sick, he warned. And I did. In fifteen minutes I was dehydrated. I came down with fever, fatigue and exhaustion after only an hour or two of working the plough. Farmhands, men and women, do it for days, months and years. Ploughing. Sowing. Weeding. Plucking. Picking. Cutting.

The best time to be on the farm is winter. The one downside is that if there has been a price slump, you will find that the farmers have lost heart. It is like watching a child get bad marks on a tough exam despite working very hard and putting in the time.

'*Dukhale sukh manun kaam chalu aahe, bhau.*'

Ramrao is staring at losses on his leased land. He will take suffering in his stride and move on, he says. If he doesn't rise to the occasion, his daughter will crumble. He needs to be strong for her sake.

By September end, the monsoon is beginning to withdraw and a long dry spell is set to spoil the crop. I accompany Ramrao to the Borgaon farm that he has leased. We park our vehicle by the side of a slender road and walk along the shrubs to his farm—it is a ten-minute walk. We greet an old man perched atop a tree branch shooing away the birds eating his jowar grains. He throws stones at them and makes loud noises to scare them off.

Ramrao tells me the birds will similarly eat all his grain too—his food earmarked for the coming months—if he does not come to the farm regularly.

'*Buddha katak hay,*' he quips. The old man is sturdy.

We leave the road behind and finally reach Ramrao's field. There is no one else around, just us standing in a field of white. This farm is awash with cotton. It is a lovely plot of land, like a tabletop. Eight acres full of white gold.

Ramrao thinks wild animals—boars or nilgais—may be around, grazing. For safety, he picks up a wooden stick as soon as we step on the farm, just in case an animal crosses our path.

'Rain or water. These plants need moisture at this moment.' Without rain, the plants will wilt. Ramrao does not have access to water here. There's no source. This is rain-fed land, dependent on the rains for irrigation, and the monsoon has withdrawn this year. But the perpetual optimist that he is—quite ironic considering that he is a suicide survivor—Ramrao invents a weather forecast.

'I heard there's a cyclone in Andhra Pradesh, so it might rain here soon.' Then he laughs, as if he knows the joke's on him.

For about half an hour he walks through the rows of cotton, observing the flowers, the bolls, the roots, searching for the presence of pests. He finds black scars beneath a few bolls and immediately knows that pink bollworms have drilled through.

No use now, mutters Ramrao. The plants won't grow any more.

We walk back, get into the vehicle and return to Ramrao's home, where Alakya complains about the lack of money. They need to buy rations. Ramrao quietly smiles. I'll arrange for it, he tells her.

He hasn't got a crop loan this year like many other farmers of Maharashtra. He did not get the loan waiver the government announced in 2017.

'How do you decide to lease more land?' I ask.

'Gut feeling. I thought I had time on my hands, a friend came with the offer that he would share expenses. So, I took the offer.'

The 8 acres of Borgaon land that he has leased will yield no more than 30 quintals of cotton this year, he predicts. The crop will be worth ₹1,50,000, equal to the amount they spent on producing it. It is a zero-sum game.

Ramrao then reiterates an old saying: '*Sau ka saath karna, baap ka naam chalana*.'

You convert ₹100 into ₹60, just to keep your father's name alive.

'We know it's a drought when small quantities of things get stolen from our farms,' Ramrao smiles at me.

Someone stole 10 to 15 kg of cotton from him. He says the thief is someone who knows the farm owner won't mind.

'*Bhay pareshan hay lok*.' People are so desperate.

It is mid-October when I visit Ramrao. It's a special day for him. He is performing a ritual called Sitadevi. No one has any idea why it is called that or why it is significant. Most probably, the term 'Shet Devata'—the farm deity—transformed into 'Sitadevi'.

Ramrao tells me that farmers have performed this ritual for ages to signal the harvest of cotton on their farms. Everyone does it irrespective of caste and creed.

It is not yet harvest time for most farmers, except those who have the good fortune of groundwater to irrigate their farms. In regions like Marathwada, farmers are digging deeper and deeper to extract water and grow atrocious quantities of sugarcane or irrigate orchards. Ramrao has an open well for his 5 acres, so his crop is ready for harvest. But for the rest of his leased farms, he will have to wait for a month or so before cotton lint can be picked from the bolls.

Farmers perform Sitadevi mostly during Navratri, around Dussehra, Ramrao informs me as we—Alakya is with us today—walk to his farm. Alakya is carrying the paraphernalia for the puja—a coconut, some milk, water, vermillion and incense sticks. We will pick the flowers from his farm; the marigolds are in bloom now. I reached Hiwara early morning as he told me the puja must be done around that time of the day.

Alakya and Ramrao sit down between the rows of tall cotton plants whose bolls have burst open, displaying fluffy white lint. Ramrao makes a small swing-like structure from the leaves and a cotton cloth and ties it across the bottom of the plants' stalks. He makes a small idol from the freshly picked cotton—that's symbolic of goddess Sita, daughter of mother earth. He sprinkles some milk and water, breaks open the coconut for prasad, lights the incense sticks and moves them clockwise thrice—this is meant to spread light and fragrance—and tucks them in the soil by the base of that tiny swing. Then he offers a few marigold flowers, some coconut and jaggery. He bends down to touch his forehead in front of the idol and prays for the well-being of his family and farm.

'Vimal used to perform this puja when she was alive,' he tells me. Alakya, he says, should do it, but she refuses because she thinks that as a widow it would be inauspicious for her to do so. She is embarrassed with the explanation. I insist too, reasoning with her that god will understand.

'*Chal chal,*' Ramrao begs her. 'Do it.'

Alakya reluctantly performs the puja but looks happy about it.

'Tomorrow the women will start picking the cotton,' Ramrao announces happily. He is hopeful this is going to bring him some income that will enable him to settle his labour wages. He is happy that he might manage to repay some of his loans despite this being a bad year. He won't be debt-free yet, though.

Cotton prices are hovering at around ₹5,500 a quintal, which is not bad but it is not great either. They have been stable for the past five years. This year, farmers predict, the yields will plummet.

Once the Sitadevi ritual is over, farmers start selling their cotton to the small traders at the village level or to the ginning mills. There was a time in the 1990s and the early 2000s when carts laden with cotton would line the roads outside the cotton markets in winter, waiting for their turn to off-load the produce for it to be procured by the agents of the state-run cotton marketing federation. Today, you drive a little tempo into a market or a ginning-pressing unit and sell cotton for a cash payment.

Over the next three months, Ramrao will harvest anything between 40 and 45 quintals of cotton from his 5 acres. From Golemwar's 7 acres, he expects about 25 to 30 quintals; the profits they make will be split between them. The Borgaon gamble has come a cropper. The rains abated early, causing the plants to remain stunted. From the 8 acres he cultivated, he expects a yield of only 20 quintals—just enough to recover the production costs and pay wages.

Alakya heads home after performing the Sitadevi ritual. She picks fresh cotton and marigold flowers and collects them in a bag. She is going to place them in front of her mother's photo at home.

Over the next two days, Ramrao employs his regular women labourers, including Meerabai—Alakya joins them too—to pick the cotton on his farm. The women chit-chat, share their concerns and trade gossip on the farm through the day, only taking a break for lunch and to drink water. They each pick 50 to 60 kg of cotton. Seven or eight of them together pick about 3 to 4 quintals of cotton a day. Ramrao will pay them a picking wage of ₹5 per kg—this goes up to ₹10 per kg during peak picking season in December, when the demand for farmhands goes up. For a quintal, that's anything between ₹500 and ₹1,000. He will sell the cotton to a ginning mill near Pandharkawda, or to his friend Sandeep Chintawar, an aggregator for cotton traders, or to owners of the ginning mills around Pandharkawda. From there, Ramrao has no idea how his cotton will travel ahead—will it become apparel, or be packed into mattresses, maybe even travel out of the country and end up with a foreign user.

EARLY NOVEMBER, I AM back in the village during Diwali.

Hiwara is quiet. All along the highway, I don't see any festivity. This is a drought year. In most farms, cotton is not yet ready for harvest. Farmers are staring at a sharp dip in their incomes and the mood is despondent. The Pandharkawda market is quiet too. Some of my shopkeeper friends here tell me there's no money with the farmers; Diwali is going to be 'thandi' (sluggish) in these parts.

Come evening, Hiwara shows signs of just modest festivities. It is yet another black Diwali for the villagers. No festive fervour, no lighting, no decorations around any house. The cotton plants look exceptionally stunted—a glaring sign that inadequate rains, delayed sowing and re-sowing, and the long dry spells in between have impacted the yields. Less cotton means less income, which means lower wages for labourers. So, no crackers or new clothes for the children. I notice a bare-bodied boy, about six or seven years old, living in the hut opposite Ramrao's home, scavenging through the paper splinters of crackers someone burst at the village square the previous night. He is probably looking to see if he can find a live cracker.

'There is hardly any money in our village,' Alakya says when I reach their home. Ramrao is on the field as usual.

She is busy washing clothes in the porch outside the toilet when I arrive. Ramrao, she tells me, is on the farm because he is planning to spray pesticide on his tur plants. There is a pest attack, she says. The Borgaon farm is not going to yield a good crop. It's going to be a year of losses, she adds. They sold 25 quintals of cotton from his 5-acre plot to pay wages before Diwali. Cotton grows in spurts and needs to be picked twice, thrice, sometime even four times over five months—mid-October through February. The money Ramrao will make from his own farm will counter the not-so-good yields from the other two farms.

The first room of Ramrao's home has cotton stacked along the wall, reaching up to the ceiling. It's about 10 quintals of cotton from the Borgaon field. Farmers in Hiwara and all over Vidarbha fill their homes with cotton picked from the fields and sell it in parts through the season.

All over the southern parts of Yavatmal, the fields are a scene of all that is wrong with farming—stunted and anemic cotton plants, frail and poor tur plants.

I sense a liquidity crunch ahead.

In Marki village, 30 kilometres south of Hiwara, farmer activist Bandu Parkhi tells me this isn't a cotton year.

'I think there is a problem with the seeds. And with the rains too. Only those with assured irrigation will get some returns.'

Vidarbha had only 3 per cent cotton under protective irrigation—that land which has well or canal irrigation—in 2005. There is no codified data on it but the Vidarbha Irrigation Development Corporation says the figure has gone up to 15 per cent now. For the other 80 to 85 per cent, the uncertainties are massive. There are no bolls on the cotton plants. And those that have look wilted. Marli, Mangli, Mukutban—everywhere farmers tell me this is another devastating year for them. And as Ramrao told me last month, there is a sudden spurt in petty thefts all over.

THE NEW YEAR IS here and Ramrao looks more confident, even if he remains indebted. When I met him late in December, half of the front room of his house was filled with cotton. Now the room is full.

In the first week of January, Ramrao sells 30 quintals of cotton at ₹5,100 a quintal. That is from his friend Golemwar's farm. The income will be split evenly between the two. January is the month when Ramrao usually goes to the market to sell the cotton and tur harvested in the previous two months. By now, he is through with planting for the winter on his well-irrigated 5 acres.

It is a wintry, pleasant day in mid-January. Ramrao calls off the plan to fill up the pick-up truck to take his cotton to the market for sale because he learns that the prices are not rising. He decides to wait for a week to see if prices go up. Instead, he tells me, he will use the time to separate the chaff from the pigeon pea produce stashed in his barn. He instructs one of his labourers, Bhimrao, to do that work. And we head for Ramrao's farm, where he has planted wheat, chickpeas and some jowar. It is exceptionally cold out in the farm, and Ramrao has put on two shirts to protect himself from the chill.

'This is a drought year, but prices are going down. How is this happening!' he wonders.

I tell him international markets are flush with cotton and pulses, and that is driving the prices down.

He says, sounding a bit exasperated, 'What all do we worry about now? Monsoon, markets, lenders, politicians ... and monkeys!' he adds, and suddenly lunges forward, picks up a big stone and hurls it towards a tree on which I spot a herd of monkeys looking at us.

'Bastards!' Ramrao picks up another stone and throws it at the tree. The monkeys pretend like they will run away, but don't.

As we are in a drought year, there is no water in the forest or on the farms, no food, no foliage. The wild animals are devouring the standing crops whenever they can. They are eating into the cotton bolls too, Ramrao says. Very few farms are green at this time. And Ramrao's is one in a vast stretch of lands where cotton plants have been left to dry, but he has removed them on a portion to plant winter crops because he has water.

Curious, I ask, 'In your life, which crops have you planted?'

Ramrao's eyes light up as he begins to list them out.

'Cabbages. I grew cabbages once, but when I took them to the market, the prices were so low that I found no buyers. I once sowed sesame seeds and got a bumper crop. By the time I took the produce to the market, prices had fallen from ₹100 to ₹45 a kg.

'I plant moong dal ever so often. Again, I get a yield of 5 quintals on an acre and fetch ₹4,000 to ₹5,000 a quintal.

'I planted brinjal and onions. I broke even on that.'

I interrupt him and ask, 'When did you make a profit, on which crop?'

He thinks for a moment. 'Chillies. I got a good price for chillies in the early 2000s but later burnt my fingers.' Around the same time, the Andhra farmers who had leased adivasi lands around Hiwara to grow chillies too left this region because they made huge losses with the volatile markets.

Ramrao goes on recounting the crops he has ever planted: 'Flaxseed, spinach, cucumbers, potatoes—my land is not fit to grow potatoes—capsicum, tomatoes, okra ...'

He mentions over three dozen crops he has cultivated. The lack of canal irrigation and markets for the produce limits his choice of crops. He never raised a dairy, though—even after he spent money to dig a well on his field in the late '90s, an important prerequisite for keeping milching cows or buffaloes. The well helps irrigate his 5 acres but not his leased arid lands.

'I can grow anything if there's water and a price for it in the market.'

As the summer sets in and the 2018-19 agriculture year comes to an end, Ramrao makes money on his farm but farmers are in the doldrums all over the region because of the prevailing water scarcity and the raging drought. Ramrao has made just enough to recover his production costs from the lands he leased. He has received his annual salary from the agriculture officer for managing his farm, and he is set to repay ₹3,00,000 to ₹4,00,000 of his outstanding debts to his lenders. That leaves him with nothing.

For his fellow villagers, it's going to be a long, harsh summer.

In 2014, Ramrao wanted to quit farming. He is more hopeful now, focused on providing a life for Alakya and Varshini but still buried under debt. He is determined to repay every dime of his borrowings. Quitting—from life or farm—is not an option or what he wishes for any more.

9

JANUS

FIVE YEARS HAVE GONE by since Ramrao swallowed two bottles of Coragen in a bid to kill himself, and survived.

It was a normal monsoon in 2014, but Ramrao didn't want to go back to his farm. Then came 2015. He was still depressed and, all over Vidarbha, Marathwada and north Maharashtra, the monsoon failed, and nearly half the state was in the grip of a drought. The following year, he picked up the plough again, driven by necessity—his elder son-in-law dead by suicide. But that year, despite his cotton and soybeans being ready to enter the market, demonetization adversely affected him and his co-farmers in more ways than one. He struggled. The only relief was that the state government asked cooperative and nationalized banks to restructure crop loans that year. Ramrao had his loan restructured —in official parlance it meant his was a running and not a defunct crop loan account—but he didn't get any fresh bank loans.

The year 2017 witnessed an average monsoon, but the pink bollworms made a comeback in Vidarbha and destroyed the cotton produce. Then, 2018 was a drought year. The monsoon failed, which meant Ramrao did not get good yields from his leased lands as they don't have protective irrigation. He made up for his losses with what he grew on his own farm, which has an open well.

In these years, hundreds of reports of farmers taking their own lives—consuming pesticides, hanging themselves, drowning in wells or lakes or, in some cases, jumping onto pyres—have come in from all parts of the country: prosperous Punjab, water-scarce central Maharashtra, the belly of the Cauvery, arid Bundelkhand, forested Odisha, Rayalaseema, north Karnataka … it is a long list. Thousands have quit farming to migrate to towns, cities or simply to any place where they may find work, better wages and relief from perpetual indebtedness.

A majority of them end up as farm labourers. Farmers' suicides are now occurring in previously untouched regions; the agrarian distress has become more uniform and ubiquitous in terms of states and crops. Earlier, paddy farmers hardly ever took their own lives; now many of them do. Between 2014 and 2019, going by statistical trends, at least 84,000 farmers may have died by suicide, clocking an annual average of 14,000. In Maharashtra, the figure would be around 21,000, if we take the long-term annual average of 3,500. Vidarbha would have seen about 10,000 of these suicides.

In five years, the Modi government has not been able to assuage the pain of farmers, but they continue to have faith in the man. They queued up during demonetization for days, faced unprecedented hardships, bore losses, but believed the move would bring them prosperity in the long run.

Every day, Ramrao is aware of the value of the life he has got, thanks to his family and friends. It is March again. In Hiwara, there is a hint of summer in the air. The winter cold has receded.

Mornings are pleasant, but they won't be in a week's time when the mercury starts soaring. Farmlands will turn hard, forests will run thin, leaves will desert trees, and the only thing standing firm, lining the farms, will be the prickly, thorny subabul trees.

Hiwara still has some jungle left, but the highway that winds down from Nagpur to Pandharkawda has more billboards than trees today. Trees have been felled for the widening of the highway—for the cause of the nation's 'development'. Some villages around Hiwara, connected by dirt roads, are tiny, but surrounded by teak and shrub forests. They too are slowly losing their density with tree thefts for cash. The poor and beleaguered farmers there eke a sustenance out of the tiny fragments of land where they grow cotton, soybeans and jowar.

In Hiwara, Bhagavata Saptah is in progress. The week-long event running up to Holi serves as a reminder to Ramrao of that near-death event in his life.

What do you even call that? An anniversary?

During this period, he has become acutely aware of the people around him who have been kind and supportive. He is grateful to his elder brother. He thanks Bhaskar with a ₹100 bill once in a while that the guy invariably loses in gambling. He thanks the almighty. He remembers his wife and adores his granddaughters, who, he says, give him an immense sense of gratification. He prays for both his daughters and hopes that Akalya will find the strength to face her life's challenges and luck will smile on her again. The thought of Alakya and her well-being never deserts him these days. He gets emotional in his solitary moments when he broods over his daughter's fate.

Despite all his troubles, Ramrao is grateful. Destiny has largely been kind to him, he says. He tells me, rather innocuously, how better off he is compared to most villagers. Look at Bhaskar, he says, the chap has not been able to put a new roof on his house; look at the Kolams, most of the tribe don't have resources to eat two square meals; or the landless, reduced to living a hand-to-mouth existence for years and years. He goes on and on to compare his own modest life with the lives of some of the poorest people in the world to remind himself that, despite his troubles, he has a lot to be thankful for. He reminds me that he has the land many would covet.

That is why, whenever he can, he spends money on his fellow villagers—he funds their trips to the town, or to a temple, or a fair. He takes fifteen to twenty boys from the Kolam tribe and other poor families every year without fail during the nine-day Navratri festival to Kelapur village, 20 kilometres away on the Hyderabad highway, to enjoy the annual fair and circus. He knows most of them will never get a chance to travel beyond the village. He hires an auto, stuffs them all into it and they go spend a day at the fair. A few of the older boys help him manage the younger ones. It is due to this unconditional love for his community that the villagers call him a pure soul, a man sent by the almighty.

'I AM PRIVILEGED,' RAMRAO says. 'You have an even better life. Never crib about it.'

We are walking to the temple where the Bhagavata Katha is being narrated. The Hanuman temple has grown in the past five years, brick by brick. Another kiosk selling tobacco and cigarettes has popped up in the village, but the health centre that could reduce the suffering of the villagers remains closed on most days for want of grants and doctors, who don't want to serve in rural areas because life here is difficult and treacherous.

As we get closer to the temple, the sound of the recital gets louder. It's blaring from the loudspeaker that hangs from a thick bamboo stick tied to the temple dome so that the entire village can listen to the katha. I hear the narrator singing in his not-so-mellifluous voice, his tone harsh, the volume loud.

Ramrao says, as though he can read my mind, 'It's loud and noisy.'

The arrangements for the saptah this year are sober. No big fanfare. No daily prasad. No pandal or shamiyana. There is only one mike, one loudspeaker.

'Why, you know?' Ramrao asks me in his usual rhetorical tone.

By now, he has taken it upon himself to educate me on every event, every detail about the village, and the ways of rural life. He knows I appreciate his insights. He always begins with, 'You know why?'

And invariably every time I ask, 'Why?'

'Dushkal! This is a drought year,' Ramrao explains. 'People don't have money. You see that, right? We had to manage with the small donations raised from the broke farmers. This year, people gave no money because they don't have any.'

Drought means different things to different people in rural parts. It could be low or erratic rainfall, crops losses due to a variety of reasons, depleting groundwater, lack of hard cash or a combination of mostly man-made factors.

In Hiwara, crops came a cropper because the monsoon was erratic and inadequate. Where they should have reaped 10 quintals of cotton, most farmers got only 4. Where they should have reaped

5 quintals of pigeon pea, they got 2. With the exception of a few people like Ramrao, nobody in Hiwara was able to plant the winter crop. Labourers did not find enough work. And there is no guarantee people will get any forest work this summer—the forest department commissions seasonal works such as tending to forest nurseries, cleaning wild weed, harvesting some teak plantations and so on, apart from the usual tendu leaves collection.

'Yes, I see that,' I tell him, so that he knows I got the point. 'How much did you contribute?' I ask him.

Ramrao smiles. 'Don't ask me that.' After a pause, he chuckles, 'A lot.'

I know he's exaggerating. He has no money to spare for lavish donations, but it is possible that he gave away whatever he has. He won't think twice before giving everything away on an impulse to the temple but, I am sure, Alakya must have applied the brakes.

Where did he get the money from, I wonder.

'I donated what I earned from my winter green gram.'

'How much?' I wait for him to answer but don't push.

He evades the question.

We are now at the newly built temple auditorium. It has been whitewashed, but there is no plaster. The hall is open. It has a new grill-gate to the inner sanctum. I can smell the fresh black paint applied to it. The devout villagers have installed idols of Lord Ram, Sita and Laxman made of white marble. People donated money to the temple even in a drought year. I learn from Ramrao that a local leader from Chalbardi pitched in.

The storyteller this year is very young, perhaps in his early thirties, and charges a modest fee—not as much as someone with more experience would.

Today is the third day of the saptah.

Ramrao tells me in hushed tones that the storyteller—the maharaj—is a novice, unlike the one who came the previous year with his battery of assistants, actors and shiny costumes. That maharaj has built an ancillary business around his craft—he rents microphones, speakers, and the system and charges a lump sum for all of his services.

In a few years, the new maharaj too will become adept at performing these religious events and eventually charge an exorbitant fee. All over Vidarbha and perhaps in Maharashtra, there is a growing tribe of such storytellers-turned-seers who do brisk business with the village devotees. Some of them even make their devotees wash their feet and revere them as though they themselves are avatars of Lord Vishnu.

The week-long event costs anywhere between ₹2,00,000 and ₹5,00,000 if the village decides to do it in a modest style. Costs can go up as high as ₹20,00,000 with lavish arrangements. I ask Ramrao why people spend money on religious functions rather than building tanks or farm ponds that might do wonders to the village's economy and help tackle a drought.

'*Bhiti*,' he replies, almost instantly. Fear.

'People who commit sin after sin live with guilt. They think they will wash their sins away by doing this. Some people are superstitious. They think if they don't do it, a curse might befall them. Very few people are genuinely spiritual.'

In the break, I find the young narrator too follows the old rules. He makes people bow and touch his feet, pats them on their back to bless them, or simply folds his hands and appears to close his eyes in meditation. He is very theatrical—Ramrao agrees with me but says the devout villagers won't. They are under a spell.

Ramrao whispers to me that this baba must drink a pauvva—a quarter bottle of liquor—at night. An old villager sitting beside Ramrao hears the remark too. He smiles, as if he too agrees, baring his few still-standing tobacco-stained teeth. Ramrao laughs along with the old man. I look at the narrator in his colourful new clothes and marvel at his grandeur and demeanour. Ramrao and the old man know the fallacy of this arrangement, but they also know the necessity of its existence. They need it to get over their troubles. It is their momentary succour.

After sitting there for a while, we get up and leave, putting the narrator, the mythology and the rapt audience behind, and return to our mortal worlds where problems abound.

As we walk past the village square, Ramrao tells me that he kept a distance from the reception committee of the Bhagavata Saptah even though he is one of the main donors this year.

Then he asks the customary 'You know, why?' and I smile and answer 'Why?'.

'I could not have devoted any time for the arrangements,' he reasons, as if to indicate he has been awfully busy, doing something I don't know. He knows I will ask questions. He waits. But I decide not to for now, keeping it for a later time in the day. I instead deflect his attention to another question. Ramrao is irritated because he expected me to probe! He decides to tell me the reason without waiting for me to ask.

'*Thye nahi ka, tumhale phone kelto!*' Ramrao reminds me of a conversation we had a few days back.

He calls me ever so often if he doesn't hear from me, merely to exchange pleasantries and update me with the goings-on. Sometimes it could be news about the weather, or the new pests he has sighted on his farm, or a bit of news he wants to share.

That day, about a fortnight ago I think, he had called to inform me that his cousin Venkanna had asked him for money. When Ramrao had needed money for his wife's medical treatment in 2012, Venkanna—his cousin in Telangana—had lent him about ₹2,00,000. It remains unpaid. 'Something needs to be done, Venkanna needs money for his son's wedding.'

The farming season is long over, though some cotton on his farm is still unpicked. Some farmers have to keep their cotton unpicked if they don't have cash to pay wages. Cotton plants and stalks stand for as long as you want. Farmers will raze and burn them in May, when the preparation for the new farming season starts.

'That cotton will fetch me some money,' he had said over the phone, making some quick calculations. I had murmured in agreement. 'My cousin is in need of the money he gave me, but I do not have a dime to pay him at this moment,' Ramrao had kept reiterating to me over phone.

I asked, 'So what are you going to do?'

'I don't know. That's why I called you.' Then he had hung up.

We have spoken several times since then, but I never had the heart to ask him about it. Now, he is eager to tell me that story.

'So, did you arrange for the money?' I check with him as we reach his home, where Alakya greet us with tea.

'Yes,' she chimes in with a smile. She overheard our conversation about Venkanna's money and knew Ramrao had already told me about it. 'He arranged it somehow.'

Ramrao falls quiet as Alakya brings two cups of very sweet black tea with a dash of ginger. I wait for his answer but sense he has again borrowed money to pay his cousin.

'Did you sell anything, Ramrao?' I prod.

'No, I mortgaged something,' he says nonchalantly. 'Alakya's gold, the ornaments she had kept safe from her in-laws.'

IN FIVE YEARS, NOTHING much has changed in the Vidarbha countryside—farmers suicides continue, incomes remain embarrassingly low. These issues don't make the prime time news. We talk about doubling farmers' incomes without finding out what has happened to real incomes. We revel in announcements from the new government—a Jal Yukt Shivar (a programme on in-situ water conservation in Maharashtra) or a Pradhan Mantri Sanman Yojana, which promises a princely dole of ₹6,000 annually, or ₹16.44 a day, to 12 crore farming households in India.

The central and state governments' focus remains vague: sometimes they announce they want to push processing; other times they say they are going to transform rain-fed farming into irrigated farming; these days they talk about forming farmers' producer companies. In the seven decades since India became independent, the primary producer status of the peasantry in this part has remained unchanged, with virtually zero allied sector income.

Farmers grow cotton and sell it. They grow soybean and sell it. They grow lentils and sell it. That's it. The region produces cotton but no cloth or apparel. Soybean extraction plants produce crude oil but not edible oil—something that the region can become popular for and pass on the price leverage to its farmers, stabilizing prices and incentivizing the cultivation of varied edible oil crops, not just soybean. Farmers earn once a year, but expenses on the farm, food, healthcare and education are shooting up exponentially every year. Most of Vidarbha's farmers depend solely on farming—rain-fed, small and marginal lands. No dairy, no poultry, no goat rearing, no horticulture or floriculture, no fishery or sericulture. And that is the problem.

Of late, unorganized goat rearing and backyard poultry farming have gained some traction in parts of the region thanks to the dogged perseverance of several voluntary organizations or a few committed individuals who took the plunge and now work in this backward region, having given up their cushy jobs. Farmers need alternative income sources to offset the vagaries of nature and markets.

Outlining the causes of famine in Berar, Professor Laxman Satya in his book *Cotton and Famine in Berar: 1850–1900* writes:

> Colonial officials from the time of Captain Meadows Taylor (1858) strongly believed that the deep black soil of Berar was naturally rich and therefore did not need much irrigation. This became the standard line of reasoning in the official opposition to investment in public irrigation projects, he writes further (pp 279). The state interest in agriculture basically lapsed outside cotton cultivation. And since cotton did not need too much water, the need for any general irrigation scheme seemed unnecessary and the colonial anti-irrigation attitude seemed to be justified.

One cannot help but feel a sense of déjà vu.

Only 1.65 per cent of cultivated land fell under assured or protected irrigation all through the colonial period and the same philosophy continued post Independence, particularly after Vidarbha became part of a unified Maharashtra. The state invested huge sums of money in the so-called rain-shadow or low-rainfall zones in the central and western parts, where sugar cultivation proliferated with the push to cooperatives and brought about an economic and cultural revolution of sorts. But the eastern region was kept deprived of funds to harness water in the Godavari sub-river basins such as Wardha, Wainganga, Katepoorna or the Indravati.

Until a decade ago, 97 per cent of western Vidarbha's cotton acreage was rain-fed dryland agriculture with abysmal productivity, as highlighted in the report of the Planning Commission's Adarsh Misra-led fact-finding committee of 2006 on Vidarbha's backwardness and agrarian distress in the face of continuing farmer suicides. In a decade or so, the land under irrigation went up marginally, but farmers who could afford it began to dig wells to extract groundwater to irrigate their farms.

In five years, barring recent piecemeal efforts or paltry sums in direct support, income inequality has grown across India, as the reports of Oxfam International regularly show. The agrarian economy is sagging, but in the face of the new political and social rhetoric that India has embraced for some years now, the mainstream media has averted its eyes away from this crisis. Farmer leaders, who would earlier push forward thousands of protest emails and cry hoarse at the news of a farmer suicide, have fallen silent or joined the self-assured ranks of experts, think tanks or ministers. And new farmers' voices are not emerging, at least in Vidarbha.

The rural downturn—a crisis of Indian society, as P. Sainath prefers to put it—is no longer considered a national calamity.

While Ramrao has recuperated and resurrected his confidence, his financial problems remain the same. Many farm families torn by suicides, distress and devastation hang on by the morsels of dole or through the charity extended by good Samaritans.

For me, nothing is more heart-wrenching than meeting benumbed parents who have lost their teenaged children to suicide. Fifteen-year-old Vishal Khule consumed poisonous weedicide in his shanty in Dadham village of Akola district in the November of 2015. Eighteen-year-old Monika Bhise hanged herself to death at her home in Bhise-Wagholi village, Latur district in Marathwada, the following year in May. Both belonged to debt-ridden farm households that were in deep financial mess. Both had dreams and simple, bare minimum needs—they wanted to study and better their lives. Alas, they could not dream or harbour hope.

Dadham is 25 kilometres from Akola city. Bhise-Wagholi is 20 kilometres from Latur city. But the respective cities and villages are two different worlds, almost different planets: the former an epitome of affluence and shiny newness—though there too poverty abounds among the working classes and migrants—the other of life stuck in the medieval ages, filled with constant drudgery and orthodoxy.

Vishal did not leave a note, but Monica did. In her beautiful, neat handwriting, she wrote to her father asking him not to consume liquor, and arguing against selling their land to raise dowry for her marriage. She questioned why their family could not make enough from their small farm. Both of them saw no future for themselves and were exhausted by the status quo.

Their premature deaths were a cry for change. They wanted more than their ravaged villages and wretched circumstances could afford. They wanted to hope, to dream and to escape lives filled with such grave inequality.

That summer, when Latur ran out of water and had to be supplied water by a train from the town of Miraj, I sat at Monica's two-room home listening to her devastated mother. She had

Monica's two younger siblings by her side and told me that their daughter made them confront their bitter reality—that they were poor, too poor to be able to even afford their children's modest education. Monica wanted to become a nurse, fend for herself and support the education of her siblings but her father wanted to sell his 1-acre land and marry her off. They wanted to get rid of what they considered their filial duty. Their orthodoxy did not allow them to consider her aspirations as valid.

'Truth came at a cost,' her mother, in tears, told me. Tankers ferried water to her village that day as we sat grieving her daughter's death. 'She gave up her life, wrote us a letter and opened our eyes.'

With a little financial help from their neighbours, the Bhises got rid of their hand loans, folded up their farm and house in the village and shifted to Latur for good with one resolve: they would do everything within their power to keep their two younger children in school. When I last spoke to Monica's father, he was working as a daily wager. He is firm that he will never farm again. His marginal and small landholding could not support his children's education. In Latur, the husband and wife earn much more from their labour work than they ever earned from an acre of their farm.

In Dadham, Vishal's mother barely spoke. She was still in a state of shock when I met them in December 2015. His father, Vishwanath, spoke of his pain. Parents cremating their child isn't natural; it is against the order of things, he said.

Akola did not get good rains that year. The Khules' 3-acre rain-fed farm had no yield, just like the other farms in the village. It would be eight months before a new crop could be planted in Dadham. And there was Vishal, angry and perturbed at the sight of his father and mother having to borrow from a private moneylender to meet their nominal expenses.

He consumed a bottle of weedicide his father had bought to spray on his farm, to end what he felt was a meaningless life. His father could not get him a new uniform or new clothes for Diwali. He saw his father unable to repay his mounting debts year after year, experienced inequality up close, daily. His classmates would bring scrumptious tiffins while he never had the luxury of carrying a meal to school. He had to wear torn, patched-up shirts, while his friends wore new white shirts ever so often. During the Diwali holidays, when he would work on the farm, they would go off on vacations. He shared his troubles with his uncle, a retired clerk living opposite their shanty.

Vishal belonged to a scheduled tribe called Andh that does sustenance farming in rural Akola.

'He would often talk to me about the village, its poverty and the difference between him and his schoolmates,' Jankinath Khule, or Khule kaka, as Vishal used to affectionately call him, told me. 'He spoke of his parents' troubles and was resigned to the fact that his situation would never change.'

'This is the darkest period of our life,' Vishwanath had said in a low, soft voice. A humble, god-fearing man, he held his composure as he spoke. 'He collapsed here,' he told me, pointing to a spot beneath the window of the two-room shanty where the family lived. 'His mother was in the adjoining kitchen, making chapatis. I was out there,' he said, gesturing towards the front yard. When her son collapsed with a thump, Sheela Khule rushed out and found Vishal lying on the floor, 'a white fluid oozing out of his mouth'. The can of weedicide lay by his side, empty. Vishal died before reaching the hospital.

What would he do if he were alive? He would be on the farm helping his father face another biting drought, repay mounting loans, postpone buying new clothes or a new mobile. The Khules' lives remain the same. They still live hand to mouth. Their eldest son Vaibhav, then eighteen years old, has now moved to Akola town, where he works as a footloose labourer to make enough money to take care of his own needs and support his parents with a share of his wages.

Vishal's was not the only suicide of its kind. In October 2014, in Latur, not far from Monica's village, seventeen-year-old Swati Pitale, daughter of a farmer and a junior college student, committed suicide. In her last note, she explained why she was choosing death. She could no longer watch her father suffer, she wrote in Marathi, and didn't want to be a burden on him. She would soon be of marriageable age and knew her father was going to incur huge expenses on her wedding. In the note, she pleaded to the banks and lenders to whom he owed money to not harass him. She said he would surely repay all his debts once her elder sister was married.

Swati had to stop attending college for a while, her monthly bus pass had expired and her parents had no money to renew it. Her mother finally borrowed ₹260 from a neighbour for the pass, but Swati had missed crucial classes and wasn't able to take the exam. When Swati consumed pesticide in her family's field in Kingaon village, her father had left home for Karnataka in search of work. Once he returned in March or April, he had planned to raise money for Swati's wedding.

While there is no specific data on suicides by children (under eighteen, or by youth under twenty) in India as a result of agrarian distress, several studies and reports—from the 2005 door-to-door study commissioned by the Maharashtra government to subsequent studies on farm distress and suicides by the Tata Institute of Social Sciences and the Indira Gandhi Institute of Development Research—have pointed to the impact of debt and distress on children in peasant households. My own study under the Child Rights and You (CRY) National Media Fellowship in 2008 showed me the far-reaching impact of farmers' suicides on their children. Many adolescent children of farmers inherit their parents' debts and are forced to take on adult responsibilities, dropping out of school, tilling fields, succumbing to depression, and, in the case of girls, being married off early so the family has one less mouth to feed.

Over the past decade, I have documented several such suicides, particularly in households where a suicide has already occurred. Sometimes farmers' children commit suicide because they fear that if they don't their parents will. In one particularly poignant case in 2005, nineteen-year-old Neeta Bhopat hanged herself in Aasra village in Vidarbha's Amravati district.

In a neat, handwritten suicide note, she wrote in Marathi and I translate: 'If I don't commit suicide, my father will. My family can't earn a thousand rupees a month. I have two younger sisters. My parents can't bear the burden of our marriages when we don't have enough to eat. So, I am taking my life.'

In 2006, Dadham, where Vishal lived, was in the news for the lynching of a schoolteacher. He had a moneylending business and had demanded sexual favours from the wife of one of his borrowers. He was stabbed by a furious mob of Dadham's farmers till he dropped dead. The incident was a culmination of the long exploitation and powerlessness marginal farmers endure, generation after generation.

Across Vidarbha, private moneylending continues unabated even as farmers and the rural poor continue to grapple with institutional credit, which is hard to come by. An internal working group (IWG) set up by the RBI said in its report in September 2019 that despite a plethora of initiatives and schemes for financial inclusion over the past decade, only 40.9 per cent of small and marginal farmers were covered by commercial banks. This means that vast sections of small farmers borrow from private sources. The money comes at exorbitant interest rates, or at the debilitating loss of assets, or, as the Dadham incident showed, from highly exploitative lenders.

Led by Deputy Governor M.J. Jain, the group reviewed agricultural credit in India and reported that a third of agricultural households still avail credit from non-institutional sources only. The panel said that as of 2015-16 the number of accounts under the small and marginal farmer (SMF) category was 51.38 million, but the total number of small and marginal farmers as per the agriculture census the same year stood at 125.63 million. This indicates that more than 70 million such farms are not serviced by banks.

'There is a need to increase the coverage of SMF by banks as they constituted 86.21 per cent of total operated holdings and have 47.34 per cent share in the operated area,' the IWG said.

Why do so many farmers remain outside the institutional net? The RBI panel listed out some probable reasons. Their credit demand could be for consumption purposes; or they could be tenant farmers, sharecroppers and landless labourers who are not able to offer collateral security to avail bank credit; or they are involved in unviable subsistence agriculture, so the banks do not find them creditworthy.

The All India Rural Financial Inclusion Survey (NAFIS) 2016-17 of the National Bank of Agriculture and Rural Development (NABARD) found that the share of non-institutional credit in 2015 was 28 per cent. As against this, the share of institutional credit in agriculture increased from 10.2 per cent in 1951 to 63 per cent in 1981 and thereafter the share of institutional credit was hovering in the range of 63 to 65 per cent during the period from 1981 to 2013. NAFIS found in 2015 that the share of institutional credit was approximately 72 per cent.

According to the Jain panel report, the total number of operational holdings in the country was 146 million and the total operated area was 157.14 million hectares (ha) in 2015-16. The small and marginal holdings taken together (0.00 to 2.00 ha) constituted 86.21 per cent, while their share in the operated area stood at 47.34 per cent in 2015-16. The average size of landholding in 2015-16 was 1.08 ha. Regarding regional disparity in agricultural credit, the RBI panel reported that some of the states were getting a much higher share—as high as 10 per cent—of total agricultural credit, compared to other states getting as low as 0.5 per cent.

Annual crop credit outlay reports of NABARD show inter- and intra-state variations in credit offtake, with regions like Vidarbha far behind others in consumption and repayment of crop credit, indicative of the wide variations between the scales of economies of farmers.

The panel proposed a number of steps to fix the issue, including replacing interest subvention schemes with Direct Benefit Transfer (DBT) and crop loans only through Kisan Credit Card (KCC) mode to boost and improve the reach of institutional credit. It asked governments to avoid loan waivers.

Over the past few years, the central government has shied away from a blanket countrywide loan waiver scheme on the lines of the 2008 waiver doled out by the UPA government, but several state governments have given loan waivers at their expense to the farmers in the state. Maharashtra has spent around ₹35,000 crore over two years. It did benefit the farmers to the extent of relieving them of their immediate financial burdens, but incomes have not gone up. Punjab doled out ₹5,000 crore, but farmers continue ending their lives with alarming alacrity. Uttar Pradesh issued a waiver worth thousands of crores of rupees, but farmers remain in distress. In Madhya Pradesh, Chhattisgarh, Rajasthan, Karnataka, Tamil Nadu, Andhra Pradesh and Telangana, loan waivers were part of political promises but they did not fix the farm economy or provide permanent relief. India's agriculture economy remains sluggish. Farmers' incomes have tanked, rattled by economic policies and ecological calamities, and pushed further into a downward spiral by Prime Minister Narendra Modi's note-ban decision of 2016.

Ramrao is a textbook example of how the exclusion of thousands of peasants from the formal bank network takes place. He remains a defaulter. His bank loans remain unpaid, making him ineligible for new ones. If he cannot borrow money from his relatives or friends, he resorts to borrowing from private lenders in Pandharkawda, at high interest rates and with stiffer repayment schedules. That kind of moneylending is usually usurious.

~

IT'S A HOT AFTERNOON, late May 2019.

'We have to get back Alakya's jewellery.' Ramrao talks about going to court if her in-laws refuse to give her the rightful share of land or return her ornaments and other belongings—that includes two buffaloes, a cow, a few goats. Of course, he has no idea what exactly going to court entails. But that consoles Alakya for a moment. She thinks he will help her get back her precious jewellery.

'It may not be much in value,' she says, her voice rising in tone and tenor, 'but it belongs to me.'

'I am okay if they don't want to part with their land, but they must at least return her belongings—her clothes, her utensils, her jewellery,' Ramrao reasons with me, lying on his bed.

Ramrao and Alakya are desperate to retrieve her belongings from her in-laws. 'I've tried,' she says and looks at Ramrao. 'We could go to the community heads.'

Alakya wants to petition the Yelmi Jaat Panchayat, Adilabad's informal caste court that adjudicates on internal community issues, from intra-family feuds to land disputes to match-making.

Alakya is cooking food in the kitchen and talking to us from there. Ramrao is trying to catch forty winks. 'My uncle knows someone there,' she says, confident that they will help her get her belongings back.

'My in-laws should at least think about my daughter. She is their granddaughter after all, and she has a right to a share in the ancestral land. If my husband were alive, they would naturally have given him a share.'

Over the past two years, Ramrao and his relatives in Hiwara have made several attempts to convince her in-laws to return her jewellery and give her rightful due so that she can support Varshini, but their pleas have failed to move her in-laws.

Alakya thinks she has a right to Rahul's share of land. She is right. 'They say you give us Varshini and you stay away. How is that possible? How can I give them my daughter?'

'I am not remarrying,' she says, bringing us plates piled with potato curry and hot, swollen chapatis.

'My in-laws fear I will marry another man and give away my money to him and dump my daughter. They think I will stoop that low. And here I am, struggling every day for Varshini.'

Alakya falls silent after her emotional outburst. She sits in the chair, sighing, wiping her tears with the corner of her sari.

Varshini, she says, has begun to ask questions about her father, and why they don't longer live with her grandparents in Telangana.

Ramrao is quietly eating, his face reflecting his sadness. He looks as if he could start crying any moment.

Three years have passed since Rahul's death. Alakya had forgotten to be herself. This is the first time I see her express herself, speak about her rights. She is angry, but she sounds more confident and vocal than I have ever seen her.

For Alakya, jewellery and a share in the land mean precious memories, a sense of belonging and her daughter's future. For Ramrao, it would mean something to pawn to raise cash.

THIS LOOKS LIKE A particularly harsh summer. It set in early, and all over Maharashtra there is a growing clamour for drinking water. Hiwara has no drinking water problem but many villages around and further south find themselves staring at a drought—Marathwada is on the brink, so is western Maharashtra, and neighbouring Telangana too. Herds of cattle are wandering in the fields of Hiwara, searching for fodder and water. Ramrao tells me farmers from the surrounding villages have either deserted or abandoned their livestock because they have no money or water this year. He counts six or seven villages around Hiwara where farmers are in deep crisis. Only last month, he says, he bought dry stalk and fodder worth ₹15,000 and collected the leftover groundnut crop from his field to feed his cows. When people desert their cattle it is a sign of distress, Ramrao explains. In the evening we walk around the villages and chat with people, they tell us about their growing hardships and troubles emerging out of crop failure and the lack of water, fodder and work in the entire vicinity.

In New Delhi, in the meantime, Narendra Modi returns to power late May. The country gives him a bigger mandate than before. He has promised to double the income of farmers by 2022.

On his field, Ramrao opts for a crop change. He decides to plant turmeric, something he had hinted at earlier. One of his friends from Jhari gave him turmeric seeds to plant. Turmeric, he thinks, will give him better returns—better than cotton or soybeans anyway. Some of his farmer friends are reaping a good harvest of turmeric, and he has tried his hand at this crop in the past. He feels it's better than many other crops, including cotton. Cotton is for dry land, turmeric for the irrigated.

Rains do not come until July end. Ramrao has started to panic.

'What's plan B?' I ask him.

'None,' he quips.

There is no plan A, B or C for farmers in case of a bad or delayed monsoon. They decide spontaneously, planting whatever they think might work at that moment.

By early October, though, after the initial scare that the rains might not come, it actually turns out to be a heavy monsoon. In

Maharashtra, floods have wreaked havoc—in Satara, Kolhapur, Sangli, Pune, elsewhere too. The rains are showing no signs of abating. August and September more than make up for the loss of rainfall in June and July.

By mid-October, when I go back to Hiwara to catch up with Ramrao and Alakya, I see marigold flowers in full bloom. Ramrao's farms are bursting with turmeric, cotton, marigold, lentils and a range of other crops. His farms resemble big splashy portraits—several shades of grey, green, ochre, light blue and white. Swathes of blood red too. The soil itself is soggy, brown.

Ramrao expects a good crop but one never knows until harvest. Crop prices need to be stable for him to actually make money, most of which he will have to use to repay loans.

He doesn't talk about quitting farming any more. The thought of suicide is far behind him. He has got a second lease of life and wants to make the most of it.

Towards the end of September, Alakya and Ramrao went to Adilabad to petition the Yelmi Jaat Panchayat to mediate on their behalf to help get back her jewellery from her in-laws, but they came back without success.

'The panchayat had its elections when we went,' Alakya tells me. But her in-laws voluntarily sent Alakya ₹35,000—they had promised to support Varshini's education. They haven't returned her jewellery and other assets, forget giving her a share of the land that belonged to her husband. Chances are they never will. Meanwhile, Alakya enrolled as a beneficiary of the widows' pension scheme in Telangana. It will provide her a monthly dole of ₹2,000. She must go there every three months to pick up her money.

'Telangana has a good support system for women,' Ramrao says. 'We [Maharashtra] are way behind.'

Ramrao wants more stable income for his daughter—he says he will try to buy a buffalo or two so that Alakya can sell milk or make curd and ghee to sell in the Pandharkawda market. Alakya is also considering rearing some goats and chickens for staggered income. She has bought a sewing machine to help Nalini. They will split the work among them to make small sums of money. Varshini has settled in her new school. As she grows older, she will become alert to the world around her, and to the harsh realities of her mother's life.

Ramrao wants Alakya to become financially independent. If something happens to him, she shouldn't suffer.

'After me, who will take care of them?'

Anuja, his younger daughter, is expecting. She will deliver her second child in early 2020. He falls quiet, tears in his eyes. How happy Vimalbai would have been, he says, if she were alive to welcome her grandchild. Ramrao then walks me to his farm, where we pick some marigold flowers that are in full bloom.

IN HIWARA, HEAVY AND unabated rains in late October and a few more spells in the first week of November destroy the white cotton lint that had come for fruition and the harvested soybean. Too much rain leaves the crops wet and soggy. High moisture content brings down the quality, and therefore the prices of the farm commodities drop too. Traders either don't buy it or pay less.

'I got ₹4,500 for a quintal of cotton today,' Ashokrao tells me on 13 November, when I visit Ramrao. He went to a Pandharkawda ginning mill and sold 5 quintals, and came back home crestfallen because of the poor price his produce fetched. This year, thousands of farmers across Maharashtra have taken a hit due to excessive rain. The agriculture department estimates the loss to be spread over 92 lakh hectares of land. That is nearly half of the farmland in Maharashtra.

Sugarcane, cotton, lentils, perishables, horticulture plants—all kinds of farm commodities have suffered from an extended spell of rain since September.

According to the National Sample Survey Organization's 2019 report, rural consumption is down. The Modi government does agree. The clamour for compensation and relief among the peasantry has begun.

Farmers are broke, Ramrao, who does not sound optimistic about fetching a good price or a good yield now, tells me. 'Last year,' he reminds me, 'it was drought, and this year it is excessive rainfall.' For two years he waited for a loan waiver, but for reasons that are not clear to him he did not get the benefit.

This year, crop loan disbursement in Hiwara was abysmal, only a few farmers got crop loans, that too partial. In 2000, banks would disburse ₹5,000 as crop loan to a dry-land farm for growing cotton; it has gone up five times today, but that does not even cover the entire production costs. Ramrao suffers from capital crunch all round the year. He has no money to invest in his farm, to innovate, or to put it into an allied activity such as dairy or poultry, forget making improvements to his thatched home. All around the region, the situation is no different; banks did not meet the targets of the crop loan disbursements.

Ramrao's overall loan liability stands at approximately ₹15,00,000. This year he mortgaged some of Alakya's remaining gold ornaments and took hand loans to foot his farm costs. He hopes to retrieve his daughter's gold when he sells his turmeric some time in March 2020. The repayment of loans will have to wait.

When I meet him in mid-November, Ramrao has not yet begun to pick his cotton in full swing. He picked 8 quintals from the Borgaon farm to pay for the wages of the labourers. The excessive rains were not good for cotton or lentils but helped the turmeric crop.

He stares at me and laughs when I ask him when he will fully repay his loans. There is no escaping the loans, he says. Old loans will go away. New ones will come.

'Loans are a part of life,' Ramrao tells me late November at his barn, where he has stacked his cotton—muggy, wet and yellowish due to the moisture content.

He picks up some cotton that is lying around to show me how the rains have affected its quality. 'Don't know what will become of this when it reaches the market. Maybe this will go into a mattress,' he envisions.

'But,' I persist, 'you must have considered a time frame to repay your loans. When will you finally be relieved of your burden?'

He looks at me intently and sits on the stack of cotton.

'*Dole mitlyavar*,' he quips with a suggestive smile.

When I close my eyes forever.

EPILOGUE

'SOMEONE KILLED MY CHICKS.'

Ramrao sounds disturbed by the fact that someone has poisoned the chickens in his cattle shed. He is pained no end by the very thought that someone could harm him in this manner.

'I have never harmed anybody. Who could have done this to me?'

Two months ago, Ramrao bought some seventy or eighty desi chicks from the nearby weekly market for a few thousand rupees. Alakya wanted to raise a small poultry for side income to meet domestic needs.

But, on a recent morning, Ramrao and Alakya were shocked to see some of the birds lying dead. Thirty-odd, they counted.

They suspected that someone had poisoned them, perhaps through their feed. The dead chicks lay listless on their backs, legs facing skyward, beaks open.

'I am at a loss to know who must have done this horrible sin,' he tells me repeatedly when I visit him in January 2021, after a long gap. We have been in touch every so often over the phone, but he did not inform me about this incident.

When we last spoke some weeks ago, he had broached the topic of bollworms. In recent months, the bollworm infestation on cotton has been particularly profuse, as bad as it was in 2017. The bollworm traps did not work, it seems. He had mentioned to me the death of Kisan Ranganeniwar, Alakya's father-in-law, in August 2020, and that her mother-in-law, Sushila, is terminally ill with cancer. He told me that despite being troubled by them after her husband's death, Alakya went with her daughter to her marital home and spent a month there in the period of mourning, looking after her ailing mother-in-law. He spoke about his younger daughter Anuja delivering her second child, a boy, last summer. He spoke on a couple of occasions about his soaring loans—the old and new ones—and the uncertainties villagers faced due to lack of work and how hard 2020 had generally been for them. But he did not speak about his chickens being poisoned.

He shows me a small closet that he had made in his cattle shed for the chickens. Backyard poultry does not need a lot of money or attention, he thought, Alakya could easily do it.

'If someone had stolen the chickens, I would not have felt bad—at least the person would make money—but why kill the birds?'

Ramrao is rattled by this incident. He thinks it could be the handiwork of an outsider. Some birds remain, and Alakya is now trying to rear them in the vicinity of their home.

THE WINTER OF 2020 was moderate; the summer of 2021 promises to be harsh. One can feel the hint of summer already in the first week of March. And the fear unleashed by the Covid-19 pandemic—which has taken the world by storm for over a year now, with no end in sight—still looms as many regions are witnessing the coming of a second wave of the virus.

Luckily, Hiwara hasn't reported a single case so far.

Maybe, Ramrao chuckles, '*Konale houn gela asan tari ka kalte ithe gavat.*' Who knows, probably someone has had it but it went undiagnosed.

In 2019, Ramrao had planted turmeric on a quarter acre of his land, which was to be harvested in March 2020, around the time India went into a harsh lockdown. He harvested about 40 quintals of wet turmeric and, after drying it, the weight reduced to 8 quintals. Turmeric proved to be a sturdy crop and quite suitable for his own land. It faces no threat from the raiding wild animals or monsoon variations, but the coronavirus struck right at harvest time.

Ramrao could not have seen the Covid crisis coming—none of us did. The world plunged into an unprecedented health emergency that also destroyed people's social and economic lives. And when he was preparing to uproot the turmeric plants, process them and sell the yield, the markets got disrupted, and he could sell with much difficulty. He sold 7 quintals of it in a staggered manner—at an average of ₹5,000 a quintal. Had he managed to polish the turmeric, he says, he could have earned ₹8,000 to ₹10,000 a quintal under normal circumstances. But because of the lockdown and consequent restrictions, he could not.

Nonetheless, the returns on that small piece of land exceeded what he would otherwise get from cotton or lentils or soybeans. He replanted some of his turmeric in the 2020 kharif season on around 1.5 acres of his farm. He expects a yield of 15 to 20 quintals of dried turmeric by April 2021. The problem is the market. This being the cotton belt, there is no major buyer for turmeric in this part. Unless a substantial number of farmers grow turmeric, the crop will not attract big buyers to come and purchase it at the doorstep or at the nearest agriculture produce market committee (APMC) at Pandharkawda. Selling it in small quantities does not fetch the kind of returns that one would expect. Ramrao has found a small-time trader who is interested in buying his turmeric. He will process it into powder and supply it in the local retail market.

'Let's see if it works out,' Ramrao says.

The summer of 2020 went in waiting for the lockdown to be lifted and for life to return to a new normal. Ramrao and the other villagers stayed home, brooding over the new health crisis, and the kharif. For the time being, other worries subsided.

They also saw a lot of men who had migrated out of Hiwara and the neighbouring villages for work return from their workplaces—Mumbai, Adilabad, Hyderabad, Chennai and elsewhere.

Ramrao once told me over phone in April 2020 that some villagers had put up water and food kiosks along the highway for the migrants walking back home from the south up north. People were walking in hordes—men, women, children—from Hyderabad to Nagpur and from there to eastern and northern India, trying to return home.

'*Bhay pareshani aahe*,' he had said. There's a lot of hardship.

WHEN PRIME MINISTER NARENDRA Modi shuttered the country into a lockdown at four hours' notice, it triggered panic and chaos. Millions of migrant workers scrambled to reach their native places across India by undertaking risky journeys as they lost their jobs and there was uncertainty over how long the lockdown would last. Thousands walked, hitch-hiked, rode their bicycles or boarded trucks and essential vehicles to reach their homes as trains and other buses came to a standstill. Poignant stories about their plight came out on social media. Several commentators described what was unfolding as a migration that had parallels only in India's Partition of 1947.

More than a crore migrants returned to their home states on foot during March–June 2020, the Centre told Parliament in a written reply in mid-September 2020 during the monsoon session. Independent estimates pegged this number at around 3 to 5 crore. However, replying to another question in Parliament, the government said there was no data available on the number of migrant workers who had lost their lives during the lockdown. But there were deaths all over, regardless.

The sudden lockdown had left thousands of poor migrants stranded and starving across India, without social or economic security and vulnerable to the virulent epidemic. Nagpur was no different. In the first two weeks of the lockdown, hundreds of labourers walked all across the Vidarbha region, exasperated, to reach their homes in Madhya Pradesh, Chhattisgarh, even Rajasthan. In the last week of April, I spoke to a group of men and women at a prominent square in Nagpur. They walked briskly, lugging along their belongings in sacks. They were seething and were in no mood to speak at first. One of them reluctantly spoke for a couple of minutes. They were walking back to their village in Gondia, the far eastern district of Maharashtra, from Hyderabad—a distance of 700 kilometres or more. They had been walking for seven days.

A week earlier, a group of boys in their late teens reached Nagpur from Visakhapatnam on their way back to Karauli in Rajasthan, hitch-hiking, tired and petrified. They worked in a company there as casual workers, now dumped by their employer. They had covered 800 kilometres already and had another 800 kilometres or more still left to go. Local policemen alerted the authorities, who took them to a shelter home of the Nagpur Municipal Corporation where they waited for a month for permission to go home.

Close to 10,000 migrants from Chandrapur district were reportedly stuck in the different districts of Telangana and Andhra Pradesh, unable to cross over, during the summer of 2020. There were men, women and children who had to wait in the fields in makeshift shanties in different villages to be allowed to go back home.

Stories abounded of the excruciating pain migrant workers faced in the wake of an unannounced complete lockdown. A pregnant woman, for instance, had come from Gondia with her young daughter for a check-up at the GMCH in Nagpur on 20 March and got stranded in the city, away from her family. She spent time at a shelter home with her daughter, food served from a central kitchen facility that the civic body had set up. A young man who worked at a sugar factory in Ahmednagar reached Nagpur in a private bus on 22 March, the day India observed a 'janata curfew', and reached his village in Saoli teshil of Chandrapur district walking non-stop for two days. Another migrant labourer reportedly committed suicide miles before his native place in Gondia on 1 May, International Labour Day. He was fatigued and frustrated from walking for days.

The pandemic is yet to end even a year later. For a while it seemed to have peaked in September 2020. India also began its vaccination drive in January 2021, bringing much relief to a beleaguered people. But just a couple of months later, the country is in fact now in the throes of a second, more deadly wave of the virus, deepening the health, economic and humanitarian crisis. In mid-April 2021, India's figures stand at more than 1.3 crore reported cases and over 1.7 lakh deaths, with the numbers rising rapidly on a daily basis.

Demonetization, the flawed implementation of the Goods and Services Tax (GST), and now the Covid-19 pandemic have broken the country's back and the poor man's economy.

As if the Covid-19 pandemic, the shattered economy and the resultant hardships were not enough, the Modi government moved three ordinances in September 2020, subsequently bulldozed through Parliament in its winter session, to amend three different pieces of legislation. This was done in the garb of agriculture reforms, unsettling farmers, particularly in the northern states of Punjab, Haryana and Uttar Pradesh, and forcing them to take to the streets. Simultaneously, the Centre also brought about changes in the labour laws, making hire-and-fire the mainstay of the labour code.

The subsequent farmers' agitation rekindled the kind of protests India had seen in opposition to the Citizenship Amendment Act (CAA) before they had to be abruptly called off in the face of the pandemic and the subsequent lockdown. In this case, though, the farmers' protests, which first began in Punjab and later spread across the cow belt, did not seem to abate even in the face of the pandemic. In a matter of months, protests broke out in all parts of the country. Some three hundred farmers who took part in the protests died during the first hundred days, some of whom sadly committed suicide at the protest sites to draw national attention.

The three controversial laws passed by the Modi government are: the Farmers' Produce Trade and Commerce (Promotion and Facilitation Act), 2020; the Farmers (Empowerment and Protection) Agreement on Price Assurance and Farm Services Act, 2020; and the Essential Commodities (Amendment) Act, 2020. Each of these would hurt them in many different ways, the farmers hold. They call them black laws that they never demanded. Besides, the laws seek to dismantle the three-pillar structure that helped the country usher in the Green Revolution in the 1970s: a guaranteed MSP for commodities; quality inputs; and assured timely procurement of the produce by the government or its agencies. The new laws seek to bring in private players without a level playing field for a farmer or small-time trader, who is closely tied to the existing system.

The Modi government has been adamant. It says it is ready to make some changes in the laws or hit the pause button on their implementation but won't withdraw them. The farmers have made it clear they will not settle for anything short of the laws being repealed. The impasse continues.

Critics and most non-BJP governments in states have rejected the laws for two reasons: one, they were not consulted; and two, the farm sector and markets are their subject and the Centre should not step into their domain. The BJP-run state governments welcomed the laws, while singing paeans to the PM's visionary leadership.

Some commentators such as Jean Dreze explained these laws as a precursor to the ultimate dismantling of the food security law and apparatus. It would hurt the poorest of the country the most. The procurement of food grain by the state helps run the public distribution system and feed the poor in times of exigencies, such as the one we witnessed in the Covid-19 lockdown. It was only due to a vast network of fair price shops that the governments could supply food to the struggling masses.

There are some damning sections in the laws that farmers genuinely fear will take away the last vestiges of state support, bulldoze the APMCs and in the long run do away with the MSP regime, which currently applies to twenty-three commodities.

For instance, Section 13 of the Farmers' Produce Trade and Commerce (Promotion and Facilitation) Act, 2020 (the one aimed at hitting the APMCs) says: 'No suit, prosecution or other legal proceedings shall lie against the Central Government or the State Government, or any officer of the Central Government or the State Government or any other person in respect of anything which is in good faith done or intended to be done under this Act or of any rules or orders made thereunder.'

As P. Sainath wrote in his critique of the laws:

> Sure, there are other laws that also exclude prosecution of civil servants for carrying out their legal duties. But this one goes way over the top. The immunity given to all those in respect of anything acting 'in good faith,' whatever they do, is sweeping. Not only can they not be taken to the courts for a crime they may have committed 'in good faith' – they're protected against legal action for crimes they are yet to commit ('in good faith' of course). Just in case you missed the point – that you have no legal

> recourse in the courts – Section 15 rubs it in: 'No civil court shall have jurisdiction to entertain any suit or proceedings in respect of any matter, the cognizance of which can be taken and disposed of by any authority empowered by or under this Act or the rules made thereunder.

It does not stop there. Section 19 of the Act states: 'No civil Court shall have jurisdiction to entertain any suit or proceedings in respect of any dispute which a Sub-Divisional Authority or the Appellate Authority is empowered by or under this Act to decide and no injunction shall be granted by any court or other authority in respect of any action taken or to be taken in pursuance of any power conferred by or under this Act or any rules made thereunder.' This section strikes at the constitutional right to a legal recourse.

The Supreme Court took suo motu cognizance of the protests and passed an order in mid-January 2021 staying the implementation of the three contentious laws until an amicable solution is found. The apex court constituted a four-member expert committee, but one of its members recused himself in a few days citing personal reasons. The farmers' unions politely rejected the intervention by the court and said they had not approached the court for any recourse and that their battle with the government would go on until the three farm laws were repealed and MSP was made a legal guarantee vide another law.

Back in Hiwara, Ramrao quietly pulls on.

In 2020, the monsoon was better than normal, he says, but it was very erratic. Heavy rains in short spans, with long gaps between them. Bollworms were back again, turmeric did fine, and

Alakya returned from her marital home after spending a month with her ailing mother-in-law. Varshini did not go to school the whole year. The village children were all home as the schools were shut. Online systems weren't working for the kids in the village. Some young men migrated out, mostly to Hyderabad, for work.

When I last visited him in late February 2021, Ramrao's farm was flush with turmeric, its fragrance in the air. The last of the cotton on his friend Golemwar's farm that he tends to remained un-picked. He had planted groundnut on an acre towards the other end of his farm, and Bhaskar was at work to prepare for the sowing of jowar as the summer crop on a small patch that had been cleared after harvesting lentils. The jowar would come to harvest in two months. He would keep the grain for his own consumption. The green foliage would be the cattle feed.

As March approached, farm work was drying up in Hiwara. After spending the afternoon on his farm, while we chatted at his home, he reminded me that Holi would come soon.

'Come over in the last week of March,' he said. The village may not hold the Bhagavata Saptah this year because of the Covid restrictions, the looming uncertainties and lack of money. Maharashtra, in the grip of the second wave of the virus mid-March, saw many cities impose lockdown-like restrictions, affecting normal life yet again.

Alakya continued to hope that she would get her rightful share in her husband's land, an asset that would help her in bringing up Varshini. Her gold ornaments were still pawned with a jeweller in Pandharkawda as Ramrao could not repay the loan he took in 2019 against them. He would try and repay it later in the year once he sold his turmeric. Her sewing machine lay idle because she had no orders.

Hiwara backed, distantly though, the protests by farmers in Delhi. Ramrao too hoped some good would come of the movement. He was not depressed any more. Only worried. He remembered how close he had come to his end seven years ago, the anniversary of which he would mark in a couple of weeks. He said he would go to the Hanuman temple—the way he does every day—and pray for his and others' well-being. He would try to repay his debts but knew there would be no escape from borrowing more to keep moving, to improve his income, to support Alakya and Varshini the best he can. His bank account had no money. He had no savings to fall back upon.

Ditto is the case with most small farmers in his village. Across Vidarbha's dryland agriculture areas, barring a few cases of exceptionally good farmers and collective efforts, a general sense of despondency prevails over the rural peasantry. Farmers' suicides continue—in Vidarbha and across the country.

Away from the humdrum of the national political discourse and economic debates, Ramrao's lonely struggle on his farm—and that of his fraternity—for a decent life goes on.

Nagpur
April 2021

A NOTE ON SOURCES

In the course of my reporting from Vidarbha since 1996, I have referred to several relevant reports, policy briefs, reportage published in newspapers, working papers, and books on the issues of agrarian crisis, cotton, and farmers' suicides. Other than that, personal interviews with women farmers, children, farmers' leaders, and experts over two decades have helped me get insights into the daily lives of peasants and farmers in the region. All of this helped me write this book. Below I enlist some of the rich literature that I have extensively drawn from that researchers and readers might find useful should they want to delve further. This is not an exhaustive list but an assorted one.

A Fact-finding Report on Agrarian Crisis and Regional Imbalances in Vidarbha, led by Adarsh Misra, Principal Secretary to the Planning Commission of India, 2005. (The data pertaining to poor crop loan outlays, irrigation backlog, and regional imbalances has been taken from this report.)

Door-to-Door Survey of Villages in Six Cotton-growing Districts of Vidarbha, submitted to the Government of Maharashtra by the Divisional Commissioner, Amravati, 2005-06.

Causes of Farmer Suicides in Maharashtra: An Enquiry, final report submitted to the Bombay High Court by the Tata Institute of Social Sciences, Rural Campus, Tuljapur, 15 March, 2005. The report is available at: http://vnss-mission.gov.in/docs/farmers_suicide_tiss_report-2005.pdf.

Suicide of Farmers in Maharashtra, a report submitted to the Government of Maharashtra by the Indira Gandhi Institute of Development Research (author: Srijit Mishra), January 2006. The report is available at: http://vnss-mission.gov.in/docs/FinalReport_SFM_IGIDR_26Jan06.pdf.

Compilation of various government resolutions about special packages at http://vnss-mission.gov.in/htmldocs/spl_pck.htm.

Agrarian Scenario in Post-reform India: A Story of Distress, Despair and Death, a working paper by Srijit Mishra, Indira Gandhi Institute of Development Research, January 2007.

Farmers' Suicide and Debt Waiver: An Action Plan for Agricultural Development of Maharashtra, a report submitted to the Government of Maharashtra by Dr Narendra Jadhav, Vice-Chancellor, University of Pune, July 2008.

Report of the High-level Committee Headed by Shri Vijay Kelkar on Balanced Regional Development Issues in Maharashtra, Government of Maharashtra, Planning Department, 2013.

Chief Minister's and Prime Minister's special development packages and schemes for the six worst suicide-affected districts of Vidarbha—data, reports and government resolutions at the

Vasantrao Naik Shetkari Swavalamban Mission website: http://vnss-mission.gov.in/.

Reports of the Commission for Agricultural Costs and Prices (CACP) for the crops sown in 2014–19: http://cacp.dacnet.nic.in.

Reports of the National Commission on Farmers, 5 volumes, led by Professor M.S. Swaminathan, 2006–08.

Union Budget 2008-09 and Agriculture Debt Waiver Scheme, RBI, Circular and Scheme Document, 2008: https://www.rbi.org.in/Scripts/BS_CircularIndexDisplay.aspx?Id=4190.

All India Financial Inclusion Survey, NABARD, 2016-17: https://www.nabard.org/auth/writereaddata/tender/1608180417NABARD-Repo-16_Web_P.pdf.

Protest, Prices and the Peasantry: Mobilizing around 'Agrarian Crisis' and Suicides in Vidarbha, India, a PhD thesis by Silva Lieberherr, Zurich and India, 2016.

Peasant Movements in India, 1920-1950, D.N. Dhanagare, New Delhi, Oxford University Press, 1983.

Peasant Movement in India by P. Venkateshwarlu, International Journal of Multi-disciplinary Advanced Research Trends, IISN: 2349-7408, Vol. II, Issue 2(2), September 2015.

Banking Sector Liberalization and the Growth and Regional Distribution of Rural Banking, Pallavi Chavan, 2005.

Reports of the Ashok Dalwai Committee on Doubling Farmers' Income, Volumes I to XII, Niti Aayog, New Delhi. All reports at: https://agricoop.nic.in/en/doubling-farmers.

Budget and Economic Survey documents, Government of India and Government of Maharashtra, 2000-01 to 2020-21.

The Economic Effects of a Borrower Bailout: Evidence from an Emerging Market, Xavier Giné and Martin Kanz, World Bank, Review of Financial Studies, 2017.

Lessons from Agricultural Debt Waiver and Debt Relief Scheme of 2008, a brief by R. Ramakumar.

Report No. 3 of 2013: Performance Audit of Civil on Agricultural Debt Waiver and Debt Relief Scheme of Union Government, Ministry of Finance, Comptroller and Auditor General of India, New Delhi.

Report of the Expert Group on Agricultural Indebtedness, Banking Division, Department of Economic Affairs, Ministry of Finance, Government of India, New Delhi, July 2007.

Every Thirty Minutes: Farmer Suicides, Human Rights, and the Agrarian Crisis in India, Center for Human Rights and Global Justice, NYU School of Law, New York, 2011.

Farmer Suicides in Maharashtra, a report by the Agro-Ecology Research Centre, Gokhale Institute of Politics and Economics, Pune, January 2017.

Understanding Under-development in Vidarbha, a pre-publication paper by Sanjiv Phansalkar, Water Policy Research, IWMI-Tata.

Slow Agriculture Growth and Agrarian Crisis, A. Vaidyanathan, Hindu Centre for Politics and Public Policy, Policy Watch 4.

Agriculture Census Reports, Agriculture Census Division, Department of Agriculture and Cooperation (now Farmers Welfare), Government of India, 2005-06, 2010-11, 2015-16.

Instability and Regional Variation in Indian Agriculture, Policy Paper 26, National Centre for Agriculture Economics and Policy Research, ICAR, New Delhi.

Farmer Suicides in India, Durkheim's Types, special article by B.B. Mohanty, Economic and Political Weekly, 25 May 2013, Vol. xlviii, No 2.

Farmers' Suicides in India: Magnitudes, Trends, and Spatial Patterns, 1997-2012, K. Nagaraj, P. Sainath, R. Rukmani, and R. Gopinath, Review of Agrarian Studies, Vol. 4, No. 2, 2014, available at http://www.ras.org.in/farmers_suicides_in_india.

The Effect of VISHRAM, a Grass-roots Community-based Mental Health Programme, on the Treatment Gap for Depression in Rural Communities in India: A Population-based Study, Rahul Shidhaye, Vaibhav Murhar, Siddharth Gangale, Luke Aldridge, Rahul Shastri, Rachana Parikh, Ritu Shrivastava, Suvarna Damle, Tasneem Raja, Abhijit Nadkarni and Vikram Patel, Lancet Psychiatry, 2017, available at: http://dx.doi.org/10.1016/ S2215-0366(16)30424-2.

On Bt. Cotton:

Cotton Varieties and Hybrids, CICR Technical Bulletin No. 13.

Genetic Modification Technology Deployment: Lessons from India, Sachin Sathyarajan and Balakrishna Pisupati, FLEDGE, India, 2017.

Report of the Special Investigation Team (SIT) Constituted by the Maharashtra government to probe the deaths and illnesses caused by pesticide contact poisoning during the praying operations in Yavatmal, March 2018.

Pesticide Poisonings in Yavatmal District of Maharashtra: Untold Realities, Pesticide Action Network, India, October 2017. The press release and reports here: https://pan-india.org/untold-realities-of-pesticide-poisonings-in-yavatmal-district-in-maharashtra/; https://www.pan-india.org/wp-content/uploads/2017/10/Yavatmal-Report_PAN-India_Oct-2017_web.pdf

The Food and Agriculture Organization (FAO) of the United Nations on Monocrotophos being highly or acutely hazardous: http://www.fao.org/news/story/en/item/180968/icode/#:~:text=Monocrotophos%20is%20an%20organophosphorus%20pesticide%20that%20is%20considered,serious%20risk%20to%20human%20health%20and%20the%20environment; and http://www.fao.org/3/w5715e/w5715e04.htm.

Writings by K.R. Kranthi, the then director of CICR, in Cotton Statistics and News, Cotton Association of India, 2015–17.

The Three Mistakes in Cotton's Life: http://www.cicr.org.in/pdf/Kranthi_art/3-Mistakes.pdf.

Agrarian Crisis: http://cicr.org.in/pdf/Kranthi_art/Agrarian_Crisis_Part-2_Ap_2015.pdf.

Cotton Season: Predicaments of 2016: http://www.cicr.org.in/pdf/Kranthi_art/cotton_predicaments_2016.pdf.

'Unlearn a few, learn some new', a two-part article: http://www.cicr.org.in/pdf/Kranthi_art/learn_unlearn.pdf; and http://www.cicr.org.in/pdf/Kranthi_art/learn_unlearn_part2.pdf.

BT Cotton Twenty-20?: http://www.cicr.org.in/pdf/Kranthi_art/20-20.pdf.

Cotton in India at Bt Crossroads: http://www.cicr.org.in/pdf/Kranthi_art/Bt_cross_roads.pdf.

Old issues: https://www.caionline.in/site/publications.

For other writings on cotton and the science of it: http://www.cicr.org.in/profiles/kranthi_articles.html.

A paper by Dr K.R. Kranthi and G.D. Stone in 2020 looks at the other corresponding changes in Indian agriculture to argue that the increased use of fertilizers and other inputs has contributed to the rising cotton yields of India—and not adoption of Bt cotton alone, as was being claimed by agri-biotechnology companies: https://pubmed.ncbi.nlm.nih.gov/32170289/.

BT Cotton Q&A, a handbook by Dr Keshav Raj Kranthi, 2012, http://www.cicr.org.in/pdf/Bt_Cotton_Q&A_Kranthi%20 2012.pdf.

Other material:

Long-term Analysis Shows GM Cotton No Match for Insects in India: https://phys.org/news/2020-03-long-term-analysis-gm-cotton-insects.html.

Pink Bollworm May Eat Up Half of Maharashtra's Cotton Crop, Alok Deshpande, 17 November 2017, https://www.thehindu.com/news/cities/mumbai/pink-bollworm-may-eat-up-half-of-states-cotton-crop/article20493492.ece.

For the chapter titled 'Marigold', in addition to news articles, research papers and so on, I have sourced information from a collection of agreements between Indian seed companies and Mahyco Monsanto Biotech India Ltd that permit the former to commercially sell the latter's transgenic varieties of cotton seeds.

Outside the Relief Net, Dionne Bunsha, 28 March 2008, *https://frontline.thehindu.com/cover-story/article30195071.ece.*

Bhishi Investment Scheme Pronounced Illegal by Law: R.R. Patil, Vishal Manve, https://www.dnaindia.com/mumbai/money-bhishi-investment-scheme-pronounced-illegal-by-law-rr-patil-1965033. The late home minister of Maharashtra R.R. Patil went so far as to say that usurious moneylenders won't be let off and they should be skinned alive if they are found guilty of troubling peasant farmers saddled by informal debts.

Replying with Bullets, Jaideep Hardikar, 6 January 2007, http://indiatogether.org/articles/vidfiring-agriculture. One farmer died and several others were injured when police opened fire as protests broke out over the inordinate delay in the procurement of their cotton at the APMC market in Wani town of Yavatmal in December 2006.

Bt Cotton: Government Admits Monsanto Never Had Patent in India, Shishir Arya, 17 February 2016, https://timesofindia.indiatimes.com/city/nagpur/bt-cotton-govt-admits-monsanto-never-had-patent-in-india/articleshow/48674689.cms.

Order by the CCI in Reference Case No. 2 of 2015 and Case No. 107 of 2015 between MMBL and other seed companies: https://www.cci.gov.in/sites/default/files/Ref%2002-2015%20and%20107-2015%20-26(1)%20order_10.02.2015.pdf.

Bt Cotton: The Facts Behind the Hype, 18 January 2007, https://grain.org/en/article/582-bt-cotton-the-facts-behind-the-hype.

Is Pink Bookworm Pest Developing Resistance to GMO Bt Corn in India?, Bhavika Jain, 7 July 2017, https://geneticliteracyproject.org/2017/07/07/pink-bollworm-pest-developing-resistance-gmo-bt-corn-india/.

The Twisted Trajectory of Bt Cotton, Sujatha Byravan, 10 September 2020, https://www.thehindu.com/opinion/op-ed/the-twisted-trajectory-of-bt-cotton/article32566091.ece.

My stories on the Yavatmal pesticide deaths:

The Storm Brewing in India's Cotton Fields, 2 May 2018, https://ruralindiaonline.org/articles/the-storm-brewing-in-indias-cotton-fields.

Lethal Pests, Deadly Sprays, 2 March 2018, https://ruralindiaonline.org/articles/lethal-pests-deadly-sprays.

Fumes and Fear in Yavatmal, 9 March 2018, https://ruralindiaonline.org/articles/fumes-and-fear-in-yavatmal.

SIT Report: Pest Attack Unprecedented, Ferocious, 16 March 2018, https://ruralindiaonline.org/articles/sit-report-pest-attack-unprecedented-ferocious.

The Indian Farmers Falling Prey to Pesticide, 5 October 2017, https://www.bbc.com/news/world-asia-india-41510730.

My reports and papers:

Agrarian Crisis and Women (and Seasonal Migration), a CWDS working paper, 2018.

Death along the Famished Road, a compendium, Prem Bhatia Memorial Fellowship, 2006, https://www.scribd.com/document/80238053/pmbt-book.

Inheritors of Debt, Burden and Distress, CRY National Fellowship, 2010, https://www.cry.org/resources/pdf/NCRRF/Jaideep_Hardikar_2008_Report.pdf.

More than 200 stories in DNA, The Telegraph, India Together, IANS, People's Archive of Rural India (PARI) and other publications. Some assorted links below:

Farmer Suicides: Now It Is the Turn of Their Children, 7 November 2005, https://www.dnaindia.com/india/report-farmer-suicide-now-it-s-the-turn-of-their-children-8872.

'The Darkest Period of Our Life', 7 May 2016, https://ruralindiaonline.org/ur/articles/this-is-the-darkest-period-of-our-life/.

CAG Report Slams Vidarbha Waiver Package, 10 May 2008, http://indiatogether.org/theesri-government.

Maharashtra's Vidarbha Set to Face Acute Economic Distress Due to Climate Change, World Bank Warns, 25 September 2018, https://www.news18.com/news/opinion/maharashtras-vidarbha-set-to-face-acute-economic-crisis-due-to-climate-change-world-bank-warns-1888037.html.

Writings by or on P. Sainath:

More than 200 stories/articles in The Hindu, People's Archive of Rural India, Seminar, The Wire, and many other publications.

Some other stories and talks by P. Sainath here:

It's More Than an Agrarian Crisis: P. Sainath, 24 June 2019, https://www.thehindu.com/news/national/kerala/its-more-than-an-agrarian-crisis-p-sainath/article28122414.ece—on how the Centre fiddled with farmer suicide data since 2013.

Women Are the Single Largest Exclusion in India's Farmer Suicides Data: P. Sainath, 31 January 2020, https://www.newindianexpress.com/nation/2020/jan/31/women-are-the-single-largest-exclusion-in-indias-farmer-suicides-data-p-sainath-2097231.html.

NDA's Crop Insurance Scheme Bigger Scam Than Rafale: P. Sainath, 3 November 2018, https://www.business-standard.com/article/news-ians/nda-s-crop-insurance-scheme-bigger-scam-than-rafale-p-sainath-118110300875_1.html.

Books:

Widows of Vidarbha: Making of Shadows, Kota Neelima, Oxford University Press, 2018.

A Frayed History: The Journey of Cotton in India, Meena Menon and Uzramma, Oxford University Press, 2017.

Empire of Cotton: A Global History, Sven Beckert, Vintage Books, 2014.

Cotton: The Biography of a Revolutionary Fiber, Stephen Yafa, Penguin, 2005.

Kapus Kondyachi Gosht Sangu Ka, a Marathi booklet of essays by Vijay Jawandhia, published by Focus on Global South, 2010.

A Field of One's Own: Gender and Land Rights in South Asia, Bina Agarwal, Cambridge University Press, 1994.

Cotton and Famine in Berar, 1850–1900, Laxman D. Satya, Manohar Publishers and Distributors, 1997.

A note on the CAG report of 2008:

The Comptroller and Auditor General of India (CAG) conducted a performance audit through its Maharashtra-II Civil Office of the two special packages—the CM's and the PM's—announced in 2005 and 2006 respectively, for the distress-ridden farmers of the six cotton-growing districts of Vidarbha. The Government of Maharashtra tabled the report on the last day of the budget session of the state legislature on 27 April 2008.

My analysis of the CAG report here: http://indiatogether.org/theesri-government.

In its introduction, the CAG report said:

> The sharp increase in the number of suicides in six districts of the Vidarbha Region from 146 in 2003-04 to 455 in 2004-05 led the Government of Maharashtra (GOM) to announce a package called 'Special Package for Farmers' earmarking Rs 1075 crore in December 2005. The suicides, however, continued unabated and the number increased to 1414 during 2006-07.
>
> The performance audit of 'Farmers' Packages' was conducted with a focus on four principal themes, viz., assessment and handling of agrarian distress, immediate (short term) relief measures, long term measures for income augmentation and monitoring, reporting and the impact.
>
> Government of India (GOI) also declared (July 2006) a package called 'Special Rehabilitation Package' to mitigate the distress of farmers in 31 districts in four States, of which

six districts were in the Vidarbha Region of Maharashtra. The package involved Rs 3750 crore, to be spent over three years. The packages included long term and short term relief measures for alleviating rural distress and preventing farmers' suicides in the six most suicide prone districts of Vidarbha, viz., Amravati, Akola, Buldana, Wardha, Washim and Yavatmal. These packages consist of various components like rescheduling of loan/debt relief to farmers, seed replacement, assured irrigation facilities, financial assistance to farmers for increase in production, community marriages, immediate relief to the family of the deceased, ex-gratia assistance for education and medical needs from the Prime Minister's National Relief Fund. Principal Secretary, Relief and Rehabilitation (R & R) wing of Revenue and Forests Department, was responsible for extending relief measures to the farmers in distress. Director General, Vasantrao Naik Sheti Swawalamban Mission (VNSSM), Amravati, was to monitor the relief measures taken up under the packages, assisted by the Collectors at district level.

INDEX

ACKNOWLEDGEMENTS

I AM ETERNALLY INDEBTED AND thankful to so many people that it would be impossible for me to name all of them here.

But my formal thanks are in order to some of them.

First and foremost, the book would not have been possible if Ramrao Panchleniwar had not opened his doors for me. After spending countless hours with him, I would come out thinking that I would like to be more like Ramrao the good Samaritan. Cumulatively, I spent close to a hundred days with him over seven years, aside from our numerous telephone conversations. He was welcoming. Always.

My thanks also to the residents of Hiwara for being forthcoming in sharing their insights and hosting me generously from time to time.

To my friend and fellow traveller Shrikant Barhate, for setting aside his own worries and challenges, for being magnanimous in extending every kind of help possible and taking me on board for a very important project in the region with regard to water commons.

To Professor Neeraj Hatekar, economist, economic historian, and econometrician, an elder brother who encouraged me and stood firmly by me when I was down, mentally and physically.

The late Meghnad Bodhankar, my first editor and mentor. He left without giving me an opportunity to bid him farewell. When in doubt, he would ask me to go back to the fundamental question: journalism for whom and for what. That lesson is at the root of the idea for this book.

To Meena Menon, my old friend, who first goaded me to write a book on Vidarbha. 'It's there with you,' she had said during a conversation in Nagpur. 'You have just got to figure it out.'

To M. Rajshekhar, a dogged reporter and among India's frontline journalists, for helping me structure the book. It was thanks to him that I was able to give some order to the narrative.

Dear friend Silva Lieberherr and my well-wisher and former Sunday magazine editor at *Lokmat Samachar* Prakash Chandrayan, for spending a lot of time reading the first drafts and sharing their invaluable feedback that helped remove anomalies.

Vijay Jawandhia, farmers' leader and my mentor, for those countless discussions and the rich insights he brings to us from time to time about the world of farming and farm life.

Kishor Tiwari of the Vidarbha Jan Andolan Samiti, for helping me with data and numbers.

Sandeep, my '*sarathi*' for all times. He has never shied away from driving me through the dusty countryside for years.

To the friends at the Centre for People's Collective in Nagpur—Prafulla Gudadhe, Pravin Mote, Sajal Kulkarni, Gautam Nitnaware, Ajinkya Shahane and others—for meaningful brainstorming.

Siddhesh Inamdar, my editor at HarperCollins, for publishing this book and believing that it would work out.

Palagummi Sainath, for being there, like a polestar, as an inspiration, as an editor, and as a journalist leading by example. He gave me one of the most important lessons in reporting—not of a technical nature but a profound one: 'Your eyes cannot see what your heart does not feel.' But for him, I may not have been the journalist I am, chronicling the small world around me—a world removed from the buzzing metros. My thanks to him for teaching us, his students, to carefully look at the processes rather than mundane events. For taking me along on his own journeys into the countryside.

My doting parents, for making me finish the tasks on hand.

And last but not the least, Varada, my companion of eighteen years, for everything. Without her, I won't be able to manage any damn thing, forget taking up and completing a project like this. And our daughter, Nimisha, for bringing an endless joy into my life.

ABOUT THE AUTHOR

Jaideep Hardikar is a Nagpur-based senior journalist, writer, researcher and a core member of the People's Archive of Rural India. He has reported extensively from Vidarbha on farmer suicides and the cotton crisis for more than a decade. He has worked with *DNA* and *The Telegraph* among other publications.

Jaideep is the winner of several journalism fellowships and awards, including the Sanskriti Award for young journalists, which he received in 2003 for his reportage on rural issues. In 2009, he travelled to the US under the Alfred Friendly Press Fellowship programme and worked with *Sun Sentinel* in South Florida.

He is also the author of *A Village Awaits Doomsday* (2013) on the lives of people displaced by government and private projects across the country. It was born of his travels under the K.K. Birla Foundation Media Fellowship in 2001. He won the prestigious New India Foundation fellowship in 2021 for research for his next book.